ross the Ocean: Nine Essays on Indo-Mediterranean Trade

Columbia Studies in the Classical Tradition

VOLUME 41

The titles published in this series are listed at *brill.com/csct*

Across the Ocean: Nine Essays on Indo-Mediterranean Trade

Edited by

Federico De Romanis and Marco Maiuro

BRILL

LEIDEN | BOSTON

er *illustration*: Codice Magliabechiano XIII 16, ff. 88v–89r, Biblioteca Nazionale Centrale di Firenze. On
cession of the Ministry of Culture/Biblioteca Nazionale Centrale di Firenze.

rary of Congress Cataloging-in-Publication Data

of Two Worlds: Comparative Perspectives on Indo-Mediterranean Commerce (I–XVII c.) (Conference
lumbia University : 2011)
cross the ocean : nine essays on Indo-Mediterranean trade / edited by Federico De Romanis and Marco
uro.
pages cm. — (Columbia studies in the classical tradition, ISSN 0166-1302 ; volume 41)
This volume is a collection of papers delivered at the conference "A Tale of Two Worlds: Comparative
spectives on Indo-Mediterranean Commerce (I–XVII c.)," held at the Center for the Ancient
literranean, Columbia University, March 4th–5th, 2011"—Acknowledgment.
ncludes bibliographical references and index.
SBN 978-90-04-28919-2 (hardback : alk. paper) — ISBN 978-90-04-28953-6 (e-book) 1. Mediterranean
ion—Commerce—History—Congresses. 2. Mediterranean Region—History—476–1517—Congresses.
e Romanis, Federico. II. Maiuro, Marco. III. Title.

IF3750.7.T35 2011
82.0937'01824—dc23

201404744

s publication has been typeset in the multilingual "Brill" typeface. With over 5,100 characters covering
n, IPA, Greek, and Cyrillic, this typeface is especially suitable for use in the humanities.
more information, please see www.brill.com/brill-typeface.

I 0166-1302
N 978-90-04-28919-2 (hardback)
N 978-90-04-28953-6 (e-book)

s book is printed on acid-free paper.

Contents

Acknowledgements

This volume is a collection of papers delivered at the conference "A Tale of Two Worlds: Comparative Perspectives on Indo-Mediterranean Commerce (I–XVII c.)," held at the Center for the Ancient Mediterranean, Columbia University, March 4th–5th, 2011.

We express our gratitude to the Center for the Ancient Mediterranean for financial assistance for the conference, and especially to William V. Harris for his intellectual, scholarly, and practical support. Our sincere thanks also go to the contributors for their promptness, cooperation and, above all, patience. An anonymous review offered pertinent suggestions, and Shinu Abraham provided helpful comments. Finally, we thank Jane Botsford Johnson; without her intelligent, accurate, and stimulating editorial assistance this book would not have been published.

List of Table, Figures, and Maps

Table

Figures

Maps

Abbreviations

Greek and Latin authors, as well as inscriptions, papyri, ostraca, journals, and encyclopaedias of classical scholarship, are cited, when possible, in abbreviated forms according to the conventions established by the *Oxford Classical Dictionary* (4th edition). Other abbreviations are taken from the *Checklist of Editions of Greek, Latin, Demotic, and Coptic Papyri, Ostraca and Tablets*, and from the *Electronic Archive of Greek and Latin Epigraphy*. European, Arabic, Persian, and Chinese sources are quoted with the simple name of the author or the title of the work.

In addition, the following may be noted:

ANTT	Arquivo Nacional da Torre do Tombo
CA	Pato, R.A. Bulhão and H. Lopes de Mendonça, (1884–1935). *Cartas de Affonso de Albuquerque, seguidas de documentos que as elucidam*, 7 vols. (Lisboa).
CIMRM	Vermaseren, M.J. (1956–1960), *Corpus Inscriptionum et Monumentorum Religionis Mithriacae*, 2 vols. (Hague).
CVR	*Cartas dos Vice-Reys da Índia.*
DUP	(1960–1973), *Documentação ultramarina portuguesa*, 7 vols. (Lisboa).
I.Cos	Segre, M. (1993, 2007), *Iscrizioni di Cos*, 3 vols. (Roma).
I.Delphinion	Kawerau, G., Rehm A., and Wiegand Th., (1914), *Das Delphinion in Milet*, (Berlin).
I.Ko.Ko.	Bernand A. (1972), *De Koptos à Kosseir*, (Leiden).
I.Pan	Bernand A. (1977), *Pan du désert*, (Leiden).
I.Priene	Hiller von Gaertringen, F. (1906), *Inschriften von Priene* (Berlin).
LÄ	Helck, W. and W. Westendorf (eds.) (1975–1992), *Lexikon der Ägyptologie* (Wiesbaden).

Introduction

Federico De Romanis and Marco Maiuro

One key feature that distinguishes classical and Islamic civilization is the way the two societies conceptualized themselves in relation to the maritime horizons with which they interacted. While the former mainly represented its inhabited world as existing around an inner sea (the Mediterranean),[1] the latter set its 'land of Islam' between two seas, the sea 'of the Romans' and the sea 'of the Persians (or of the Habashat, or of the Chinese)'.[2] This contrast hardly needs elucidation. Despite Alexander's conquests, the Mediterranean Sea always remained the heart of the political horizon of the Greeks and the Romans, and its centripetal connectivity was the core of the intense cultural interchanges that characterized the Roman Empire.[3] It was a different sense of the world that induced the Abbasids to move the seat of the Caliphate from Damascus to Baghdad, and with it the barycentre of the Islamic world.[4]

Nevertheless, the Mediterranean centre of the Graeco-Roman world was not completely closed into itself. In particular, it was never impervious to the influence of the Indian Ocean world,[5] and over time Graeco-Roman society developed views of the greater world that were comparable to Islamic ones. When Cosmas Indicopleustes describes the *oikumene* as 'invaded' by four 'gulfs' (the Mediterranean, the Red Sea, the Persian Gulf, and the Caspian Sea), he is much closer to the perspective of Arab geographers than to that of Plato.[6]

In modern historiography, the first efforts to explore the nature of the interactions between the ancient Mediterranean and the Indian Ocean arose from an interest in the impact of the India trade on the economy of the Roman Empire. These attempts, not coincidentally, go back to the early eighteenth century, when it was thought that Roman trade with India could offer a

1 Plato's metaphor (*Phd.* 109b) is only too famous. Geographers like Strabo or Mela, or Pliny's geographic books organize their accounts by following the coastal lines of the Mediterranean and of the outer sea.

2 See Qur. LV 22 and other texts in De Romanis 2002.

3 Horden and Purcell 2000.

4 Brown 1971, 200–203.

5 Given the focus of this book, it goes without saying that when we speak of the Indian Ocean we refer especially, if not exclusively, to the western part of it.

6 Cosmas Indicopleustes 2.29.

 | DOI 10.1163/9789004289536_002

historical comparandum for the contemporary activities of European trading companies. Written at the request of Jean-Baptiste Colbert right after the foundation of the *Compagnie française pour le commerce des Indes orientales* (and published several decades later, when John Law's bank was about to create the new *Compagnie des Indes*), Pierre-Daniel Huet's *Histoire du commerce et de la navigation des anciens* was meant to be the scholarly work of a 'savant universel'.[7] Yet it did not fail to emphasize (and optimistically twist) the sole literary text by which the ancient India trade is quantitatively evaluated. Among Pliny's famous remarks about the India trade's financial implications,[8] Huet chose to focus on the claim that Indian commodities were sold in Roman markets at a price a hundredfold higher, taking this as the measure of the Roman profits.[9] The *arrière-pensée* of Huet's emphasis is only too clear and aims at a creeping decontextualization of Pliny's complaint. Pliny deprecated the high prices of the Indian commodities as a menace to morals no less than to the socio-economic order of the empire. Huet pointed out to his readers what he thought to be a startling gap between investments and revenues, a kind of paradise for a mercantilist state.

The popularity of Huet's work must have drawn the attention of Richard Cantillon to the India trade of the Romans. In his *Essai sur la nature du commerce en général*, published in 1755, but written around 1730, the history of Rome is represented as a typical evolution of a state which 'by Violence and Arms' increased the quantity of money actually circulating in the empire and eventually declined as a result of an inexorable 'fury of Luxury', which created the deficit quantified by Pliny.[10]

---

7 The book was published in 1716. However its *Préface*, addressed to Colbert, alludes to F. Charpentier, *Discours d'un fidèle sujet du roy touchant l'establissement d'une compagnie françoise pour le commerce des Indes orientales* (Paris 1664) as a recent publication. In 1717, Huet will publish, anonymously, *Memoires sur le commerce des Hollandois, dans tous les états et empires du monde. Où l'on montre quelle est leur maniere de le faire, son origine, leur grand progrès, leurs possessions & gouvernement dans les Indes.*

8 Plin., *HN* 6.100.

9 Huet 1716, 388: 'Ce que je vois de plus remarquable dans tout ce traité de Pline, c'est ce qu'il dit qu'il n'y avoit point d'année que les Romains ne portassent aux Indes du moins pour cinq millions de marchandises, & qu'on ne gagnât le centuple sur celles qu'on en raportoit.'

10 Cantillon 262–263 (II 8): 'La fureur du luxe augmenta toujours; & du tems de Pline l'Historien, il sortoit de l'Empire tous les ans au moins cent millions de sesterces, suivant son calcul. On n'en tiroit pas tant des Mines'; 417–418 (III 7): 'Ce Tresor de deux milliards sept cents millions de sesterces, laissé à la mort de Tibere, fut dissipé par l'Empereur Caligula son Successeur dans moin d'un an. Aussi ne vit-on jamais à Rome l'argent si

Huet's and Cantillon's thoughts about Roman trade with India are the unrevealed interlocutors in several passages of Montesquieu's *De l'esprit des lois* (1748),[11] in which an entire chapter is devoted to the subject of Roman trade with Arabia and India. Montesquieu is sceptical about the gap between initial and final prices of Indian commodities; he makes it clear that Roman trade with India cannot provide the ultimate validation of mercantilist theories for the simple reason that, unlike the Portuguese kingdom, it did not import to re-export to other states, but to supply internal consumption: the profits, if real, were made at the expense of the empire's economy.[12]

Montesquieu echoes the arguments of the advocates for a de-moralisation of luxury,[13] and replaces Cantillon's moralism with anthropological insight: the unbalanced trade with India, both ancient and modern, was due more to the cultural otherness of the Indians and their indifference to Western goods than to the Western passion for luxury.[14] Cantillon's argument is there, minus

---

abundant. Quel en fut l'effet? Cette quantité d'argent plongea les Romains dans le luxe, & dans toutes sortes de crimes pour y subvenir. Il sortoit tous les ans plus de six cents mille livres sterlings hors de l'Empire pour les marchandises des Indes; & en moins de trente ans l'Empire s'appauvrit, & l'argent y devint très rare sans aucun démembrement ni perte de Province.' On the ubiquitous theme of luxury in the eighteenth century literary debate, cf. e.g. Berry 1994, chapter 6.

11 In *Considérations sur les causes de la grandeur des Romains, et de leur décadence* (1734) no association appears between the decadence of the Romans and their India trade. The link between Pliny's deficit figures and the billon coinage confirms that Montesquieu read Cantillon's manuscript in the meantime. (Cf. Hayek 1991, 289: 'it still can scarcely be doubted that he was familiar with his manuscript.')

12 Montesquieu, *De l'esprit des lois* XXI 16: 'Pline dit que les marchandises qu'on en rapportait se vendaient à Rome le centuple. Je crois qu'il parle trop généralement: ce profit fait une fois, tout le monde aura voulu le faire; et, dès ce moment, personne ne l'aura fait. [...]Que si les marchandises de ce pays se vendaient à Rome le centuple, ce profit des Romains se faisait sur les Romains mêmes, et n'enrichissait point l'empire.'

13 Ibid.: 'On pourra dire, d'un autre côté, que ce commerce procurait aux Romains une grande navigation, c'est-à-dire une grande puissance; que des marchandises nouvelles augmentaient le commerce intérieur, favorisaient les arts, entretenaient l'industrie; que le nombre des citoyens se multipliait à proportion des nouveaux moyens qu'on avait de vivre; que ce nouveau commerce produisait le luxe, que nous avons prouvé être aussi favorable au gouvernement d'un seul que fatal à celui de plusieurs; que cet établissement fut de même date que la chute de leur république; que le luxe à Rome était nécessaire; et qu'il fallait bien qu'une ville qui attirait à elle toutes les richesses de l'univers, les rendit par son luxe.'

14 Montesquieu, *De l'esprit des lois* XXI 1: 'Les Indiens ont leurs arts, qui sont adaptés à leur manière de vivre. Notre luxe ne sçauroit être le leur, ni nos besoins être leurs besoins. Leur climat ne leur demande ni ne leur permet presque rien de ce qui vient de chez nous. Ils

his apocalyptic overtones: the Roman deficit in the India trade resulted in a general scarcity of silver, which compelled the Romans to increase the value of their specie by establishing base coin.[15]

It is not by chance that a more resolute move away from Cantillon's link between the India trade and Roman decline occurs in the first volume of Edward Gibbon's *History of the Decline and Fall of the Roman Empire* (1776), which appeared at a time when Indian imports to Britain were balanced by less and less bullion.[16] To such a thorough investigator of the Roman decline, Cantillon's diagnosis looked grossly simplistic and fallacious. The silver scarcity claimed by Montesquieu was disproved by simply comparing the ratios of gold to silver in the first and fifth centuries CE,[17] after which Gibbon's conclusion was straightforward: 'whatever might be the amount of the Indian and Arabian exports, they were far from exhausting the wealth of the Roman world.'[18] Far from being the secret cause of its decline, the Roman Empire's trade with India was yet another indicator of its prosperity and sophistication.

The conclusion of this debate on the impact of the India trade in ancient times—just a retrospective chapter of the debates on the impact of the India trade on European economies—dismissed forever any mechanical subordination of the history of the Roman decline to that of the Roman Oriental trade, and it is to Gibbon's credit that no one thereafter seriously renewed Cantillon's thesis. However, Gibbon's rebuttal also had less positive collateral effects. Gibbon thought to present a modern, objective evaluation of Rome's

---

vont en grande partie nuds; les vêtements qu'ils ont, le pays les leur fournit convenables; et leur religion, qui a sur eux tant d'empire, leur donne de la répugnance pour les choses qui nous servent de nourriture. Ils n'ont donc besoin que de nos métaux, qui sont les signes des valeurs, et pour lesquels ils donnent des marchandises, que leur frugalité et la nature de leur pays leur procure en grande abondance. Les auteurs anciens qui nous ont parlé des Indes, nous les dépeignent telles que nous les voyons aujourd'hui, quant à la police, aux manières et aux mœurs. Les Indes ont été, les Indes seront ce qu'elles sont à présent; et, dans tous les temps, ceux qui négocieront aux Indes y porteront de l'argent, et n'en rapporteront pas.'

15 Ibid. 16: 'On peut mettre en question s'il fut avantageux aux Romains de faire le commerce de l'Arabie et des Indes. Il faloit qu'ils y envoyassent leur argent, et ils n'avoient pas, comme nous, la ressource de l'Amérique, qui supplée à ce que nous envoyons. Je suis persuadé qu'une des raisons qui fit augmenter chez eux la valeur numéraire des monnaies, c'est-à-dire établir le billon, fut la rareté de l'argent, causée par le transport continuel qui s'en faisait aux Indes.'

16 Prakash 1998, 273–274.

17 Neither Montesquieu nor Gibbon could have been aware that mostly gold coins were exported.

18 E. Gibbon, *History of the Decline and Fall of the Roman Empire*, Chapter II.

trade with India by contesting Pliny's perception of it, which he alleged was overblown and distorted. On this contention, he found more followers than he should have. The unaltered economic prosperity of the Roman Empire up to the period of the Antonines, as outlined by Gibbon, set the stage for the notion that Roman trade with India was an essentially peripheral epiphenomenon of a flourishing Roman economy. As a consequence, its study became a marginal intellectual detour, an idle exercise in erudition for scholars with an antiquarian taste for curiosities and oddities. It is as if the India trade of the Romans, as a subject of inquiry, had to pay for its failure to provide an explanation for the fall of the Roman Empire.

There is an implicit (quite seldom fully articulated) narrative about the India trade that permeates historical scholarship: that Europe's long-distance trade with India gained prominence—that is, became quantitatively relevant—only during the early modern period. Confined as it must have been (so the assumption goes) to the fringes of Roman economic life, the elite, demand–driven markets for Indian merchandise were in classical times quantitatively negligible relative to the Mediterranean commerce in food and staples. It has also been assumed that trade with India grew in prominence only over the course of later centuries, ultimately becoming the core of the foreign policies of Portuguese and Dutch monarchies. This narrative is thus a linear history of growth: the ancient world is credited with the *discovery* of the India trade, its maritime routes and the monsoon patterns, but that trade remained confined to the realm of curiosities or marvels and was never fully exploited in Antiquity.

New data, randomly piled up by the investigations of many researchers in different fields, especially during the last decades, urge for a reassessment. Many particular issues—from demand, to taxation, to the role of the State, to outflows in precious metals, credit, naval technology, and economic information—have recently been subjected to detailed historical reappraisals. What this means is that the scholarly community can now address the question of Indo-Roman trade armed with a stronger evidentiary database that includes the new archaeological data from projects along the Red Sea and in India. Consequently, we have become very much more aware of how substantial the imperial taxation on Indian commodities was; we now see how deeply consumption of these goods penetrated into the imperial societies, and how vibrantly their dissemination all over the Roman Empire enhanced the economic dynamics.

Trading in the Indian Ocean has been an economic feature of developed economies since Hellenistic times, and—albeit not *the* fundamental component of agrarian pre-modern economies—it was certainly a vital factor of these economies. Long-distance trade is a lens through which we can analyse certain economic parameters, such as the demand for luxury goods, the quantity of money exacted as customs dues or taxes across frontiers, the outflow and inflow of gold and other precious metals, the role of credit and maritime loans, and naval technology and infrastructures. Insights can be derived about geographical knowledge, the circulation of economic information, and the role of states and other public powers in promoting lucrative economic activities. Finally, trade serves as a magnifying glass on the social players. It reveals important things about the actors on stage: the merchants and their organizations, the capitalists, and the counterparts of this commerce in India.

Moreover, the heuristic potential of an exploration of Roman trade with India is not limited to the acknowledgement of how intimately the economy of the Roman Mediterranean was interconnected with the Indian Ocean. It also opens windows wide on the long history of the Indian Ocean itself, putting in perspective later moments of the relations between the 'West'—be it the Roman Empire, Islamic West Asia, or Atlantic Europe—and South Asia. No matter which period we are dealing with, one can argue that the India trade functions as an informative proxy for the socio-economic complexities of any given society. This holds true as much for the Roman Empire as it does for Fatimid Egypt and the Netherlands in the seventeenth century, and indeed it is the only methodological premise that makes such comparisons intellectually worthwhile. This is why Roman trade with India will be most productively studied by comparisons with trade centered on the Indian Ocean from other periods.

This is the kind of comparative history we tried to promote when we organized the conference of which the papers here collected are a partial reflection. Specialists of different historical periods have been asked to contribute to produce an overview of a subject—trade in the western Indian Ocean between the Roman conquest of Egypt and the industrial revolution—that is geographically, chronologically, and culturally compact. If what we encouraged may be nonetheless defined as 'comparative history', that is only because we looked for a more intense interaction between narratives that in the current practice, due essentially to academic specializations, proceed autonomously from each other. The scope of our project was, therefore, one or more steps behind what has recently become the methodological trend for comparative history, as applied to ancient history.

Ever since it was first hailed as the frontier for historical research on the ancient western world, capable of leading to fresh insights in a field notoriously short of good hard data, comparative history has become more evident in the research of social and economic historians. Paraphrasing Benedetto Croce, we could say that any social and economic history of the ancient world is ultimately comparative. The benchmark of other, better-known periods or places has always served comparative-minded historians, especially those reluctant to confine themselves within the Pillars of Hercules of the classical Mediterranean basin. From the Meyer–Bücher debate to the recent explosion of studies prompted by Finley's *The Ancient Economy*, one will often find the element of comparison—overt or implied—with other epochs and places employed as a rhetorical or heuristic device.[19] Moreover, one could argue that no real intellectual attack has ever been levelled against the methodological validity of the comparative approach to ancient economic history; in fact, while some scholars do question the comparability of ancient and medieval/early modern economies, none has ultimately questioned the comparative method itself, as has happened in other disciplines.

Nevertheless, recent attempts to make systematic comparisons among pre-modern empires have resulted in a certain degree of scepticism[20]—all the more so because such efforts generally put together scholars from distinct and highly specialized backgrounds with little or no attempt to standardize disciplinary jargon. The outcomes are understandably somewhat disappointing, even for the pioneers who seek to bridge the comparative gap. The attentive reader finds, at best, intellectual oranges and apples in the same basket or, at worst, mental confusion and philological sloppiness. But a caveat is in order here: single-authored books spanning multiple epochs or civilizations are rare today. Few contemporary scholars command the twin skills of comparative historical research: both a mastery over primary and secondary sources for multiple civilizations or periods,[21] as well as a recognition of which questions are historically answerable in a comparative approach and through document-based study.

One must accept, therefore, that comparing, say, monetary stocks, demographic tallies, and productive outputs between pre-modern empires is a risky endeavour: it means relating the obscure with the obscure. Only if we are prepared to ignore the uncertainties that undermine our precarious historical

19 See Bang 2008 on the history of comparative method in recent historiography of the ancient world, esp. 24–5 for a list of recent works. Pleket 1990 is the fullest attempt to systematically compare ancient (i.e. Roman) and early modern economies; a 'primitivist' rebuttal of Pleket in Bang 2008, 35 ff.

20 E.g. Vasunia 2011 and Chaussende 2011 on Scheidel 2009a; see the work in progress of Scheidel (http://www.princeton.edu/~pswpc/pdfs/scheidel/041305.pdf) who lucidly confesses the limits (but at the same time exalts the potentialities) of this approach.

21 Bang's remarkable attempt (2008) has had, as far as we can see, a negligible impact on scholarship and cannot be taken as a model.

conclusions about such macroeconomic factors—and to take the conclusions of specialists of histories distant to our own domain as indisputable truths—can this fascinating intellectual exercise be credited with any scholarly utility.

We present this collection of papers as a contribution to the ongoing intellectual and scholarly project of re-examining and re-evaluating afresh Indo-Mediterranean trade. We have started, as it is clear from the papers that follow, from a re-appraisal of the evidenciary basis. We deem that any fresh insight that can be gained about this topic should necessarily combine evidence and models, and inductive and deductive methods. An attentive scrutiny of the evidence at hand, when interrogated with relevant historical questions, would yield, and indeed has yielded, a generous harvest of new insights. This in turn will stimulate, we hope, further debates on this central issue of world history.

•••

The papers collected in this volume reflect, in part, the talks delivered at the conference 'A Tale of Two Worlds', held at Columbia University in March 2011, under the aegis of and generously sponsored by the Center for the Ancient Mediterranean. The collection as a whole is more centered on the ancient time period than the conference was. The first section focuses on the critical region of the Red Sea and addresses key questions about the quality of the interactions between the Mediterranean and the Indian Ocean. Andrew Wilson examines the role of the State in Indo-Roman trade, from its fiscal policy to the water supply along the caravan routes of Egypt's Eastern Desert. The function of a major infrastructure feature, the *Traianos potamos*, is the focus of the chapter by Jean-Jacques Aubert. Katia Schörle reconstructs the trade of a typical commodity, the pearl, with its peculiar socio-economic implications. The extent and scope of Nabataean trading activities in the Mediterranean region is reviewed in the chapter by Taco Terpstra. And Dario Nappo collects and analyses the evidence for Roman expansion in the Red Sea during the second century CE.

The second section explores topics of broader import and across epochs. Harry Falk's paper on gold references in ancient Indian literary sources deals with the cultural context that fostered the export of western gold coins to India. Jairus Banaji emphasizes the tenacious persistence of the Arabian Sea trading network from Antiquity to the Middle Ages, calling into question the characterization of the big merchants of the pre-modern Arabian Sea. Federico De Romanis' chapter presents a comparison of Roman and Portuguese trade, outlining the geographic and anthropological contexts of Malabar pepper production and the quantitative dimensions of its export. The chapter by Martha Howell analyses the reasons why the Dutch East Indies Company (the VOC) succeeded so spectacularly in monopolizing the spice trade during the seventeenth and eighteenth centuries. Finally, Elio Lo Cascio remarks on the book's overarching topic, and the insights offered by the author of each chapter.

PART 1

The Cradle of the Ancient India Trade: The Red Sea

CHAPTER 1

Red Sea Trade and the State

Andrew Wilson

This paper examines evidence, both documentary and archaeological, for State interest in Indo-Mediterranean trade via the Red Sea in Antiquity, focusing on the creation of infrastructure to facilitate trade, measures taken to protect trade and traders, and the extent of the State's interest in the trade principally as a result of customs dues, which it is argued formed a significant and hitherto under-appreciated source of income for the Roman State.

The development of Indo-Mediterranean trade in large volumes via the Red Sea route in the Augustan period was the result of a combination of at least four main factors: (1) the creation of overland routes between the Nile and the Red Sea, obviating the need for ships to beat all the way up the Red Sea to the Gulf of Suez against strong northerly winds;[1] (2) the discovery of the monsoon winds, enabling a more direct passage to and from India;[2] (3) the transfer of Mediterranean shipbuilding techniques to the Red Sea, allowing the construction of ships that could carry a burden of several hundred tons and ride out the high seas in monsoon conditions, thus enabling the *exploitation* of those monsoons; and (4) the incorporation of Egypt into the Roman Empire after Actium, which plugged these long-distance eastern trade routes into a vast pan-Mediterranean market under a single political control and with increasingly—though not entirely—convergent legal and financial institutions. The flourishing of this trade for several centuries under the Roman Empire relied on effective protection of these routes.

The first piece of this jigsaw was put in place in the Hellenistic period under Ptolemy II Philadelphus, with the foundation of Berenice and the creation of regular overland routes across the Eastern Desert between Coptos and Edfu on the Nile and the ports of the Red Sea. Strabo gives us the basic details:

> Thence [i.e. from Coptos] one crosses an isthmus, which extends to the Red Sea, near a city Berenice. The city has no harbour, but on account of the favourable lay of the isthmus has convenient landing-places. It is said

1 On Red Sea sailing conditions, see Cooper 2011.

2 Casson 1980; Tchernia 2005.

 | DOI 10.1163/9789004289536_003

> that Philadelphus was the first person, by means of an army, to cut this road, which is without water, and to build stations, as though for the travels of merchants on camels, and that he did this because the Red Sea was hard to navigate, particularly for those who set sail from its innermost recess. So the utility of his plan was shown by experience to be great, and now all the Indian merchandise, as well as the Arabian and such of the Aethiopian as is brought down by the Arabian Gulf, is carried to Coptos, which is the emporium for such cargoes. Not far from Berenice lies Myos Hormos, a city containing the naval station for sailors; and not far distant from Coptos lies Apollonos polis, as it is called, so that on either side there are two cities which form the boundaries of the isthmus. But now it is Coptos and Myos Hormos that have high repute; and people frequent these places. Now in earlier times the camel-merchants travelled only by night, looking to the stars for guidance, and, like the mariners, also carried water with them when they travelled; but now they have constructed watering-places, having dug down to a great depth, and, although rainwater is scarce, still they have made cisterns for it. The journey takes six or seven days. On this isthmus are also the mines of smaragdus, where the Arabians dig deep tunnels, I might call them, and of other precious stones (17.1.45; trans. Jones LCL 1935).

Five principal routes have been traced archaeologically between the Nile Valley and the Red Sea: a northerly one from Kainepolis (Qena) to Abu Sha'ar, a central route from Coptos (Qift) to Myos Hormos (Quseir al-Qadim), two southerly routes, from Apollonos polis Magna (Edfu) to Marsa Nakari (perhaps the ancient Nechesia), and from Edfu to Berenice, and a longer route running south-east from Coptos to Berenice (*Maps 1.1* and *1.2*).[3] It is not entirely clear which route Strabo means by the one he says was built by Ptolemy Philadelphus; a straightforward reading of the passage would suggest that he means the Coptos–Berenice route, although in fact the road stations along the central section of this route, where it is not shared with the Coptos–Myos Hormos road or the Edfu–Berenice road, have produced largely Roman material and very little Ptolemaic pottery, whereas the Coptos–Myos Hormos and Edfu–Berenice routes both have Ptolemaic road stations.[4] It seems likely that

3 On Ptolemaic infrastructure for transport across the Eastern Desert, see Sidebotham 2011, 28–31.

4 Generally, see Murray 1925; Sidebotham and Zitterkopf 1995; Sidebotham, Hense, and Nouwens 2008, 192–4 and 329–43. Kainepolis-Abu Sha'ar: Sidebotham, Zitterkopf, and Riley 1991. Coptos–Myos Hormos: Zitterkopf and Sidebotham 1989; Cuvigny 2003a. Coptos-Berenice: Sidebotham 1999; Bagnall, Bülow-Jacobsen, and Cuvigny 2001.

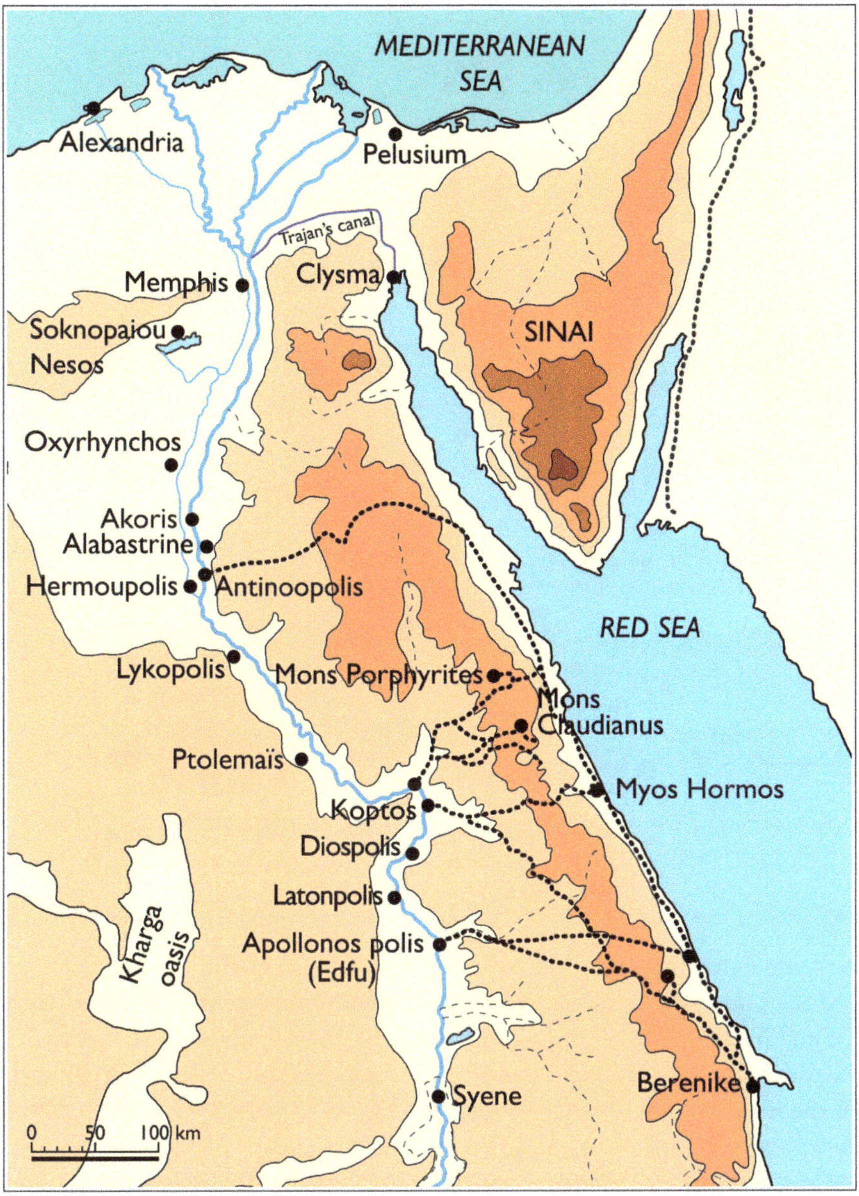

MAP 1.1 *Routes between the Nile and the Red Sea (M. Anastasi / A. Wilson, based on a map by J.-P. Brun).*

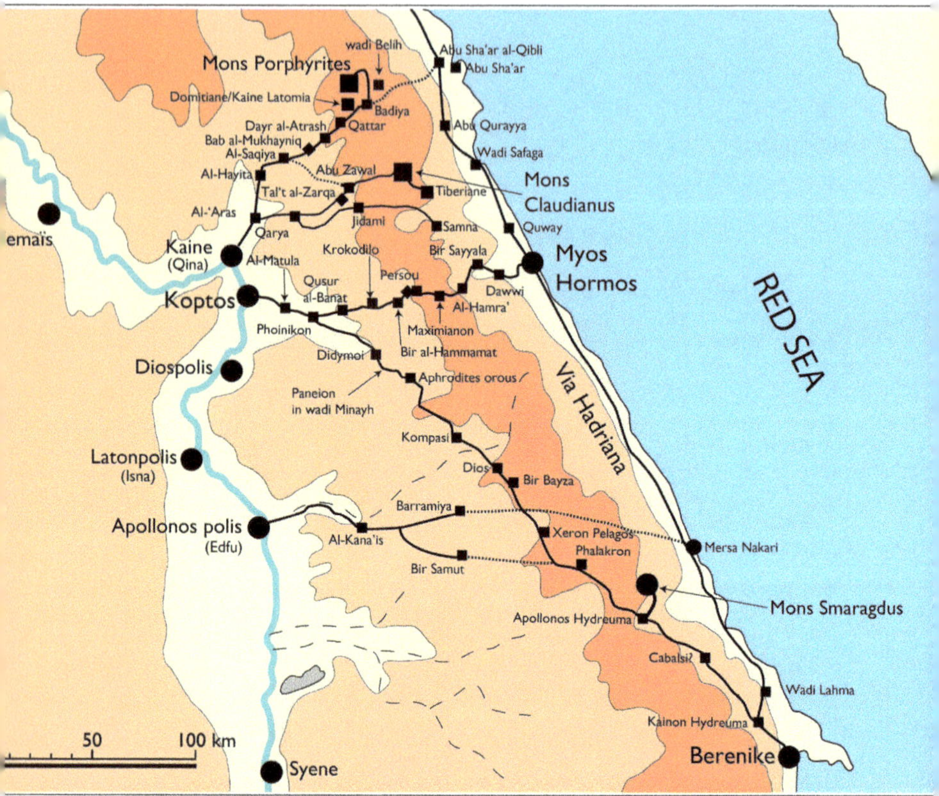

1.2 *Routes across the Eastern Desert, and their forts and watering points* (*M. Anastasi / A. Wilson, based on a map by J.-P. Brun*).

in the Ptolemaic period, the two shortest routes between the Nile and the main Red Sea ports, from Edfu to Berenice and from Coptos to Myos Hormos, were the major ones for Ptolemaic trade. Over time, as we shall see, the emphasis on the different routes shifted, according to changes in the condition of the ports on the Red Sea, and perhaps also in the security of the desert through which they passed.

Crucial to these overland routes from the Nile to the Red Sea were the watering points or *hydreumata* created along them. One of these Ptolemaic road stations has been identified at Bir 'Iayyan on the road from Edfu to Berenice, a watering point with Ptolemaic pottery and an inscribed distance stone (461 stadioi from the Nile = 97.7 km) dated to 257 BCE. The site has cisterns; no ancient well has been discovered, but there is a modern well 100 m to the north.[5]

5 Bagnall et al. 1996. On rain-runoff collection ('rainwater harvesting') for cisterns at such road stations, see Krzywinski 2007.

This site seems broadly to confirm Strabo's testimony, and gives us a better chronological fix, showing that at least one of the routes was in existence in 257 BCE.

The creation of these watering points not only made this overland desert transport easier but also cut the costs: caravans no longer had to carry reserves of water for the full six or seven days of the journey, but only for the distance from one watering point to the next. This freed up capacity to carry saleable goods rather than the water needed simply for survival. The effect was to increase the ratio of the weight of saleable cargo to the number of animals and people in the caravan, and thus the profitability of each trip.

The *hydreumata* cannot have functioned without a means of raising water from deep wells in quantities sufficient to feed desert caravans; although rain runoff and wadi floodwater collected in cisterns certainly supplemented wells at some sites,[6] dependence on rainwater harvesting alone would have been precarious and could not be relied upon to support a regular caravan traffic without the use of wells in addition. The Hellenistic invention of *saqiyya* technology will have facilitated the extraction of groundwater from deep wells at some of the road stations, thus enabling the intensification of overland trade along the Nile–Red Sea route. Of the various water-lifting machines used in Antiquity, the *saqiyya* is the only one suited to lifting water in large quantity from deep wells. It consisted originally of a series of wooden compartments or boxes on a metal chain, later re-engineered (from the late third century CE onwards?) in cheaper materials as a chain of pots on a rope, looped over a wheel which is driven via a right-angled gearing by an animal walking in a circle around the well.[7]

The invention of the *saqiyya* has been placed by Michael Lewis, on the evidence of Philo of Byzantium who clearly knew of it, in the window 280–220 BCE,[8] and it may probably be narrowed further to the earlier part of this period. Right-angled gearing was sufficiently well developed by *c.*240 BCE for Archimedes to use it in his hodometer cart.[9] In other words, the technology existed, as a recent invention, during the reign of Ptolemy Philadelphus, and it is difficult to believe that it was not used on this desert route.

The evidence for the use of the *saqiyya* at the *hydreumata* of the Eastern Desert, however, is not clear cut. The Ptolemaic installations are not known in detail, and in the case of those Roman *hydreumata* where details of the wells have been published, most have large wells that now present themselves as a

6 Krzywinski 2007.

7 Oleson 1984, 350–85.

8 Lewis 1997, 32.

9 Vitr. 10.9.1–4; Sleeswyk 1979; 1981; 1990; Lewis 1997, 37–8.

collapsed erosion cone, sometimes 16 m in diameter. In some cases there are traces of a spiral ramp or staircase up and down which people—or animals—went to carry water in skins or jars; in other cases it is possible that an originally much narrower well has progressively collapsed and been cut back in a cone shape to retard further collapse of the walls. These wide wells, which are clearly not *saqiyya* wells in their present form, are found at some of the Roman praesidia on the route from Coptos to Myos Hormos and also at the *hydreuma* of Siket and Wadi Kalalat, supplying water to the port of Berenice. Both are in unstable piedmont wash gravels through which it was difficult to cut a narrow enclosed well; at Wadi Kalalat a staircase leads down into the well.[10] Details on the morphology of most of these wells are scant in the published literature (the project which investigated sites on the Myos Hormos route was primarily interested in finding inscribed ostraca), and there are no explicit statements either on the presence or the absence of *saqiyya* pots at the sites on the road to Myos Hormos.[11] However, since it was only in the third century CE that *saqiyya* pots replaced the wooden boxes used until then, and most of these *hydreumata* were abandoned by that time, this is not a decisive argument; if these sites had been supplied by *saqiyya* machines in the first and second centuries CE, the *saqiyyas* would have used wooden boxes which would be unlikely to survive archaeologically.[12] *Saqiyya* pots have, however, been found at some sites in the Eastern Desert, including Didymoi, on the road from Coptos to Berenice.[13]

Ptolemy II opened the overland route between the Nile and the Red Sea with the idea of enabling the supply of war elephants from the Sudan, but the routes clearly facilitated subsequent commercial traffic with the Red Sea and the southern Arabian Peninsula. Following the discovery of the monsoon winds and the incorporation of Egypt into the large market of the Roman Empire, the intensity of trade with India via the Red Sea increased. Strabo says that under the Ptolemies only some twenty ships per year left Myos Hormos for India, but

10 Cuvigny 2003a: figs 1 (Bir Sayyala, Abu Qurayya, al-Zarqa = Maximianon), 35 (Krokodilo), 58 and 59 (Bir al-Hammamat); Sidebotham 2000, 359–363; Sidebotham, Hense, and Nouwens 2008, 311 (Wadi Kalalat).

11 Six ostraca from the praesidium of Maximianon, on the route from Coptos to Myos Hormos, mention payments called *kykleutikon* to women there; these were initially thought to have something to do with the operation of a *saqiyya* (*kykleuma*) (Cuvigny 2003b, 389–93), but have more recently been reinterpreted as payments to prostitutes who made the circuit (*kykleuein*) of the garrison in a desert fort (Cuvigny 2010).

12 Cf. Malouta and Wilson 2013.

13 Sidebotham, Hense, and Nouwens 2008, 322–3.

'now' (i.e. 27 or 26 BCE, when he accompanied Aelius Gallus on his expedition to Ethiopia), 120 ships did.[14] A corollary of this was that over time it was necessary for the Roman State to intensify the infrastructure on the Ptolemaic routes through the Eastern Desert to support increased traffic between the Nile and the Red Sea, and indeed the construction of new *hydreumata* is attested by inscriptions.

The roads themselves were relatively simply constructed—cleared passages, marked with cairns and sometimes overlooked by watch-towers; occasionally short stretches were cut through passes or supported on embankments. The complete lack of milestones, remarked upon by previous commentators as strange for Roman roads,[15] may in fact be explained by the fact that these roads were not for wheeled vehicles, but were caravan routes, and the miles could therefore not be measured off by a vehicle fitted with a hodometer, as seems to have been the normal practice elsewhere (cf. Vitr. 10.9.1–4).[16] As Gates notes, official inscriptions commemorating construction are concentrated instead at forts and *hydreumata*, but it is nonsense to say (apropos of the lack of milestones) that 'This change in treatment of the road almost certainly reflects a hesitancy to claim the road tracks and surfaces as controlled, familiar spaces', or that the roads were intended in some way to be 'hidden' from desert nomads.[17] The forts, watchtowers, and marker cairns along their routes were substantially more conspicuous in the landscape than milestones.

The road between Edfu and Berenice appears to have largely fallen out of use soon after the start of the Roman period; the road stations between Edfu and Dweig (the junction with the Coptos–Berenice route) have produced mainly Ptolemaic and very early Roman material, with minimal amounts of late Roman and early Islamic pottery.[18] By contrast, early and late Roman material is found along the route from Coptos to Berenice, with very little Ptolemaic pottery in the central section between Phoinikon and Dweig, and evidently the longer route from Coptos to Berenice was preferred over the route from Edfu in the Roman period. At first sight this seems strange—Sidebotham and Zitterkopf note that 'There is no apparent reason for the Roman preference

14 Strabo 2.5.12; cf. Brun 2003, 192.

15 Gates 2006, 318; Sidebotham, Hense, and Nouwens 2008, 46; Sidebotham 2011, 147–9.

16 Cf. note 9 above.

17 Gates 2006, 319.

18 Sidebotham and Zitterkopf 1996, 452.

for the alternate, and longer, route to Qift'[19]—but we shall return to a possible explanation for this shortly.

Ptolemaic and Roman pottery are both found along the route from Coptos to Myos Hormos. Strabo's testimony suggests that by the Augustan period both the Coptos–Myos Hormos and the Coptos–Berenice routes were in use, with the Coptos–Myos Hormos road being preferred, presumably because it was the shortest link between the Nile and the Red Sea; he implies that Myos Hormos was also the principal port of departure for the ships heading towards India.[20] Over the next century or so, however, the balance shifted in favour of the longer route from Coptos to Berenice, probably largely because of the silting of the lagoon that formed the harbour of Myos Hormos. Myos Hormos itself seems to have ceased to function as a port around the end of the second century CE or the start of the third century, and the road stations on the road from Coptos to Myos Hormos were abandoned around the same time.[21]

During the course of the first century CE, improvements were made to the infrastructure along the roads from Coptos to Myos Hormos, particularly from Coptos to Berenice.[22] The rock shelter near Menih al-Heir on the Coptos–Berenice road has graffiti left by travellers and merchants, some of which are dated to 6 BCE, 2 CE, and 44 CE, attesting the use of this route from the Augustan period onwards.[23] An inscription at Coptos dated possibly as early as the reign of Augustus records the construction of cisterns (*lacci*) at Apollonos Hydreuma, Compasi, and Berenice, and the building and repair of a camp at Myos Hormos.[24] The sites mentioned in that inscription are among those mentioned by Pliny as lying along the Coptos–Berenice route;[25] fortified wells and cisterns were added at other sites in 76/77 CE by the prefect of Egypt, Julius Ursus, as is made clear by one well-preserved inscription from the fort at Wadi Sikayt near Berenice, and fragments of closely similar texts from the forts at Didymoi and Aphrodites.[26] In addition to the forts protect-

19 Sidebotham and Zitterkopf 1996, 452; cf. Sidebotham 1997, 388, suggesting the abandonment of the shorter route might have been due to a drop in the water table, but without supporting evidence.

20 Strabo 17.1.45, quoted above.

21 Brun 2003, 201–2.

22 For the most recent synthesis on the routes across the Eastern Desert in the Roman period, see Sidebotham 2011, 125–74.

23 Sidebotham, Hense, and Nouwens 2008, 192–3.

24 *ILS* 2483; Kennedy 1985; De Romanis 1996, 219–24; Bagnall, Bülow-Jacobsen, and Cuvigny 2001; Kennedy 1985, 330.

25 Plin., *HN* 6.102–3.

26 *O.Ber.II*.120; Bagnall, Bülow-Jacobsen, and Cuvigny 2001; Cuvigny 2003c 356.

ing the water sources along the routes, caravans were provided with armed escorts (privately hired?) for protection against the desert nomads.[27] On the authority of the Prefect of Berenice, tax collectors who farmed the taxes from the *arabarchs* levied charges on travellers for permits to use the routes, and the revenue presumably defrayed some of the costs of maintaining this infrastructure.[28] Although the State's interest in roads across the Eastern Desert was also motivated by the need to transport granite and marble from the desert quarries, and by the exploitation of some gold mines and the beryl/emerald mines near Berenice,[29] the main quarries and gold mines lay to the north of the roads under consideration here; the primary motive for the upkeep of the Coptos–Berenice and Myos Hormos routes was clearly to sustain these roads as trade routes.

This idea is supported by an examination of Trajanic policy in the region, which included the construction of the Via Nova from Aila to Bosra linking the northern Red Sea with southern Syria;[30] the dredging and rehabilitation of the Clysma canal together with the creation of a river port at Babylon (Old Cairo) enclosing the junction of the canal and the Nile;[31] and the stationing of a fleet in the Red Sea.[32] This followed the annexation of the Nabataean kingdom and seems to be a systematic set of measures designed to maximise the takeover of Nabataean trading interests in this area.[33] Under Hadrian a road linking Antinoe to Berenice via the smaller harbours of the western Red Sea

27 The second-century CE 'Muziris' Papyrus (*PVindob*. G 40822) stipulates the conveyance of goods through the desert under guard.

28 Sidebotham 1986a, 80–81. Details of charges for these permits to travel are given in the Coptos Tariff of 90 CE: *OGI* 674.

29 Schörle 2008; 2011; cf. Schörle this volume for pearls; Sidebotham 2011, 167–74.

30 Sidebotham 1986a, 154.

31 Canal: Bourdon 1925; Ball 1942, 15, 58–59, 110, 130; Sijpesteijn 1963; Redmount 1995; Mayerson 1996; Cooper 2009. Trajanic harbour at Old Babylon: Sheehan 2012. Aubert (2004; and this volume) unnecessarily confuses the seasonality of navigation along the canal with the idea that the canal cannot really have been used for navigation in Antiquity, in a series of forced arguments which involve specious dismissals of the ancient evidence pointing to its use, and made in ignorance of the recent archaeological work at the port of Old Babylon at the junction of the canal with the Nile.

32 Eutr. 8.3.2; Jer. *Chron*. 220 *Olymp*.; cf. Nappo, this volume (though I cannot see that the ostraca from the Nikanor archive which he cites necessarily prove the existence of a fleet in the Red Sea, rather than the odd patrol vessel).

33 Sidebotham 1986a, 148–55, *contra* Young 2001, 117–9. Cf. Terpstra, this volume.

coast, the Via Nova Hadriana, was constructed to facilitate regional communications and supplies between the important main ports of Myos Hormos and Berenice (*Map* 1.1).[34] This was an unpaved but cleared route through the stony desert, marked by cairns and equipped with wells, way stations, and forts, as an inscription of 25 February 137 CE proclaims, stressing that the road runs through safe and level places (διὰ τόπων ἀσφαλῶν καὶ ὁμαλῶν).[35] In the mid second century a detachment of troops (and ships) was stationed on the Farasan Islands in the southern Red Sea, well to the south of any Roman land frontier.[36] This may represent an extension of the sphere of operations of the fleet which Trajan had stationed in the Red Sea; in any case, the purpose of this unit must have been principally to protect trade shipping entering or leaving the Red Sea from piracy off the coast of the Arabian Peninsula.

Why did the Roman State go to such lengths to invest in the physical infrastructure for the Red Sea routes, and protection along them? The answer seems to lie principally in the customs revenue that the State derived from Indo-Mediterranean trade. Customs tariffs across the empire's frontiers were, at least on the eastern frontiers where we have direct evidence, set at 25 per cent until some time perhaps in the early third century CE, and this may have been the case universally.[37] Strabo, writing about why Augustus did not bother to invade Britain, stresses the high revenue derived from customs dues on cross-Channel trade, which exceeded the likely revenue from tribute exacted under direct rule, once the costs of enforcing that rule are deducted (*Geography* 2.5.8 and 4.5.3).[38] The importance of these passages is that—whether or not Strabo's

34 Sidebotham, Hense, and Nouwens 2008, 42–60. Murray (1925, 150) says 'One gets the impression that the Via Hadriana, circuitous and, in the northern half, waterless, was little used except for local traffic between ports. It was probably planned however as a great trade-road to divert the traffic from all the ports to Antinoe in order to give that artificial foundation a solid commercial basis.'

35 *OGI* 701.

36 Villeneuve 2004; Villeneuve 2009; Villeneuve, Philipps, and Facey 2004; cf. Nappo, this volume (summarising Villeneuve).

37 Duncan-Jones 2006, 4.

38 Strabo 2.5.8: 'And for governmental purposes there would be no advantage in knowing such countries and their inhabitants, and particularly if the people live in islands which are of such a nature that they can neither injure nor benefit us in any way because of their isolation. For although they could have held even Britain, the Romans scorned to do so, because they saw that there was nothing at all to fear from the Britons (for they are not strong enough to cross over and attack us), and that no corresponding advantage was to be gained by taking and holding their country. For it seems that at present more revenue is derived from the duty on their commerce than the tribute could bring in, if we deduct

analysis of why Rome did not occupy Britain in the Augustan period really results from an actual cost-benefit analysis by Augustus and his advisors—they show that Romans were capable of thinking, and that some Romans did think, in terms of such cost-benefit analyses, and that external trade was recognised as producing significant—strategically significant—income for the State via customs revenues.

This can be exemplified, of course, by the well-known second-century 'Muziris' papyrus,[39] which values the cargo of the ship *Hermapollon*, with a cargo from India, at 1,151 talents 5,852 dr. of silver, equivalent to HS 6,911,852.[40] The valuation was made after deduction of the 25 per cent customs dues, implying a valuation before tax of HS 9,215,803, and customs dues equivalent to HS 2,303,951 on this one cargo alone. If there were only one hundred such cargoes per year (almost certainly an underestimate—over one hundred years earlier, Strabo speaks of 120 ships per year leaving Myos Hormos for India), the customs revenues from the *imports* from India alone would amount to some HS 230 million, or one-third of Duncan-Jones' estimate for the total annual cost of the army in the second century.[41] To this must be added the import dues on goods coming from the Arabian Peninsula and the coast of Africa, because of course not all trade up the Red Sea had originated in India, and

---

the expense involved in the maintenance of an army for the purpose of guarding the island and collecting the tribute; and the unprofitableness of an occupation would be still greater in the case of the other islands about Britain.'

4.5.3: 'At present, however, some of the chieftains there, after procuring the friendship of Caesar Augustus by sending embassies and by paying court to him, have not only dedicated offerings in the Capitol, but have also managed to make the whole of the island virtually Roman property. Further, they submit so easily to heavy duties, both on the exports from there to Celtica and on the imports from Celtica (these latter are ivory chains and necklaces, and amber-gems and glass vessels and other petty wares of that sort), that there is no need of garrisoning the island; for one legion, at the least, and some cavalry would be required in order to carry off tribute from them, and the expense of the army would offset the tribute-money; in fact, the duties must necessarily be lessened if tribute is imposed, and, at the same time, dangers be encountered, if force is applied.' (trans. Jones LCL 1917)

39 De Romanis 1998; De Romanis 2010/1 [2012]; and this volume; Rathbone 2001; Morelli 2011.

40 Accepting the most recent reading of Morelli (2011, 214), followed by De Romanis (2012; and this volume). The reading of the *editio princeps* was 1,154 talents 2,852 dr. of silver, or HS 6,926,852.

41 Duncan-Jones 1994, 36 (Table 3.3: 643–704 million sesterces). Sidebotham's calculations (2011, 217–8) imply a much higher figure still, as he multiplies up the potential total value of the *Hermapollon*'s cargo on the basis that the itemised cargo in the Muziris papyrus may have formed only a small fraction of the ship's total cargo capacity.

the export customs dues on goods leaving Egypt for Arabia, the African coast, and India, and also the customs dues on onwards transport of many of these goods from Alexandria to other provinces (usually at 2.5 per cent). It looks as if the total State revenue for the empire may have been significantly underestimated by not taking due account of the revenues from trade, especially Indo-Mediterranean trade. This has wider implications for current debates over the size of Roman GDP and the proportion of that GDP captured by the State in taxation, and the proportion of the State's income expended on the army. It makes it much easier, for example, to understand the State's ability during the first to early third centuries CE to fund large-scale infrastructure and civic building projects to a level not matched again until the rise of nation states in nineteenth-century Europe.[42] The size of State revenues from customs taxation also suggests that the fiscal importance of trade in the Roman economy has been rather overlooked.[43]

As Dominic Rathbone has noted, the phrasing in the Muziris papyrus loan contract (on the recto) to the effect that if the merchant does not repay the loan, the financier is entitled 'to possess and own the aforesaid security and pay the quarter-tax, to convey the [three] parts which will be left where you choose and to sell or use them as security' shows that the State levied the *tetarte* (quarter-tax) in kind,[44] presumably because the value of the goods was so high that the merchants would have had difficulty in paying the tax in cash before they had sold the cargo. This left the State with the problem of selling the goods, which at a quarter of all the imports via the Red Sea must have made the State the largest single dealer in luxury goods in the dockside markets of Alexandria. No wonder, then, that the Muziris papyrus (recto, line 8) refers to the 'warehouse for receiving the quarter-tax at Alexandria'. The State had its own warehouse for the goods levied in kind as customs dues, which it must have sold to realise the dues in cash. This interpretation is supported by Pliny's information (*HN* 12.123) that 'balm-resin auctioned by the *fiscus* for 300 den. per sextarius is resold [by private traders] for 1,000 den.'—he may

42 See the debate between Scheidel 2009b and Wilson 2009.

43 Morley's otherwise excellent survey of trade in the ancient world (2007), although it mentions customs revenues in passing, makes no attempt to engage with the question of how important revenues from trade really were to the Roman State.

44 Rathbone 2000, 43. In the scenario envisaged, the lender is to pay the quarter-tax in kind and convey the three-quarters (of the original cargo) which will be left to wherever he wishes to sell them.

even be referring to auctions at Alexandria, rather than at Rome, although he is not explicit on the point.[45]

The involvement of the Roman State in the resale of commodities, albeit in a different context, is also suggested by the only plausible interpretation of the large amphora dump in Rome known at Monte Testaccio: it consists entirely of deliberately smashed olive oil amphorae, the great majority of which are Dressel 20-type amphorae from Baetica bearing a series of inscribed information or *tituli picti* which include details of the estate of origin, the name of the merchant conveying the consignment, and control marks recording the weight of the amphora and its contents. The extent of bureaucratic information (which is also different in nature from that found on amphorae containing wine or fish products), combined with the centralised discard, indicates that the State was importing vast quantities of olive oil to Rome, and since the evidence goes back a long way before the inclusion of olive oil in the *annona*, the State must have been reselling the oil, presumably as part of an operation aimed at guaranteeing the effective supply of olive oil to the city of Rome in sufficient quantities to avoid sharp price rises that might precipitate unrest among the urban populace.[46] A similar scheme for the State to resell Italian wine at controlled prices from the porticoes in the Temple of the Sun at Rome may have been introduced by Aurelian.[47]

Presumably therefore the State (or its agents) sold the quarter-tax goods in the dockside emporium at Alexandria, probably at auction, enabling it to benefit from the market prices at Alexandria while ensuring that private merchants and not the State bore the transport costs and risk of getting it there from the Red Sea coast; this was why the tax was not levied directly on entry to Egypt at Berenice or Myos Hormos. And of course, since a large proportion of such eastern luxury imports were re-exported from Egypt to other Mediterranean markets, the State will have benefited again from—usually—a 2.5 per cent customs tax on such inter-provincial transfers.[48] Presumably the sale of the goods levied as tax was managed by the arabarchs (or alabarchs), but we do not know whether they simply administered the operation, passing all profits to the State, or whether the contract for the quarter-tax was farmed to the

45 Ibid. 48.

46 For this argument, see Wilson 2008, 187–188.

47 SHA *Aurel.* 48.1–4; State-organised stocking of wine in the Temple of the Sun corroborated by *CIL* 6.1785 = 31931 (cf. Rougé 1957).

48 Duncan-Jones 2006, 4, noting that in some regions customs dues of 2% or 5% were payable, rather than 2.5%.

arabarchs, as seems to have been the case for the 25 per cent tax in Syria.[49] Annius Plocamus is said by Pliny to have bought from the *fiscus* the *vectigal* of the Red Sea trade, which is probably but not certainly the quarter-tax, in or before the reign of Claudius.[50] If the quarter-tax was farmed, the State would have been assured of a predictable and very sizeable income, and there would have been great scope for the arabarchs as individuals to make large profits. Certainly Alexander Lysimachus, arabarch in the reign of Tiberius, brother of Philo and father of Tiberius Julius Alexander (who became prefect of Egypt), was a man of extraordinary wealth; among other things, he loaned Cypros, the wife of Herod the Great's grandson Agrippa, 200,000 drachmas, and covered the nine gates of the Temple in Jerusalem with silver and gold.[51] His other son, M. Iulius Alexander, is attested on ostraca from the Nikanor archive as being involved in private trading activities at Berenice between 37 and 43/44 CE.[52]

Apart from the considerable financial profit from customs dues, there were other reasons for the State's interest in supporting and sustaining this luxury trade with India via the Red Sea. The moment at which the State gave up the fight against controlling luxury may be relevant here (Tac., *Ann.* 3.52–55). In 22 CE, the aediles at Rome reported that sumptuary laws were being ignored, and utility prices in markets were rising. The Senate wrote to Tiberius (in Campania) asking for renewed sumptuary measures; he replied that he would not do this, because:

1) Many other aspects of luxury are not controlled—the size of villas, the size of slave households, gold and silver plate, bronze statues and paintings, male and female clothing, and 'the feminine speciality—that for the sake of precious gems our currency is transferred to foreign or hostile peoples';
2) Such laws may create more problems than they solve, by being perceived as tyrannical;
3) The real concern to the State is not table luxuries, but supplying Rome with grain.

49 *IGLS* 17.1.196 is an inscription from Palmyra mentioning a councillor of Antioch who was responsible for the collection of the 25% tax; contrary to Young's opinion (2001, 149), this does not imply that the tax was *collected* at Antioch, since trade via Palmyra could easily be routed onwards to other destinations in Syria.

50 Plin., *HN* 6.84; Raschke 1978, 644 and 848, nn. 808, 811; Sidebotham 1986a, 32–33; Young 2001, 69. Cf. Schörle, this volume.

51 Joseph *BJ* 5.205; *AJ* 18.159–160; 20.100; Turner 1954, 54; Evans 1995; cf. Raschke 1978, 644 and 848, nn. 804–807.

52 Turner 1954, 59; Raschke 1978, 644 and 848, n. 805.

Wallace-Hadrill has suggested that behind this latter point may have lain the thinking that much grain came from Egypt, which was also the source of many luxury goods that provided profit for the grain traders.[53] In other words, facilitating the eastern luxury trade was an indirect way of ensuring the grain supply to Rome by incentivising the participation of private shippers in *annona* transport.

Aside from State interest in the trade at this level, Alan Bowman has argued that the imperial house was directly involved in the trade between Egypt and India, and points to attestations of the *familia Caesaris* involved in Indo-Roman trade.[54] Eivind Seland's analysis of donations of eastern spices and incense from estates in Egypt to Churches in Rome traces some of these back to imperial domains,[55] which may again suggest an involvement of the imperial house, via its estates, in the spice and incense trade with India and Arabia via the Red Sea.

The State's interest in customs revenues from the external trade with Arabia and India explains not only the creation and maintenance of the Eastern Desert routes and their water and fortification infrastructure, but also the shift from the Edfu–Berenice route to the longer Coptos–Berenice route in the early Roman period, which, as Sidebotham and Zitterkopf noted, initially seems somewhat puzzling.[56] Since the extraction of customs duties involved the goods being transported across the Eastern Desert to bonded warehouses at Coptos before being conveyed down the Nile under seal to State warehouses at Alexandria, the shift from Edfu to Coptos as the Nile terminus of the route from Berenice enabled the concentration of State resources in forts and a single customs control point on the Nile at Coptos—which of course also served the Myos Hormos road. This explanation is really an extension of the argument already advanced by Sidebotham and Young, that one of the purposes of the military presence at the forts along the routes between the Nile and the Red Sea was to control and funnel the caravan traffic along these routes to ensure that they did not evade taxation by slipping past the customs checkpoint at Coptos.[57]

It has been argued, however, that at some point the quarter-tax on external trade was reduced to a one-eighth tax (12.5 per cent), the *octava*. This is supposed to have happened after 174 CE, when the *tetarte* is still attested at

53 Wallace-Hadrill 2008, 331–2.
54 Bowman 2010.
55 Seland 2012.
56 Sidebotham and Zitterkopf 1996, 452.
57 Sidebotham 1986a, 62–3; Young 2001, 72–4.

Palmyra, and probably by 227 CE, when a *vectigal octavarum* is mentioned in a law of Severus Alexander.[58] There is some uncertainty though as to whether this is the same *octava* which had become generally applicable as tax on trade in the east by 366 CE, when it is mentioned in the Codex Theodosianus.[59] It has been generally assumed that this fourth-century *octava* was a tax on imports into the empire, and that it replaced the *tetarte*,[60] but the Codex Theodosianus does not actually say this; indeed the context seems to imply that it was a general tax on trade. *If* the eastern trade was so important to the Roman State, why halve the customs dues on imports across the frontier, especially at a time of intense fiscal pressure, when gold and silver production from the mines in Iberia had declined, the population and therefore the tax base had been reduced by the Antonine plague, and the Severan dynasty was increasing military pay to retain army loyalty? If indeed the *tetarte* was replaced by the *octava*, which is not at all certain, then the most reasonable explanation would be that the reduction was an acknowledgement by the State of its inability to maintain previous levels of protection for shipping and caravans—this would have been a measure intended to compensate traders for increased transaction costs along these routes.

Irrespective of whether the customs rates really were halved in the late Roman period, it does appear that, while until the late third century the Roman State attempted to protect and secure the Eastern Desert routes, from the third century onwards the State had increasing difficulty doing so, and may eventually have abandoned the effort. The ostraca from Krokodilo on the Coptos–Myos Hormos road record occasional hostilities with small groups of Bedouin (*barbaroi*) in the reign of Trajan and at the start of Hadrian's reign—between 108 and 118—in the wake, it seems, of Rome's annexation of the Nabataean kingdom and the reorganisation of the northern Red Sea region.[61] Ostraca

58 *Cod. Iust.* 4.65.7; De Romanis 1998, 51.

59 *Cod. Theod.* 4.13.6 = *Cod. Iust.* 4.61.7 (20 January A.D. 366): IMPPP. VAL(ENTINI)ANUS, VAL(ENS) ET GRAT(IANUS) AAA. AD ARCHELAUM COM(ITEM) ORIENT(IS. Ex) praestatione vectigalium nullius omnino nomine qu(ic)quam minuatur, quin octavas solite constitutas om(ne) hominum genus, quod commerciis voluerit interess(e, de) pendat, nulla super hoc militarium exceptione facien(da). P(RO)P(OSITA) BERYTO IIII K. FEB. POST CONS. VAL(ENTINI)ANI ET VALENTIS AA. CONSS. 'The Emperors Valens, Valentinian and Gratian to Arkelaus, Count of the East. No one shall, under any circumstances, be permitted to pay less than one-eighth in the settlement of duties on merchandise, which is the usual amount fixed for all those who desire to engage in commerce, and no exception should be made in the case of soldiers.'

60 On this question see De Romanis 1998, 48–50, arguing that the *octava* was indeed a customs tax.

61 Cf. Cuvigny 2003c, 356.

from Mons Claudianus, farther north, contain only one allusion to the Bedouin under Trajan, one in 152/153, and four referring to Bedouin attacks, or the risk of them, in the 180s.[62]

At the end of the second century or the start of the third century, the fort at Maximianon, also on the Coptos–Myos Hormos road, was abandoned, and Myos Hormos likewise seems to have ceased to be occupied on a large scale then; the route from Coptos to Myos Hormos thus ceased to be of importance.[63] The fort at Didymoi on the route to Berenice continued into the 230s though, and a new fort was built at Qusur al-Banat.[64]

The third century evidently saw increased insecurity in the Eastern Desert in the face of incursions by the Blemmyes, a desert tribe from the south. By 279/280 the Blemmyes had taken Coptos, from where Probus then drove them out (SHA *Prob.* 17.2.3; Zos. 1.71.1). They must have taken it again, since Diocletian recaptured it from them in 296. We do not know the chronology of the background to the capture of Coptos, but the abandonment of the route to Myos Hormos and the concentration of resources on the Berenice–Coptos route may well be an indication that these routes had become unsafe well before 279. We hear of further Blemmye raids on the Eastern Desert in the fourth and fifth centuries, and the shift in late Antiquity towards more northerly ports in the Red Sea may, as Federico De Romanis has suggested, be connected with the increasing instability of the desert routes.[65] However, the port of Berenice functioned into the first half of the sixth century,[66] although not necessarily under direct Byzantine control. Sidebotham has suggested that Berenice may have been taken over, like the emerald mines, by the Blemmyes; and if so, it would seem that some accommodation had been reached between the Byzantine Empire and the Blemmyes that allowed a resurgence of trade along the Eastern Desert routes in the fifth and early sixth centuries, as pottery from several of the stations along the Coptos–Berenice road suggests.[67]

Although Berenice continued to function as a port until the sixth century, its role appears to have changed in late Antiquity; by the late fifth century it seems that although there had been some revival in traffic along the Eastern Desert routes, much of the trade was passing through Aila/ʻAqaba and Clysma at the northern end of the Red Sea, avoiding the overland routes. Fifth- and

62 Cuvigny 2003c, 351–2.

63 Brun 2003, 201–2.

64 Ibid.

65 De Romanis 2002 (*non vidi*); cited in Brun 2003, 202.

66 *Martyrium Sancti Arethae* 27, 28, 29; 524/5 CE, as noted by Sidebotham and Wendrich 1999, 456.

67 Sidebotham 1997; Sidebotham, Hense, and Nouwens 2008, 342.

sixth-century sources imply that the main revenue collection for the Indian Ocean trade was now happening in the northern Red Sea, on the island of Iotabê, un-located but probably near the Arabian coast to the south of the mouth of the Gulf of 'Aqaba.[68] In 473 CE the customs collectors (*dekatelogoi*) at Iotabe were evicted by the Saracen Amorkesos, who took over the revenue collection and became rich; a punitive expedition under Romanus twenty-five years later in the reign of Anastasius re-took the island, and installed a Roman merchant community (transhipping goods from India from large vessels into smaller craft that could sail more easily up the Gulf of 'Aqaba) that produced revenue for the emperor.[69] This community may have been Jewish; certainly by 534 CE, under Justinian, Iotabe was occupied by Jews who, according to Procopius, had lived there from of old.[70] Choricius says that it 'served as a port for cargoes from India, the taxes of which were considerable', but that the Jews of Iotabê were depriving the emperor of his income by appropriating taxes on merchandise brought to the island, and that the island was retaken by the *dux* Aratius who entrusted it 'to trusted men who were appointed to levy taxes for the emperor'.[71] An edict of Anastasius (491–518), known from epigraphic fragments, also mentions a *commerciarius* (controller of foreign trade) of Clysma, who evidently exacted customs dues.[72]

This northward shift in emphasis of the receiving points of Indo-Roman trade in late Antiquity may be in part explicable by the increasing difficulty that the Byzantine State was having in securing the desert trade routes between Berenice and Coptos; it was now preferable for shipping to beat its way up the Red Sea, even against the adverse northerly winds, to Clysma and Aila.

To sum up: vast profits were to be made on Indo-Roman trade, and the Roman State took a large cut of these via customs dues. It is striking that the estimates offered above for State revenues from Red Sea trade in the mid second century CE far exceed, for example, the figure of HS 40 million given by Suetonius for the tax revenue from the Tres Galliae after Caesar's conquest of Gaul,[73]

68 Mayerson 1995a.

69 Mayerson 1992; 1996, 122–3.

70 Procop. *Pers.* 1.19.4; Mayerson 1992, 1.

71 Mayerson 1992; 1996, 123–4; Choricius, *Laudatio Aratii et Stephani* 67, ll. 17–19 ed. Foerster and Richtsteig.

72 Sartre 1982, 112, no. 9046 lines 12, 15; cf. commentary at pp. 115–8.

73 Suet., *Iul.* 25, noted also by Young (2001, 210), whose own estimate of HS 10–50 million for the income of the *tetarte* in the Flavian period, derived from Pliny, is much lower than mine for the second century.

or the port revenues from Lycia, given by the *lex portorii* of Lycia as HS 400,000 annually in the reign of Nero.[74] Even allowing for the differences in date between these comparisons, it is striking that the scale of customs revenues from the Red Sea trade appears equivalent to the total combined tax income from several provinces. Recent work has stressed the inadequacy of the concept of a luxury trade (for example, pepper and incense for religious rituals were not conceived of as luxuries);[75] but the argument presented here is that such goods, although destined for a minority of rich consumers, constituted a trade of very considerable value, the customs dues on which were of great interest and importance to the State.

The high level of the 25 per cent tax levied across at least the eastern frontier, and perhaps all frontiers of the Roman Empire in the early principate, and the fact that it applied to exports as well as to imports (not a usual feature of, for example, medieval European customs) are particularly striking features of the Roman Empire's 'tax morphology'.[76] But customs taxation involves an element of game theory; how high a level can the State exact before it inhibits levels of trade to such an extent that its overall revenue might drop, or that the rates of evasion skyrocket? Higher customs dues might be thought more tolerable if there were visible benefits provided by the State; and in the case of the Red Sea trade via Egypt, at least, this is the case. In return, the State equipped desert routes with forts and wells and provided a measure of security along them, and even, for a while in the second century, against piracy in the southern Red Sea; it built roads and even re-dug a canal linking Red Sea ports to markets in Egypt and the Levant. But it appears that the high levels of State predation on trade (via customs dues), and also of State investment to facilitate trade, could not be sustained through the third century in the face of increasing insecurity in the Eastern Desert; the effective result was the abandonment of the overland desert routes between the Nile and the Red Sea, confining trade to the sea routes up to the head of the Red Sea. It is possible, but not certain, that this rerouting of the main trade routes was accompanied by a halving of the customs rates. Only in the Ptolemaic period and to a much greater extent in the Roman period, as a result of State investment, did the routes across the Egyptian Eastern Desert, which were linked also to imperial mines and quarries, play a major and structural part in the Indo-Roman trade networks.

74 Takmer 2007.

75 See Morley 2007, 39–43.

76 The phrase is Nicholas Purcell's: Purcell 2005.

Acknowledgements

I am grateful to Nicholas Purcell, William Harris, Federico De Romanis, Katia Schörle, and Steve Sidebotham for comments on earlier versions of this paper; and Jean-Pierre Brun and Arietta Papaconstantinou for discussion and bibliographic suggestions. I thank Candace Rice for drawing my attention to the *lex portoria* of Lycia. I am especially grateful to Jean-Pierre Brun for providing the maps on which Maps 1 and 2 are based, and to Maxine Anastasi for preparing them.

CHAPTER 2

Trajan's Canal: River Navigation from the Nile to the Red Sea?*

Jean-Jacques Aubert

Commercial contacts between the Indian Ocean and the Mediterranean Sea have followed various land and sea routes over millennia. Since 1869, all ships have gone through the Suez Canal, built by the French after decades of planning and construction. The *c.*160-km long waterway used by steam- or fuel-propelled ships over the last century and a half makes one forget that during most of history the land of Egypt (and other territories in the Near East) constituted a major obstacle on the passage between East and West. Sailing around the African continent was hardly an option in Antiquity and the Middle Ages, and in so far as it was ever chosen, it was a choice made by adventurers rather than traders. Consequently, goods had to be carried overland from the Mediterranean shore to Red Sea harbours or vice versa. The overland journey was shortened thanks to the Nile, which could be accessed through several of its branches.

We also know of various ancient roads running across the Eastern Desert.[1] One of the best-attested ones connects the Red Sea port of Quseyr, currently identified as the ancient Myos Hormos or, possibly, Leukos Limen, with the Nile Valley at Coptos. While this is certainly the shortest of several roads between the Red Sea coast and the Nile Valley, it is more than 150 km long and climbs to nearly 600 m above sea level, in a deserted area poorly provided with water and vulnerable to robbers. Comparatively, the distance from the Mediterranean Sea to the Red Sea, following the course of the modern canal, is hardly longer than the desert road, and it runs through some lowlands rising no more than 20 m above sea level, between Port Saïd in the north, in the

* I am grateful to Profs. W.V. Harris, M. Maiuro, and F. De Romanis for inviting me to participate in the 2011 conference at Columbia University and for commenting on drafts of this paper. I also thank Dr. K. Schörle for comments and additional bibliographical references. This short chapter is meant as an afterthought to my 2004 articles.

1 See Sidebotham 2011, 125–74, esp. 126, Fig. 8.1.

 | DOI 10.1163/9789004289536_004

vicinity of the ancient settlement of Pelusium, and Suez in the south, close to the ancient town of Clysma (near Ptolemaic Arsinoe or Cleopatris).[2]

In Antiquity, eastward-bound cargoes had to be unloaded from Mediterranean ships and reloaded onto riverboats in harbours located near one of the mouths of the Nile,[3] possibly at Alexandria, then shipped upstream to Middle or Upper Egypt, unloaded from the riverboats and loaded onto pack animals (camels, mules, donkeys) or carts for the desert stretch, and then unloaded and reloaded onto oceangoing ships.[4] By comparison, the crossing on land over the Isthmus of Suez would have saved the trip up-river, one transfer, and the uphill-downhill stretch in the Eastern Desert. Logistical supply was also easier to provide because of the proximity of the above-mentioned settlements and others located in the Eastern Delta and the Wadi Tumilat.

The question is why ancient traders would have chosen the more difficult desert road across the hills while an easier albeit longer path was available.[5] This question becomes even more relevant considering the fact that some ancient sources report—or allude to—the existence of a man-made waterway running from the Nile to the Gulf of Suez, known in Roman times as Trajan's Canal. These written sources, epigraphical,[6] literary,[7] and papyrological,[8] are supported by some rather ambiguous archaeological evidence spread over

---

2 For the location of this/these settlement/s, see Mayerson 1995b and 1996; and Cohen 2006, 308; Nappo, in this volume, points out that according to Strabo (16.4.23) Arsinoe/Clysma was the main hub for the Red Sea fleet from the time of Augustus onward. See also Sidebotham 2011, 51 and 178–79.

3 All mouths were not equal in this respect. Cf. map in Bietak 1975, 176, Ab. 43 and in Butzer 1975, 1047, Fig. 2.

4 Such a combination of land- and river-transport for trading purposes between the Mediterranean world and the East is attested in the context of the Nabataean perfume and aromatic trade, as discussed by Terpstra in this volume.

5 This question is discussed in detail by Cooper 2011.

6 Four stelae found *in situ* and set up by Darius (/Xerxes?, *c.*518 BCE) and one by Ptolemy II Philadelphus (*c.*270) commemorate work done on the eastern stretch of the canal. Cf. Aubert 2004a, 225–27, based on previous work by G. Posener. Some of the texts are translated in Cooper 2009, 197.

7 Hdt. 2.158 (*c.*460 BCE) and 4.39; Arist. *Mete.* 1.14 (352b) (*c.*335 BCE); Diod. Sic. 1.33.8–12 (*c.*60 BCE) and 3.43–44; Strabo 1.2.31; 16.4.23; and 17.1.25–26 (*c.*24 BCE–24 CE); Plin., *HN* 6.165–167 (mid first c.); Ptol., *Geog.* 4.5.54 (mid. second c.); Lucian, *Alex.* 44 (*c.*180 CE); Egeria, *Peregrinatio* 1.7–8 (381–384); Gregory of Tours, *Hist. Francorum* 1.10 (*c.*575); Dicuil, *Liber de mensura orbis terrae* 6.12–20 (late eighth/early ninth c.); El-Maqrizi 202–3 (1364–1442).

8 *SB* VI 9545.32 = Ostracon, in W. Müller, *APF* 16 (1956) 211–12, no. 32 (Thebes, Memnonia?, 112 CE); *O.Marb.priv.* (Thebes, Memnonia? 112) = Jördens 2007, 478–80; *O.Cair. GPW* 99 (Thebes, Memnonia? 112) = P. Heilporn in Jördens 2007, 480–82; possibly some Elephantine ostraca

a long period of time,[9] namely from the late sixth century BCE to the early Middle Ages. The purpose of this paper is to examine and answer this specific question.

Trajan's Canal or *Traianos Potamos/Diôrux*, as it is known in Ptolemy's *Geography* (4.5.54) and a handful of Greek papyri, ran from Babylon/Memphis—or Phakoussa, further down the Pelusiac branch—to the Gulf of Suez, near the city of Arsinoe/Cleopatris/Clysma.[10] The partly man-made (at times demonstrably navigable) canal followed an ancient branch of the Nile running through the Wadi Tumilat, and along—rather than through—Lake Timsah and the Bitter Lakes. The name refers to the work commissioned by the emperor Trajan (98–117 CE) to reopen an existing (though silted up) channel, or to modify its path in its western section, or both. The project was financed by a special tax, seemingly levied on an exceptional basis, in Upper Egypt (and possibly elsewhere), as shown by a few receipts on ostraca found in the vicinity of Thebes and dated to September 112. Scarce papyrological evidence from the third to the eighth century CE suggests that maintenance work was at times carried out by liturgists (*tektones*) or contractors (*potamitai*). Papyri and ostraca strongly suggest that throughout its existence the project initiated by Trajan was of more than local importance, since taxes were levied in, and liturgists summoned from, various areas of Egypt, at times quite removed from the Eastern Delta. In Trajan's time, the canal may have been considered of more strategic than commercial importance, in view of the emperor's planned campaign against Arabia and Persia.

As was said before, Trajan's Canal was not a new project, in spite of its occasional name (*kainos potamos*). The ancient tradition, based on Herodotus and

---

(*O.Wilck.* 89–92; *O.Bodl.* II 871; *O.Eleph.* DAIK 18–19, all in 114) = R. Duttenhöfer in Jördens 2007, 483–85; *P.Oxy.* LX 4070 (Arabia 208); *P.Bub.* 4.69.2 (Boubastis 221); *P.Cair. Isid.* 81 (Karanis 297); *P.Oxy.* XII 1426 (Oxy. 332); *P.Oxy.* LV 3814 (Oxy. III/IV); *PSI* I 87 (Oxy. 29.6.423); *PSI* VI 689 (Oxy. 420/1–423); *P.Wash.Univ.* 7 (Oxy. V/VI); *P.Lond.* IV 1346 (Aphrodito 710); *P.Lond.* IV 1465 descr. (Aphrodito 710?).

9 First and foremost, the multi-volume *Description de l'Egypte ou Recueil des observations et des recherches qui ont été faites en Egypte pendant l'expédition de l'armée française* (Jomard E.-F. (ed.), Paris 1809–1928). Modern work is represented by Bruyère 1966; Bietak 1975; Holladay 1982 and 1999ab; Redmount 1989 and 1995; Sonnabend 1999; and Cooper 2009.

10 The scholarly literature on the subject is growing: Posener 1938; Calderini 1940; Sijpesteijn 1963; Oertel 1964; Tuplin 1991; Redmount 1995; Mayerson 1996; De Romanis 2002; Aubert 2004a, 2004b, and 2013; Jördens 2007 and 2009; Trombley 2009, with a translation of documents from the Arabic period; Cooper 2009, with an interesting study of the landscape and archaeological remains of the canal in the Eastern Delta; and Sidebotham 2011, 179–82.

expanded by Aristotle, Diodorus Siculus, Strabo, and Pliny the Elder, reports that the canal was originally designed by the Egyptian Pharaoh Necho II (610–594 BCE) in the late seventh/early sixth century BCE—not by Sesostris in the early second millennium BCE—and completed by the Persian king Darius I (521–486 BCE). The claim that it was started two and a half centuries later by Ptolemy II Philadelphus (285–246) is misleading. These literary reports are supported by a series of sixth- and third-century BCE multilingual inscriptions found *in situ* along the eastern section of the canal, where heavy work (locks, sluices, *diaphragmata*) had to be done to restore, or supplement, the ancient waterway.

If in the early history of the canal civil engineering seems to have been restricted to the easternmost section, east of the Wadi Tumilat, maintenance, remodelling, and extension in the Ptolemaic, Roman, and mostly late antique period took place in the western part. Provided that ancient authors and the drafters of papyrological documents had a precise and accurate knowledge of the area, it seems that the western end of the canal was repeatedly redesigned in its relationship with the Pelusiac branch of the Nile.

A key to understanding the making of the canal lies in the geological and hydrological structure of the Eastern Delta.[11] In a distant past the Nile had an 'eighth' branch flowing down into the Gulf of Suez, through the Wadi Tumilat and the Bitter Lakes. This branch may even have been navigable in case of high—not to say exceptional—flood. The rapidly changing geological and hydrological conditions of the Nile Delta, due to the accumulation of alluvial deposits and the proximity of the juncture of continental plates in the Suez area, suggest that the outflowing of the Nile water all the way into the Red Sea must have become increasingly rare. This natural development also affected other branches of the Nile to the west, such as the Pelusiac branch. Riverboats may have used it travelling upstream from the Mediterranean during the first millennium BCE. As the Pelusiac branch progressively dried up in the Hellenistic period, the eighth branch had to be reached further south, through another branch running further west, such as the Sebennitic or the Bolbitine branch.

At this point, let us focus on the situation in the Roman period. Numerous modern historians claim that, on the basis of the existing written evidence, from Pharaonic, Persian, or Ptolemaic times down to the Arab conquest, or at least for extended periods within these limits, ships loaded with goods and

11 Posener 1938; and Aubert 2004a, 241–44.

people travelled on a regular basis from the Mediterranean to the Red Sea.[12] Such a practice would have stopped only when the canal was intentionally filled up in 767/8 by the Abassid Caliph Abou Jaafar Al-Mansour, according to the later writer El Maqrizi (1364–1442) in his fifteenth-century *Topographical and Historical Description of Egypt*. As a matter of fact, there is only one piece of written evidence that supports this view, a passage in the short story *Alexander or the False Prophet* (ch. 44) by Lucian of Samosata, dated to 180 CE: 'The young man cruised up (ἀναπλεύσας ὁ νεανίσκος εἰς Αἴγυπτον) the Nile as far as Clysma, and as a vessel was just putting to sea, was induced to join others in a voyage to India.'[13] Interestingly, the young man was thought to have died during the boat trip on the Nile or at the hands of bandits (*lestai*), a common plague in those days. The nature of the source, a fictional narrative by a Greek satirist, lends little credit to the information—similar claims of through-navigation had been made by narcissistic rulers such as Darius I or Ptolemy II Philadelphus, and since they are self-serving, they do not weigh much on the scale of history.[14]

However, the dearth of written evidence might not be convincing enough to discard all possibility that Trajan's Canal was indeed used, at times, for river navigation in the context of long-distance trade. At this point I would like to introduce two arguments. One is based on the evidence of the 'Muziris' papyrus, the other on the respective schedules of river and sea navigation. The combination of the two will lead to the consideration of an alternative scenario that should be checked against the known archaeological record of the Isthmus area.

The Muziris papyrus contains on one side the terms of a financial arrangement between a trader and a businessman for the transport by camels of luxury goods from an unspecified Red Sea port, be it Myos Hormos, Leukos Limen, Berenice, or any other one, to Coptos:

> And I will weigh and give to your cameleer another twenty talents for loading up for the road inland to Coptos, and I will convey [sc. the goods] inland through the desert under guard and under security to the public warehouse for receiving revenues at Coptos, and I will place [them]

---

12 For instance: Raschke 1978; Sidebotham 1986a; De Romanis 1996; Young 2001. Sidebotham 2011, 179–82, esp. 181, is somewhat more cautious.

13 Trans. by A.M. Harmon, LCL 1936.

14 Sidebotham 2011, 51 rightly sees Ptolemy's claim in the Pithome stele to have imported elephants through the Eastern canal as 'a onetime public-relation stunt.'

> under your ownership and seal, or of your agents or whoever of them is present, until loading [them] aboard at the river, and I will load [them] aboard at the required time on the river on a boat that is sound, and I will convey [them] downstream to the warehouse that receives the duty of one-fourth at Alexandria and I will similarly place [them] under your ownership and seal or of your agents, assuming all expenditures for the future from now to the payment of one-fourth—the charges for the conveyance through the desert and the charges of the boatmen and for my part of the other expenses.[15]

The document is dated, on palaeographical grounds, in the mid second century CE, slightly earlier than Lucian's text quoted before. In addition, it is probably less than half a century later than Trajan's alleged major makeover of the canal (*c.*112 or within a few years after). The westbound cargo is made up of nard, garments, and ivory—all very expensive items likely to attract bandits. The arrangement alludes to security and existing accommodation along the road. There can be no doubt, then, that at the very time when the newly restored canal could have offered an interesting alternative route for the kind of commodities that would benefit from a shorter and safer trip up the Gulf of Suez and across the Eastern Delta by water, goods were transported overland through the Eastern Desert.[16] The argument that goods had to go through Coptos for fiscal reasons is unconvincing, as the administration would have had several decades to equip the Suez area with similar infrastructure, as seems to have been the case in a later period with the Arabarch of Egypt and Augustamnica.[17] Let us note finally that the shipment is westbound, which leaves open the possibility that Trajan's Canal was used concurrently for eastbound shipment, a scenario to be explored further on.

The second argument is based on known conditions of navigation on the Nile, in the Red Sea, and across the Indian Ocean.[18] First, on the Nile: if Trajan's Canal was indeed using stretches of an ancient branch, hydrological conditions were linked with the annual flood, with water rising in July and receding

---

15 *PVindob.* G 40822 = *SB* XVIII 13167, translated by Casson 1990.

16 For some evidence for the transport of pearls through the wadis, see Schörle's contribution in this volume.

17 Cf. Aubert 2004a, 239, n. 68; and Trombley 2009, 109, with reference to M. Sartre, *Inscriptions grecques et latines de la Syrie* XIII.1 (Paris 1982) no. 9046 (about a *kommerkiarios* stationed at Clysma/Augustamnica, under the jurisdiction of the *dux* of Palaestina). See also Mayerson 1996, 123.

18 Cooper 2011.

in November. Assuming that the eastern section of the canal was at all sensitive to hydrological variations, it is likely that it was the last to see the effect of the flood and the first to feel its withdrawal. If the canal was indeed open to navigation throughout, i.e. from one end to the other, riverboats using the canal could not have started before July, possibly late July, and could have carried on only until early November,[19] for an active period of three to three and a half months, which actually would have been more than sufficient since the trip along the canal lasted only a few days. Eastbound goods arriving at Clysma could have been transferred onto large seagoing ships or kept in storage space while waiting for the next ship to come by.[20]

Secondly, in the Red Sea: thanks to Federico De Romanis' seasonal maps,[21] we can visualize how difficult navigation in the Red Sea can be, given the dominant winds and currents at two different periods of the year. In July, both winds and currents seem to favour south-bound navigation for Indian Ocean-bound vessels, at least in the Red Sea if not in the Gulf of Suez. By comparison, in January, when ships would return from India, winds, though not currents (except in the Gulf of Suez), would run opposite to north-bound navigation. At all times, shallow waters and reefs made navigation in the Red Sea problematic at best; it seems that the situation must be even more difficult now than in Antiquity, the Red Sea having since receded to a level some 2.6 m lower than in Roman times.

Thirdly, across the Indian Ocean: ships departing from the Red Sea in July were able to take advantage of the southwest monsoon,[22] which occurs from June through September, while those returning from India with the northeast monsoon, occurring in the fall and early winter, arrived in the Red Sea and, eventually, in the Gulf of Suez at the worst time to sail northward toward

19 The evidence of *P.Lond.* IV 1346 (710 CE) suggests that the canal was expected to be navigable as late as the month of February. Cf. Cooper 2009, 204–5, who cites counter-evidence to the effect that the canal was closed earlier (December). Sidebotham 2011, 181 rightly notes that 'use of the canal would not have been in sync with departure times of ships from the Red Sea ports for destination in India.'

20 It is not certain that seagoing ships rather than flat-bottomed boats were used in the Red Sea, as Nappo (in this volume, ad nn. 28–30) found evidence (*O.Petr.* 279, Myos Hormos, 52 CE) for *liburnae* in the context of the Roman Red Sea fleet. The evidence for big ships involved in the pepper trade from India in the first-third centuries CE is collected by De Romanis (in this volume, ad nn. 26–28, with reference to the *Periplus Maris Erythraei* 56; Philostr., *VA* 3.35; and a graffito from Alagankulam/Tamil Nadu discussed by Tchernia 2011a).

21 De Romanis 1996, 24–27, maps 2–5. See also Cooper 2011.

22 On the history of the discovery of the monsoon by the Greeks, see Plin., *HN* 6.100–106.

Clysma and, in addition, up a more or less dried-up canal. The difficulty and the delay incurred by these unavoidable circumstances may very well have been the decisive factor in keeping the desert road open over the centuries.

If Trajan's Canal were indeed navigable, at least during the flood season (July through November) or part of it (August through October), Indo-Mediterranean trade would have suffered from the imbalance imposed by nature as a result of the lack of synchronization between the flood of the Nile and the respective monsoons. Therefore eastbound trade would have benefited from a navigable canal, while westbound trade would have to have used the desert road. This is what I would call *the one-way scenario*. It deserves some consideration, especially in view of the fact that eastbound goods were of a different nature than westbound goods. If the Mediterranean world exported wine, cereal, and metal, in coins or bullion, in exchange for spices, perfumes, and slaves, it can be argued that eastbound cargoes were more bulky than their westbound counterparts. I believe such a hypothesis to be fallacious, just as a pound of feather is no lighter than a pound of lead. If the one-way scenario is adopted, we have to imagine what the return cargo would have been on either route. The answer comes easier for the desert road: pack animals may have brought back food supply, especially grain, to the Red Sea ports.[23] I have no suggestion for returning riverboats on Trajan's Canal. Empty riverboats getting back from Clysma to Heliopolis cannot be ruled out, as the price of labour—for that is all it took—was certainly not prohibitive.

However, there are two more arguments against the regular use of Trajan's Canal for commercial river transport from the Mediterranean to the Red Sea, or the one-way scenario. The first is that river maintenance is costly, just like the supplying of the relay-stations along the desert road, and even more so if several desert roads were operational at the same time. Even with the input of liturgists and army personnel, cleaning waterways from silting, building watch-towers and cisterns, operating facilities for food and lodging, and providing security for travellers was probably more than what the thin population of the concerned areas could shoulder. The provincial government must have been eager to cut down on unnecessary expenses and focus on one land route rather than a canal plus one or more land routes.

The second argument against the regular use of Trajan's Canal is that, in so far as we can tell, transiting international trade over several centuries left surprisingly little mark in the Wadi Tumilat and the Isthmus of Suez, either in the

23 See the first century CE Nikanor archive from Coptos, with Ruffing 1993.

area of Clysma/Qulzum,[24] Ismaïlia, or Pithom/Heroonpolis/Tell El-Maskhuta. The passage of massive quantities of valuable goods attracts people and fosters settlement, such as early seventeenth-century New York City experienced to a high degree. However, there are no remains of any significant settlement on the course of the canal or in its immediate vicinity.[25] It is true that further archaeological excavations or surveys could still contradict this observation, although the urban development of the Eastern Delta from Cairo to Ismaïlia in the last century and a half makes major archaeological discoveries somewhat unlikely.

An ancillary argument could be adduced: Trajan's Canal would have had a negative ecological impact, had it been open to navigation throughout. Strong Red Sea tides would have brought salted seawater and possibly sea species into the Wadi Tumilat, at least for that part of the year when the flood was receding, which Aristotle seems to have been well aware of. One could object that sluice gates built by Ptolemy Philadelphus (according to Diodorus Siculus and Strabo) may have prevented such contamination, but they were unlikely to have been 100 per cent efficient.

My conclusion is obvious, but runs against the *communis opinio*, recently reiterated by Andrea Jördens, and to some extent Federico De Romanis, at least for late Antiquity. In my view, Trajan's Canal, just like its forerunners, the canals of Necho, Darius, and Ptolemy, was not in service for any significant period of time, if ever, provided that the term 'canal' was used to designate a navigable through-waterway connecting the Nile Valley with the Red Sea. There is no reason to doubt that some megalomaniac, such as one of the aforementioned rulers, may have entertained the hope of success where others had notoriously failed, but nature was bound to prevail. Some maintenance work was certainly carried out on a recurrent basis and on some parts of the canal, probably in the western part during the Roman period. The Nile kept reaching the Wadi Tumilat, at least during flood season. This phenomenon is accidentally attested by the pilgrim Egeria passing through in the 380s. It is likely,

24 Nappo (in this volume, ad n. 48, with reference to Ward 2007) sees a different picture, which I fail to recognize. See Mayerson 1996, esp. 123, whose overall conclusion I fully embrace.

25 Mayerson 1996, esp. 124–26, rightly underlines the relative importance of Clysma in late Antiquity and early Byzantine period in the context of religious tourism/pilgrimage mostly using land-roads from the eastern Delta toward the Sinai, Medina, and Mecca, through the fort/port of Clysma. Sidebotham 2011, 178–79 about the dearth of archaeological evidence for 'international connections' and the prospect of further surveys and excavations in the area.

but not proven, that this truncated branch of the Nile served mainly for the purpose of irrigation and fresh-water supply, and for local transportation. If long-distance trade indeed passed through the region, it must have been overland, on a north-south rather than east-west axis. Just as today the fresh-water canal built by the French before the construction of the modern Suez canal contributes to the agricultural development of the Eastern Delta, Trajan's Canal should be counted as one more example of that emperor's concern for water-management.[26]

26 This interpretation does not necessarily contradict Nappo's contention (in this volume) that Trajan's canal could be part of a larger eastern policy, with far-reaching military, administrative (including fiscal, I may add), and economic purposes.

CHAPTER 3

Pearls, Power, and Profit: Mercantile Networks and Economic Considerations of the Pearl Trade in the Roman Empire

Katia Schörle

Introduction

In the second half of the first century BCE, the end of the Civil Wars and the unification of the Mediterranean under more or less direct Roman State control brought security and enabled greater capital investments and profits to be made. A general increase in wealth combined with a rise in the demand for luxury goods can be seen as the catalyst behind Rome's involvement in the Indian Ocean trade. This upsurge of wealth is noticeable in the appearance of luxury goods in archaeological contexts, for instance in mosaics such as that from a household in *Insula VI.15.14* in Pompeii depicting a matron wearing a gold and pearl necklace and pearl earrings.[1] Luxury and Eastern goods also became intricately woven into the fabric of the early imperial literature and poetic writings of the Golden Age, particularly in love elegies.[2]

The trade with India and the East relied on substantial organisation and far-reaching and complex networks of exchange. The imported goods fetched considerable prices, engendering substantial profits for the willing, those who were capable of investing in the lucrative but also highly risky Indo-Roman trade. Both individuals and the State benefitted substantially from it—despite claims to the contrary in the literature.[3] To begin with, I will contextualise the pearl trade and look at the origins of pearls and the mechanisms of trade and

1 For finds in Pompeii and Herculaneum: Siviero 1954, esp. cat. 271 (forty-eight examples of these two pearl earring types were found); cat. n. 283 and colour plate 189 for a *crotalum*-type pearl earring (earrings with a bundle of pearls) from the House of Menander in Pompeii. Museo Nazionale, Naples, inv. 124666 for the mosaic of the matron with pearls. For a history of pearl fishing in the Classsical World, Donkin 1998, 80–104; finds in archaeological contexts, Donkin 1998, 90–91.

2 E.g., Prop. 1.8 boasts of having managed to convince Cynthia to stay with him due to his verses rather than gold or pearls from India.

3 Plin., *HN* 12.83–84: 'But it is the sea of Arabia that has even a still greater right to be called "happy," for it is this that furnishes us with pearls. At the very lowest computation, India, the

 DOI 10.1163/9789004289536_005

production (whether real or fake) within the empire, and ultimately identify those who were involved, whether the State or the merchants and families who organized the trade. As we will see, vertical integration (the absorption of various phases of production and/or distribution of a product) was a recurrent market strategy in the Roman world.[4] The general role of the State in setting up and maintaining the infrastructure in the Eastern Desert[5] is an important element for the development of the pearl trade. This is in contrast to trade with the East via Palmyra, where the local infrastructure consisted of a communal organization of goods into caravans. This trade route however benefitted from the presence of Palmyrene communities along the Euphrates and in the Persian Gulf, notably on the island of Bahrain.[6]

Pearls: Origins of the Trade

The origins of the trade in pearls, the quintessential luxury from the Indian Ocean and the East, date from well before the Roman period. A growing number of pearls found in Neolithic sites across the Arabian Peninsula suggest an early pearl-fishing tradition in the Persian Gulf. Currently, the oldest known find of a pearl in an archaeological context comes from the Persian Gulf (Umm el Quwain), and is radiocarbon dated to 5547–5477, 5410–5235 BCE.[7] Excavations at a pavilion in the royal garden at Pasargadae in southern Iran dating from the second half of the sixth century BCE revealed a cache with 244 pearls, the largest pearl measuring just under 1 cm across.[8] Pearls were imported from India, Sri Lanka, or the Persian Gulf; the awareness of the pearl in the Mediterranean basin is said to have begun at the end of the fourth century BCE, in the Hellenistic period, with Alexander the Great's conquest of the East and travels into India.[9] The early find of a pearl oyster shell (*pinctada*

Seres, and the Arabian Peninsula, withdraw from our empire one hundred millions of sesterces every year—so dearly do we pay for our luxury and our women.'

4 See Brockaert 2012 and Silver 2009 on the issue.

5 See Wilson, this volume.

6 Young 2001, 139–148, esp. 144.

7 Charpentier et al. 2012.

8 Ogden 1996, 37; Stronach 1965, pl. XIVh.

9 Ogden 1996, 37. They are mentioned in the accounts of Androsthenes of Thasos, who accompanied Nearchus, commander of Alexander's fleet, along the coast from Indus to Tigris, and Chares of Mytilene (Alexander's chamberlain) also mentions pearls found in oysters in the Indian Ocean and the Black Sea, Persian Gulf, and Arabian Gulf. (Ath., *Deipn.* 3.93).

margaritifera) in a tomb at Amathous, Cyprus (600–475 BCE), and the gradual appearance of the shell from the early Hellenistic period onwards on Cyprus, also testifies to the introduction of pearl oyster shells as objects of trade in the Mediterranean.[10]

Nevertheless, no pictorial representations of pearls are known before the Roman period. It has previously been suggested that the earliest pictorial evidence may be deduced from a wall painting in the tomb of Petosiris in Tuna el Gebel (Hermopolis Magna, Middle Egypt) from the end of the fourth century BCE, which depicts a bag full of what the author understood to be pearls examined with care.[11] Unfortunately both the colour (red) and the context make it clear that these are red bays being prepared for making perfume,[12] and not pearls. The first pictorial representations of pearls are therefore from the Roman period, whether from Pompeii, as mentioned earlier, from funerary scenes in the Fayum Portraits, or on the famous tondo of the Severans in Berlin.

Overall, the trend would seem to indicate a gradual increase in the use and trade in pearls: the novelty of pearls is particularly well reflected in poetry, and becomes a necessary reference in love elegies.[13] In the first century BCE, pearls were still considered products of considerable worth. The literary trope concerning the disapproval of their popularity develops over time; Pliny's comment that Cleopatra drank pearls dissolved in vinegar is meant to arouse feelings of disgust for her, given the cost of a single pearl;[14] Seneca complains that women wear the value of two or three estates on each earlobe. And Caligula's wife Lollia Paulina was criticized for appearing at a banquet covered with emeralds and pearls valued at 40 million sesterces and carrying the papers of ownership of the jewels—presumably to show off.[15] These texts, however, are generally not concerned with the trading networks involved in the acquisition of these goods, but with wealth, power, and prestige.

---

10 Michaelides 1995.

11 Ogden 1996, 37–38.

12 Cherpion et al. 2007, 47. To Ogden's credit, no colour prints have previously been published of the wall painting; the article otherwise presents an excellent overview on the pearl in Antiquity.

13 E.g., Varro, *Menippeae* frags. 97, 283; Tib. 2.4; Prop. 1.8; Mart. 8.81. For non-poetic texts, e.g. Cic., *Verr.* 2.4.1, 2.5.146; Vitr., *De arch.* 8, 8.3; Sen., *Ben.* 2.12; Petron., *Sat.* 55, 63, 64; Plin., *HN* 6.89.

14 Plin., *HN* 9.119–121.

15 Sen., *Ben.* 7.9; Plin., *HN* 9.117.

Pearl Imports

Pearls entered the Roman Empire via the eastern Mediterranean, in particular from Egypt and Syria. They came from India and Sri Lanka, but also from the Persian Gulf via Palmyra and Syria: sculptural portraits of Palmyrene women show them wearing jewellery which in all likelihood included pearls.[16] The light weight of pearls, as with silk, made them particularly suitable for long-distance trade across difficult terrains, and a likely source of good profits for merchants. Palmyra's trade monopoly in the east relied on the reach of its mercantile network to the Persian Gulf and its presence on Bahrain as well as in India.[17] Spasinou Charax, a recurrent destination on the Persian Gulf for the Palmyrene caravan trade, may have been a major pearl market for the India trade, leading to the continuation of a pearl market tradition in nearby Ulla during the Sassanid/early Islamic period.[18] The nomination of a Palmyrene as satrap on the island of Bahrain in 131 CE, as well as two other Palmyrenes as archons,[19] presumably further secured mercantile connections. The island was already famed for its pearls by the time of Pliny,[20] and must have been an important pearling centre by then.

Pearls also entered the Roman Empire via the Red Sea—they are recorded in the mid first century CE nautical handbook from Egypt, the *Periplus Maris Erythraei*, as an item that could be found in various ports of India and the Arabian Peninsula. Korkai on the south-eastern tip of India was celebrated for its pearls both in the *Periplus* and in Tamil literature.[21]

Pearl Fishing on the Red Sea

Although pearls typically came from the Indian Ocean, two inscriptions from the Eastern Desert of Egypt mention the pearl industry, giving us crucial information about the origin of *some* pearls much closer to the Mediterranean, namely from within the Roman Empire.[22] Both inscriptions are rock-carved dedications from the mountainous area of the Eastern Desert of Egypt, an

16 Chehade 1987.
17 Young 2001, 123–168.
18 Carter 2005, 144.
19 Gawlikowski 1994, 29.
20 Plin., *HN* 6.148.
21 Casson 1989, 59: 19.22–23, and 226.
22 De Romanis 1996, 161.

important corridor for the Indo-Roman trade and an area exploited for its marble, gems, and precious ores.[23] These inscriptions were located in sanctuaries to the god Pan along *wadis* (dried-up riverbeds) that were used as throughways between the Red Sea and the Nile.

The first document is an inscription from a shrine in the Wadi Semna (a quarrying area to the north of the Myos Hormos–Coptos route), dated to the first of Payni of the year 40 of Caesar (26 May 11 CE); it records the dedication of a shrine to Pan by Publius Juventius Agathopous, freedman of Publius Juventius Rufus, tribune of the III legion and eparch of Berenice, and supervisor of the mines of emerald, peridot, *pearls* (which are obviously not mined), and all the mines and all the quarries of Egypt.[24] The second inscription, very similar to the first, is also from a temple dedicated to the god Pan, located this time in the Wadi Hammamat, an important quarry that produced stone used for imperial portraiture and sculpture, which was continuously used from the Pharaonic period onwards.[25] The inscription records a dedication by the same Publius Juventius Agathopous, and is dated to the reign of Tiberius, 14–37 CE, specifying again that Publius Juventius Rufus was in charge of the mines of emeralds, peridot, *pearls*, and all the mines and all the quarries of Egypt.

The mention of pearls as part of the remit of Publius Juventius Rufus, along with mines and all the marble and gem quarries, may at first seem odd, but it is particularly relevant here. We have seen that pearls were usually imported from India and Sri Lanka or from the Persian Gulf, and it has been suggested that no pearls were produced in the Red Sea and that the inscription referred to pearl imports as part of the responsibility of this person.[26] I am not, however, fully satisfied with this answer. Among the various elements of P. Juventius Rufus' remit mentioned in the inscriptions—marble quarries, goldmines, and gems—the clear common denominator is geographic unity, and the inclusion of imported pearls strikes one as odd. The inclusion of peridot, which comes from St. John's Island, is not a problem here: the island was part of the same administrative district as the Eastern Desert. Consequently, the marble, gold, emeralds, and peridot in the inscriptions and all the items invoked make it clear that the eparch's responsibility concerns territorial production, not imports. The alternative proposed by Ogden, that the pearls are mentioned because the official was in charge of both local products and of goods traded

23 Schörle 2008; Sidebotham 2008.

24 *I.Pan*, 121 = *SEG* XX, 670.

25 *I.Ko.Ko.* 41.

26 Ogden 1996, 39. Furthermore, Ogden only mentions the Wadi Semna inscription.

up the Nile,[27] does not seem a viable option. As we know, considerable quantities and varieties of other goods were imported and exported via the Red Sea to and from India and Arabia; that pearls alone would have been singled out from the wide variety of such goods—frankincense, pepper, elephant ivory, gems, and other items—is less than probable, not least of all because goods coming into the Roman Empire via the Red Sea travelled under seal from Berenice to Coptos. The separation of pearls seems unjustifiable, particularly as they are mentioned amongst items that would not be subject to import taxation. A possible tax exemption cannot be envisaged; the *Digest of Justinian* mentions pearls amongst all items subject to the *vectigal*,[28] and we will see that the smuggling of pearls further dismantles this hypothesis.

The twin inscriptions of Publius Juventius Rufus suggest that diving for pearls happened on the Red Sea, and that the State controlled it. Two varieties of pearl-producing oysters from the Red Sea come into consideration: the *pinctada margaritifera* and the *pinctada radiata*. Both species produce pearls, are non-comestible, and are found in Roman contexts at the Roman Red Sea ports of Berenice and Myos Hormos.[29] The shell middens, located at the south-eastern tip of the lagoon that formed the southernmost part of the ancient harbour basin of Berenice, are currently inaccessible due to landmines, but may also contain oyster shells.[30]

In the Persian Gulf, the pearl oysters were gathered and tossed back into the sea. Nineteenth-century Bahraini pearl fleets could be out at sea for several months and go through millions of shells in a season, since ships with twenty to thirty divers could collect up to 8,000 pearl oysters per day, although the scale and market were not necessarily the same in Antiquity.[31] Pearl divers were working from the boat itself: on average, pearl oysters only yield a few small pearls for every five hundred oysters.[32] Ethnographic work by the MARES project on the Farasan Islands (Red Sea), however, suggests that pearl

27 Ibid.

28 *Dig.* 39.4.16.7.

29 Berenice: Van Neer and Erwynck 1998, 355; Van Neer and Erwynck 1999, 434; A gold and pearl earring has also been found on site (Sidebotham 2007, 165); Myos Hormos: Hamilton-Dyer 2011, 272–273; she also notes that the pearl oyster constitutes 28% of finds at Mons Porphyrites, where there was a clear manufacture of objects from it such as dishes and palettes.

30 Personal observation. I am grateful to Ross Thomas, who initially drew my attention to these middens.

31 Strack 2008, 13.

32 Ibid.

divers there preferred to bring the oysters to the shore, leaving middens.[33] So the question of whether shells were thrown out at sea or discarded in Berenice must remain open, but both inscriptions and later pearl-diving traditions suggest that pearl diving did occur in the Roman period.

While Red Sea pearls are now a rarity, the port of Quseir, close to Quseir al Qadim (ancient Myos Hormos), was a centre of pearl-fishing activity in the nineteenth century.[34] The Farasan Islands, as well as the Dahlak Islands, were important pearling centres.[35] Roman presence, in the form of the army, is attested on Farasan in the second century CE,[36] though in this case no direct document testifies to pearl diving, as is so in the Egyptian Red Sea. Fishermen's activities on the Red Sea were apparently tightly regulated, as suggested by a permit granted to Pakubis Ichthyophagos to move his ship from Myos Hormos to Philoteras.[37] It is therefore not surprising, given the worth of pearls, to find that the regulation of diving was a duty of the eparch.

Merchant Connections

The long-distance trade between India and Egypt was dependent on the monsoon winds, which regulated maritime commerce on the Red Sea and the Indian Ocean. The exotic goods that arrived via this route could produce vast sums of money: the second-century CE Muziris papyrus records a loan taken out for one such transaction, representing a portion of cargo worth some seven million sesterces.[38] Even allowing for a several-fold mark-up between India and Egypt, this suggests a trading investment only the wealthiest could afford. Prominent Italian families were therefore involved in the trade, their slaves and freedmen most often accompanying the goods to their final destination. Several families are known through inscriptions found in rock shelters along the main roads crossing the Eastern Desert of Egypt, and they serve as excellent examples of the merger of different market specializations. The Peticii, from the famous wine-producing area of Minturnae in Campania, handled

33 John Cooper. Pers. comm.
34 Ibid. 15.
35 Strack 2008, 15; Ogden 1996, 39; Kuntz and Stevenson 1908, 139, 142.
36 See Nappo, this volume.
37 Thomas 2011, 217–218.
38 Rathbone 2000; other aspects of the papyrus are referred to in the chapters of Wilson, Nappo, Aubert, and De Romanis.

long-distance commerce with North Africa,[39] and were also involved in commerce with India via the Red Sea and the Eastern Desert of Egypt. One of them, Gaius Peticius, is known from a graffito in a sanctuary of Pan in the Wadi Hammamat, on the Coptos–Myos Hormos road to the Red Sea, where the majority of graffiti date between 9 CE and 238 CE. Wine was one of the well-known exports to India; given that we know the Peticii were in the wine business, we can probably assume that Gaius Peticius was exporting wine across the Eastern Desert on the backs of camels—such as those shown on the relief from l'Aquila, which Tchernia has suggested may have belonged to one of the Peticii.[40]

The Annii family was similarly well connected and had considerable interests in the Indian Ocean trade. Annius Plocamus is known as a *publicanus* (tax collector) for the 25 per cent import tax levied at Berenice, while Lysas, his slave, known from a graffito in a cave shelter at Wadi Menih dated to 6 CE,[41] may well be the same Lysas whom Pliny mentions as Plocamus' agent in the tax collection.[42] The family was sufficiently wealthy to build the basilica Anniana in Puteoli; in the last quarter of the second century CE, we hear of a meeting in the *curia basilicae Augusti Annianae*,[43] so the building must be Augustan in date, contemporary with Plocamus. It is likely therefore that the Annii were involved in the luxury trade, and that while their main base was at Puteoli, they also organised themselves in various ports from which they controlled their local business ventures. While Puteoli was Rome's first port for all Eastern Mediterranean goods as well as the largest seaport on the Italian coast in the Augustan period,[44] the Annii were also working from Ostia, the city connected to Rome's harbour at Portus. From the Hadrianic reconstruction phase at Ostia, one thing in particular stands out: the inscription on the façade of the Casa di Annio: *Omnia Felicia Anni*.[45] The owner made his connection with maritime business very clear—underneath the words *Omnia Felicia Anni* are two terracotta plaques, one of which shows a *dolia* ship under sail. The owner

39 Tchernia 1992, 296.
40 Ibid. 298–300.
41 Meredith 1953, 38.
42 Plin., *HN* 6.84; Tchernia 2011b, 62–63.
43 D'Arms 1974, 107–108; Tchernia 2011b, 63; *CIL* X 1782, 1783 and 1786. Some of the Annii from Puteoli are also known from the Sulpicii archives (*TPSulp*. 46, 57, 121).
44 On the Red Sea / Indian Ocean trade and the Nabataean community residing at Puteoli, see Terpstra, this volume.
45 Casa di Annio III, XIV, 4.

of the house was probably Annius Felix, probably a descendant of another Annius Felix attested at Ostia during the Claudian period,[46] when the other Annii were busy with Eastern Mediterranean and Indo-Roman commerce at Puteoli. Whether the two family networks were connected remains unclear.

The Calpurnii also seem to have invested in luxury goods from the Eastern Mediterranean, and their names appear in Naples, at Puteoli, and at Rome. We can associate them with different phases of the niche pearl trade, a strategy usually referred to by economists as 'vertical integration'.[47] Several Calpurnii were involved in maritime trade, as for example L. Calpurnius Capitolinus, to whom traders from Alexandria, Asia Minor, and Syria dedicated a statue in Puteoli, along with one for his brother, C. Calpurnius.[48] (Alexandria and Syria—especially Antioch, where the tax collector of the 25 per cent tax for Palmyra's eastern trade resided[49]—were important entrance points for all eastern goods, including pearls.) Gianfrotta has suggested a possible connection at Ostia with Calpurnia Ptolemais and Calpurnius Ianuarius, whose second-century CE burial on Isola Sacra bears a terracotta plaque with a ship, referring to their maritime activities.[50] *Horrea* and commercial spaces in Ostia would certainly have been ideal selling points for Eastern goods such as pepper, silk, or pearls. Tantalizingly, the Calpurnii were not only working with merchants from the Eastern Mediterranean: the name of Laudanes, slave of Calpurnius Moschas, is also found amongst graffiti carved in the *paneion* in the Wadi Menih in the Eastern Desert of Egypt, on the Coptos–Berenice road. Laudanes was probably supervising the transport of luxury goods, such as the pearls that other members of the same family would have been selling on the Via Sacra in the Roman forum.

In Rome, most pearl sellers known to us were located in the Via Sacra, with a *margaritarius* also attested in the *Velabrum*, perhaps by the Porticus Margaritaria,[51] but Rome (or Ostia) also served as an important centre of redistribution for the empire, though the retail trade from Rome to other cities is also attested through an inscription mentioning a *negotiator margaritarius ab Roma* from Aquileia.[52] Among the eight inscriptions concerning pearl

46 Gianfrotta 2008, 75 and n. 78.

47 As noted above, n. 5.

48 Gianfrotta 2008, 74–75; *CIL* X, 1797; Tchernia 2011b, 64.

49 *AE* 1947, 180.

50 Gianfrotta 2008, 75.

51 Monteix 2013; Papi 2002.

52 *ILS* 7603. I wish to thank Hélène Rougier for pointing this inscription out to me.

sellers from the Via Sacra,[53] there are references to L. Calpurnius Antiochus,[54] L. Calpurnius Nicaei f. Cor. Antiochus, L. Calpurnius Rufus, and L. Calpurnius Strato.[55] The involvement of Laudanes as a direct supplier of goods from India or the Eastern Desert indicates backward integration (integration of the activities preceding the main commercial activity) in order to control the market and prices. Could the reference to the L. Calpurnius Antiochus Nicaeus as a *margaritarius maior* (see note 49) imply some sort of hierarchical organization amongst pearls sellers? His son, L. Calpurnius Nicaei f. Antiochus, himself *margaritarius*, may have begun operating under his father's supervision, along with Calpurnius Rufus and Calpurnius Strato.[56]

In the case of the Calpurnii, the family network or business is attested at every stage of the chain: the Calpurnii and their agents or freedmen are evident from the Wadi Menih on the route to Berenice in the Eastern Desert, through the ports of Naples, Puteoli, and Ostia/Portus, all the way to individual sellers on the Via Sacra in Rome. This suggests vertical integration and a particular investment in the pearl business, although it is likely that this was just one venture within a larger trading and investment portfolio.

Fakes, Emulation, and Smuggling

The Fayum portraits best capture the frenzy for pearls and the spirit of the times, with most portraits showing women adorned with precious gems and pearls dangling from their ears or on their necks. In Egypt and Syria, pearls may have been more accessible to a greater proportion of society than in other provinces, as there were no further transport costs, customs dues, or transaction costs involved. It is therefore not at all surprising that smuggling pearls from these areas into the Roman Empire was common. Pseudo-Quintilian

53 CIL 6.9545–9; 33872; 37804; CIL10.6492.

54 CIL 6.33872: 'L. Calpu[---/Antioch[---/ Maior m[---/ de sacra [---/ vixit a[---. The CIL suggested restorations are: L. Calpu[rnius L.l./Antioch[us Nicaeus?/ maior m[argaritarius/ de sacra [via/ vixit a[---.'

55 CIL 6. 9546: 'L. Calpurnio Nicaei f. Cor. Antiocho/ margaritario de sacra via/ L. Calpurnio L. l. Rufo/ L. Calpurnio L. l. Stratoni/ Calpurnia L. l. Egale patrono suo/ et fratribus suis et sibi fecit.' Only L. Calpurnius Nicaei f. Cor. Antiochus is specified to be *margaritarius*, the activities of his freedmen are not specified, so that they may or may not be involved in pearl trading.

56 CIL 6.33872. Though as remarked by Federico De Romanis, one cannot entirely exclude the possibility that *maior* actually goes with the name to distinguish two homonyms, rather than with *margaritarius*.

presents the judicially complicated case of a woman smuggling pearls, claiming both her feminine right not to be searched by the *scrutatores* and also that the pearls are part of her personal belongings—her *instrumenta itineris*—and therefore not to be considered taxable.[57]

When pearls became an obsession of the wealthy, the desire percolated down through the social strata.[58] Whether the pearls on the Fayum portraits or on the Palmyra sculptures were real or fabricated, these representations nonetheless serve as witnesses to an important social trend. Several Egyptian papyri refer to the many different ways one can create something resembling a pearl using various products.[59] The emergence of an industry of fakes is an indication of the growing fashion for pearls stimulated by the influx from India and the Persian Gulf, and also from the Red Sea coast of Egypt itself.

Conclusion

The trade in Indo-Roman goods presented the opportunity for remarkable profits, but also considerable risks, partly offset by the establishment of social networks, from the Red Sea across the Eastern Mediterranean and towards Rome. Indeed, we can trace vertical integration in the luxury Indo-Roman trade and the involvement of elite Italian families and merchants from Rome through the ports of Italy to the Eastern Desert of Egypt. The growth of the pearl market led to an expansion of the industry; while mainly a commodity from the Indian Ocean and the Persian Gulf, the market was supplemented by Red Sea pearl fishing, which probably resulted in pearls that could be sold for a high price even though they were obtained at a much lower cost. The State wanted to reap profits from pearl diving in the Red Sea so they closely

57 Pseudo-Quintilian, *decl. min.* 359: 'Lis publicani de unionibus. Praeter instrumenta itineris omnes res quadragesimam publicano debeant. Publicano scrutari liceat. Quod quis professus non fuerit, perdat. Matronam ne liceat attingere. Matrona iter faciens cum ad publicanos venisset, uniones habens quadringentos in sinum abdidit. Hos cum requireret publicanus, matrona scrutandi potestatem fecit. Publicanus noluit scrutari. Translatis manum iniecit et suos dicit.' As discussed by Duncan-Jones 2006, 7–8.

58 Plin., *HN* 9.114: 'cupiuntque iam et pauperes, lictorem feminae in publico unionem esse dictitantes.'

59 The Stockholm papyrus (*c.*300 CE) provides recipes for producing fakes. Recipe 18 discusses the elaborate production of a fake from ground mica, wax, eggwhite, and mercury held together by gum tragacanth. In Roman Egypt pearls are often mentioned as *pinna* or *peina*—though one text specifies 'real' pearls (*alethinopeinon*), presumably due to the commonness or popularity of fake pearls. Ogden 1996, 41; Caley 1926.

monitored it, and merchants drastically cut the risk and cost factors by obtaining pearls from Egypt in addition to India. The Indian Ocean trade had a transformative effect, both in the way the State dealt with and sought profit, as demonstrated in its dealings with the pearl trade. In addition, the regions originally at the margins of the empire became motors of production and consumption for this new market—pearls eventually reaching all levels of society—whether as real, smuggled, or artificial items.

Acknowledgments

I would like to thank Rob Carter, John Cooper, and Andrew Wallace-Hadrill, as well as Nick Ray for reading and providing useful comments to this paper. I would also like to thank the editors for saving me from mistakes, and for all their help and patience. All remaining errors are of course, my own. The paper was finished during my fellowship at British School at Rome, generously funded by Ms. Janet Gale and the Portus project, for which I am most grateful.

CHAPTER 4

Roman Policy on the Red Sea in the Second Century CE

Dario Nappo

Trajan in the East

In the summer of 116 CE, the emperor Trajan completed his Parthian campaign and reached Spasinou Charax on the shores of the Persian Gulf; when he arrived, he complained that he was not young enough to attempt the conquest of India, as Alexander the Great had done. At least, this is what Cassius Dio tells us in one of the books of his work, which survives only through the epitome of Xiphilinos:

> Κἀντεῦθεν ἐπ' αὐτὸν τὸν ὠκεανὸν ἐλθών, τήν τε φύσιν αὐτοῦ καταμαθὼν καὶ πλοῖόν τι ἐς Ἰνδίαν πλέον ἰδών, εἶπεν ὅτι 'πάντως ἂν καὶ ἐπὶ τοὺς Ἰνδούς, εἰ νέος ἔτι ἦν, ἐπεραιώθην.' Ἰνδούς τε γὰρ ἐνενόει, καὶ τὰ ἐκείνων πράγματα ἐπολυπραγμόνει, τόν τε Ἀλέξανδρον ἐμακάριζε.[1]

> Then he came to the ocean itself, and when he had learned its nature and had seen a ship sailing to India, he said: 'I should certainly have crossed over to the Indians, too, if I were still young.' For he began to think about the Indians and was curious about their affairs, and he counted Alexander a lucky man.

This anecdote can be viewed as nothing more than the usual rhetorical *topos* of Roman emperors wishing to emulate Alexander the Great; Trajan was by no means the first to be fascinated by the charismatic Macedonian king.[2]

On the other hand, an echo of Dio's text might be found in the much later reports of Eutropius, Festus, and Jordanes[3] (also in Hieronymus, though not addressed in this paper), who explicitly tell us of a fleet in the Red Sea established by the emperor (*in mari Rubro classem instituit*) in order to 'conquer'

1 Cass. Dio 68.29.1. Transl. by E. Cary LCL, 1925.

2 Parker 2008, 223–227.

3 A comparison recently made by Parker 2008, 222. See also Wilson's article in this volume.

 | DOI 10.1163/9789004289536_006

India. If we compare the three accounts it is easy to recognise their great similarity, since they use almost the same words to describe what happened and are likely taken from the same sources.

> [*Traianus*] *usque ad Indiae fines et mare Rubrum accessit atque ibi tres provincias fecit, Armeniam, Assyriam, Mesopotamiam, cum his gentibus, quae Madenam attingunt. Arabiam postea in provinciae formam redegit. In mari Rubro classem instituit, ut per eam Indiae fines vastaret.*[4]

> [Trajan] advanced as far as the boundaries of India, and the Red Sea, where he formed three provinces, Armenia, Assyria, and Mesopotamia, including the tribes which border on Madena. He afterwards, too, reduced Arabia into the form of a province. He also fitted out a fleet for the Red Sea, that he might use it to lay waste the coasts of India.[5]

> *Carduenos, Marcomedos obtinuit, Anthemusiam, optimam Persidis regionem, Seleuciam, Ctesiphontem, Babyloniam accepit ac tenuit, usque ad Indiae fines post Alexandrum accessit. In mare rubro classem instituit. Provincias fecit Armeniam, Mesopotamiam, Assyriam quae inter Tigridem atque Euphraten sita inriguis amnibus instar Aegypti fecundatur.*[6]

> [Trajan] obtained the Carduenians and Marcomedians; received and maintained Anthemusia, Persia's finest region; Seleucia; Ctesiphon; and Babylon; and, after Alexander, even reached the boundaries of India. He established a fleet in the Red Sea. He made Armenia, Assyria, and Mesopotamia into provinces, which, situated between the Tigris and Euphrates, is made equal to Egypt in fecundity by the flooding rivers.[7]

> *Traianus pene omnium imperatorum potior regnavit an. xviii m. vi. Hic enim de Dacis Scythisque triumphavit Hiberosque et Sauromatas, Osroenos, Arabas, Bosforanos, Colchos edomuit, postquam ad feritatem prorupissent. Seleuciam et Ctesifontem Babyloniamque pervasit et tenuit. Nec non et in mari rubro classem, unde Indiae fines vastaret, instituit ibique suam statuam dedicavit.*[8]

---

4 Eutr., *Breviarium* 8.3.

5 Trans. by J.S. Watson.

6 Festus, *Rerum gestarum populi romani* 20.

7 Trans. by Th.M. Banchich and J.A. Meka.

8 Jord., *Romana*, 267–268.

> Trajan, more powerful than almost all emperors, reigned for 18 years and 6 months. For this man triumphed over the Dacians and Scythians and subdued the Iberians and Sauromat, the Osdroni, the Arabs, the Bosphorians, the Colchi after they had erupted into anarchy. He invaded and held Seleucia and Ctesiphon and Babylonia. He also established a fleet in the Red Sea whence he might lay waste to the borderlands of India, and consecrated his own statue there.[9]

These three accounts present what is likely merely imperial propaganda from the time of Trajan, as they try to link the eastern campaigns to the possibility of conquering India, though they *do* provide some concrete evidence for what actually occurred. It is perhaps worth pointing out that the texts from which the above quotes are drawn are all concise chronicles of history, and that the writers dedicate no more than a few lines to each emperor. For this reason, only the most important or characteristic facts are reported. In the case of Trajan, we have seen in the aforementioned texts that the authors chose to report his conquests in Dacia and in the East, and this part is straightforward. Together with this information, they all also state as fact the first-time creation of a fleet in the Red Sea,[10] somehow related to a project to reach the limits of India. This scenario is contradicted, however, by other strong evidence, which I am going to analyse.

Evidence for the Presence of a Fleet in the Red Sea

The presence of a military fleet in the Red Sea during Roman times has been discussed by a number of scholars, so far without much agreement.[11] In principle, it would seem reasonable to imagine that a regular fleet would be stationed in the Red Sea, in order to protect commerce. This seems even more obvious considering that evidence for such an institution already exists for the

---

9 Trans. by B.T. Regan.

10 The exact meaning of the sentence *Mare Rubrum* and its Greek equivalent in the ancient sources is not always clear. The phrase can refer to the present-day Red Sea, or the Persian Gulf, or even the Indian Ocean. The analysis of the evidence presented in this work would suggest that at least for the sources included here, the *Mare Rubrum* is the Red Sea.

11 The first to postulate the presence of the Roman fleet was Rostovzev 1931, 25, followed by Kortenbeutel 1931, 70–71. Opposing opinions were expressed by Kienast 1966, 84; Sidebotham 1986a, 67–71.

Ptolemaic[12] and even for the Pharaonic period.[13] In fact, evidence for the presence of a military fleet in Roman times can be found as early as the Augustan period. Both the emperor himself and his contemporary Greek geographer Strabo tell us the story of a military expedition led by Aelius Gallus, aiming at the conquest of South Arabia. In 25 BCE Gallus set out from Cleopatris (near modern Suez) with an army of ten thousand men, comprising a *legio* plus Nabataean and Jewish *auxiliares*.[14] In his *Res Gestae*, Augustus describes the planning and achievements of the military expedition as follows:

> *Meo iussu et auspicio ducti sunt duo exercitus eodem fere tempore in Aethiopiam et in Arabiam, quae appellatur Eudaemon, maximaeque hostium gentis utriusque copiae caesae sunt in acie et complura oppida capta. In Aethiopiam usque ad oppidum Nabata perventum est, cui proxima est Meroe. In Arabiam usque in fines Sabaeorum processit exercitus ad oppidum Mariba.*[15]
>
> By my order and auspices two armies were led at about the same time into Ethiopia and into that part of Arabia which is called Felix, and the troops of each nation of enemies were slaughtered in battle and many towns captured. They penetrated into Ethiopia all the way to the town Nabata, which is near to Meroe; and into Arabia all the way to the border of the Sabaei, advancing to the town Mariba.

Despite Augustus' triumphalist words,[16] Strabo's account in fact presents the expedition as a failure.[17] He records how the expedition intended to loot Arabia's great treasures and conquer its territory. He then describes the preliminary arrangements for the expedition and explains that a fleet was set up to reach Arabia. It is this part of his account that is the most interesting for the purposes of our analysis:

> Ἐπὶ τούτοις μὲν οὖν ἔστειλε τὴν στρατείαν ὁ Γάλλος. ἐξηπάτησε δ' αὐτὸν ὁ τῶν Ναβαταίων ἐπίτροπος Συλλαῖος, ὑποσχόμενος μὲν ἡγήσεσθαι τὴν ὁδὸν καὶ

12 *OGI* 132 (dated to 130 BCE).
13 Bourdon 1925, 51.
14 Jameson 1968, 76–80.
15 Augustus, *Res Gestae* 26.
16 On the propagandistic relevance of the Arabian expedition, see Jameson 1968; von Wissmann 1976; Sidebotham 1986b; Buschmann 1991; Marek 1993; Potts 1994; Luther 1999.
17 Strabo 16.4.22–24.

χορηγήσειν ἅπαντα καὶ συμπράξειν, ἅπαντα δ' ἐξ ἐπιβουλῆς πράξας, καὶ οὔτε παράπλουν ἀσφαλῆ μηνύων οὔθ' ὁδόν, ἀλλὰ ἀνοδίαις καὶ κυκλοπορίαις καὶ πάντων ἀπόροις χωρίοις ἢ ῥαχίαις ἀλιμένοις παραβάλλων ἢ χοιράδων ὑφάλων μεσταῖς ἢ τεναγώδεσι: πλεῖστον δὲ αἱ πλημμυρίδες ἐλύπουν ἐν τοιούτοις καὶ ταῦτα χωρίοις καὶ αἱ ἀμπώτεις. πρῶτον μὲν δὴ τοῦθ' ἁμάρτημα συνέβη τὸ μακρὰ κατασκευάσασθαι πλοῖα, μηδενὸς ὄντος μηδ' ἐσομένου κατὰ θάλατταν πολέμου. οὐδὲ γὰρ κατὰ γῆν σφόδρα πολεμισταί εἰσιν ἀλλὰ κάπηλοι μᾶλλον οἱ Ἄραβες καὶ ἐμπορικοί, μήτι γε κατὰ θάλατταν: ὁ δ' οὐκ ἔλαττον ὀγδοήκοντα ἐναυπηγήσατο δίκροτα καὶ τριήρεις καὶ φασήλους κατὰ Κλεοπατρίδα τὴν πρὸς τῇ παλαιᾷ διώρυγι τῇ ἀπὸ τοῦ Νείλου. γνοὺς δὲ διεψευσμένος ἐναυπηγήσατο σκευαγωγὰ ἑκατὸν καὶ τριάκοντα, οἷς ἔπλευσεν ἔχων περὶ μυρίους πεζοὺς τῶν ἐκ τῆς Αἰγύπτου Ῥωμαίων καὶ τῶν συμμάχων, ὧν ἦσαν Ἰουδαῖοι μὲν πεντακόσιοι Ναβαταῖοι δὲ χίλιοι μετὰ τοῦ Συλλαίου.[18]

Upon these considerations, therefore, Gallus set out on the expedition; but he was deceived by the Nabataean administrator, Syllaeus, who, although he had promised to be guide on the march and to supply all needs and to co-operate with him, acted treacherously in all things, and pointed out neither a safe voyage along the coast nor a safe journey by land, misguiding him through places that had no roads and by circuitous routes and through regions destitute of everything, or along rocky shores that had no harbours or through waters that were shallow or full of submarine rocks; and particularly in places of that kind the flood-tides, as also the ebb-tides, caused very great distress. Now this was the first mistake of Gallus, to build long boats, since there was no naval war at hand, or even to be expected; for the Arabians are not very good warriors even on land, rather being hucksters and merchants, to say nothing of fighting at sea. But Gallus built not less than eighty boats, biremes and triremes and light boats, at Cleopatris, which is near the old canal which extends from the Nile. But when he realised that he had been thoroughly deceived, he built one hundred and thirty vessels of burden, on which he set sail with about ten thousand infantry, consisting of Romans in Egypt, as also of Roman allies, among whom were five hundred Jews and one thousand Nabataeans under Syllaeus.[19]

---

18 Strabo 16.4.23.

19 Trans. by H.L. Jones LCL, 1930.

Then Strabo continues with a description of how Gallus' troops were betrayed by Syllaeus, and the unsuccessful conclusion of the expedition.[20] Above any consideration of the success or failure of the military campaign,[21] what is more important here is the fact that Strabo's text is the first account of the presence of a Roman military fleet in the Red Sea, an account dating from only a few years after the formal annexation of Egypt to the Roman Empire.

We do not know whether this episode marked the beginning of the regular presence of a military fleet in the Red Sea, or if it was only linked to the military operations in South Arabia, although it has usually been assumed to be the latter. However, a new source of evidence offers proof of the presence of a fleet in the Red Sea soon after the beginning of the following century:[22] two ostraca from the archive of Nikanor report that two Roman fleet officers received provisions in ports on the Egyptian side of the Red Sea.[23]

The first one is the *O. Petr.* 296, dated to 6–50 CE, from either Myos Hormos or Berenice:[24]

> Λούκιος Κλώδιος
> τριηρ̣α̣ρκως (*l.*τριήραρχος) Νικάνορι
> Πανής. Ἀπέχω τούς
> γόμου(ς)
> οὓς επ̣ι̣θ̣ωιμ̣ε (l. ἐπιθῶμεν) σοι
>
> Lucius Clodius / *trierarchos* to Nicanor, / son of Panes. I receive the loads / that we entrusted to you.

20 Other less-detailed accounts on Aelius Gallus' expedition are provided by Plin., *HN* 6. 160–162; Joseph, *AJ* 15. 317; Cass. Dio 53. 29. 3–8. For more on Syllaeus, see Terpstra, this volume.

21 See Sidebotham 1986a, 127–128 for an interesting alternative assessment of the outcome of the Arabian expedition.

22 This hypothesis was put forward for the first time many decades ago by Rostovtzev 1931, 25, on the basis of *O.Petr.* 279, which I am going to discuss below. See also Daris 1956, 244–6.

23 The so-called archive of Nikanor belongs to a firm of transporters active on the routes between Coptos on the Nile and the ports of the Red Sea, namely Myos Hormos and Berenice. This firm operated between 18 BCE and 69 CE at least. Nikanor ran the firm for most of the years it existed, and for this reason the archive is named after him. The documents are published in *O.Petr.* 220–304, *O.Bodl.* 1968–1971, and *O.Brux.* 7. See Rostovtzev 1931, 23–26; Fuks 1951, 207–216; Sidebotham 1986a, 83–92; Ruffing 1993, 1–26; Adams 2007, 221–6.

24 First edition in Tait 1930, 125, n. 296. The text was recently republished with substantial amendments by Messeri (2004–05, 69–73). It is to her edition that I refer in this work.

The reason scholarly discussion has for so long neglected this document is that the word τριηραρκως was in fact fragmentary and has only recently been properly read by G. Messeri.[25] The *trierarchos* was the captain of a trireme, a warship used by the Roman army that was able to host a crew of two hundred.[26] His presence at either Myos Hormos or Berenice strengthens the hypothesis that in the first century CE a military fleet was located in the Red Sea, and that it was connected to international trade.[27]

A second document, from the same dossier as the previous one, adds to this reconstruction. It is *O. Petr.* 279, from Myos Hormos, safely dated to 52 CE. It reads as follows:[28]

> Σατορνῖλος τεσσαράριος λ̣υβέρ-
> νου Ἐπωνύχῳ Ἀχιλλέως χαίρειν.
> ἀπέχω παρὰ σοῦ̣ ἐπὶ Μυὸς Ὅρμου̣
> πυροῦ ἀρτάβας τρεῖς (γίνονται) γ̣. (ἔτους) ιγ Τιβ̣ε̣ρ̣ί-
> ο̣υ Κλαυδίου Καίσαρος Σ̣ε̣β̣α̣σ̣τ̣ο̣ῦ Γερμ̣α̣-
> νικοῦ Αὐτ̣οκρ̣ά̣τ̣ορο̣ς̣ Θὼθ ιθ̣.

> Satornilos *tesserarius liburnae* / to Eponichos, son of Achilleus, greetings. / I receive from you here in Myos Hormos / three artabas of grain. Year 13 of the Caesar / Tiberius Claudius Augustus Germanicus / Imperator, Thoth 19.

Unlike the previous one, this ostracon has already been quoted as possible proof of the existence of a military fleet in the Red Sea, but again, an incorrect reading of the text has affected its interpretation. The original editor has, in fact, read the first line as Σατορνῖλος τεσσαράριος κυβέρνου, i.e., 'Satornilus, tesserarius of helmsman.' The title *tesserarius* can be used either in a military context or in a civilian one.[29] However, the correct restoration of the word λυβέρνου allows us to safely rule out the possibility that he is a civilian. The *liburna*

25 Messeri 2004–05, 69–71.

26 Kießling, *RE* VII A1, 116. *trierarchos*; Casson 1971, 141–147.

27 It is universally accepted by scholars that Myos Hormos and Berenice were, through all of the Roman imperial period, the two most important Roman harbours on the Red Sea, functioning as hubs for trade with India. On Myos Hormos, see Peacock 1993; Cuvigny 2003a; on Berenice, see Sidebotham and Wendrich 1995; Sidebotham and Wendrich 1996; Sidebotham and Wendrich 1998; Sidebotham and Wendrich 1999; Sidebotham and Wendrich 2000; Sidebotham and Wendrich 2007; Sidebotham 2002b.

28 Cf. Messeri 2004–05, 73.

29 See the discussion in Sidebotham 1986a, 69.

was in fact a kind of warship originally used by pirates in the Adriatic Sea and later adopted by the Roman army. Its manoeuvrability, especially in shallow waters, would have made it suitable for operations in the Red Sea.[30] All of this enables us to affirm the *tesserarius* of *O. Petr.* 279 as an officer of the Roman army. He was a watch commander, who organised and held command over the nightly guard assigned to keep watch over the fort when in garrison or on campaign. On a normal day he could be found maintaining the duty and supervising work details or checking on the guard posts.[31]

Thus the two ostraca appear to prove the existence of an established military fleet in the Red Sea waters. It can be noted that, while Strabo points to Arsinoe/Clysma as the main hub for the fleet, the two ostraca from the archive of Nicanor suggest that the fleet was later moved to either Myos Hormos or Berenice (or possibly divided between the two ports), an arrangement that would allow it to patrol the trading area more efficiently.

From what we have seen so far it should be clear that these documents demonstrate that traces of a Roman fleet in the Red Sea can be found from the very beginnings of Roman rule in the area, and that the Roman interest in military control of this area significantly predates Trajan, actually coinciding, at the very least, with the economic boom created by Roman trade with the East under Augustus and Tiberius.[32]

The Role of Trajan in the Roman Red Sea

It should by now be clear that the interpretation of Trajan as the first ruler to set up a fleet in the Red Sea should not be accepted at face value. Therefore, there can be no doubt that the later Roman historians seem to grant Trajan special merit when defining Rome's military attitude toward the Red Sea area. Although they certainly exaggerate his role, this exaggeration must have been linked to the actual policy of the emperor, a policy that seems to have had such an impact that it was still remembered four centuries after Trajan's death, obliterating the memory of the policies of his predecessors. In fact, as I am going to discuss, there is enough evidence to argue that Trajan's campaigns marked the beginning of a new scenario in the Red Sea, and that the path opened by Trajan was most likely consistently pursued by his successors, at least up to Marcus Aurelius.

---

30 Casson 1971, 340; Höckmann 1985; Medas 2004, 129–138.

31 Von Domaszewski 1981; Speidel 2000, 65–96.

32 See Sidebotham 1986a; De Romanis 1996; Young 2001; Tomber 2008.

In order to understand what happened in the Red Sea at the beginning of the second century CE, it is necessary to quickly examine all of Trajan's enterprises in the area. An obvious starting point is the Roman annexation of the client kingdom of Nabatea, as the *provincia Arabia*.[33] Scholars do not yet agree on what led Trajan to annex the kingdom, though many hypotheses have been put forward. Some scholars have suggested that 'the annexation of the Nabataean kingdom was of an administrative nature more than a military one.'[34] This hypothesis tends to identify the death of the last Nabataean king Rebbel II—and the extinction of his dynasty—as the reason for the annexation of the kingdom. Others have suggested that it stemmed from the need to reorganise the region[35] before the forthcoming war against the Parthians.[36] Lastly, some have preferred to focus on the economic factors that might have pushed Trajan to incorporate the Nabataean region.[37]

This is not the place to dissect the scholarship on the subject,[38] but it is worth pointing out the important role played by the small kingdom in the context of international trade with Arabia. It is safe to assert, I think, that the annexation made a favourable impact on the economy of the empire, fully integrating a key strategic area for long-distance trade. A new road was quickly

33 See Speidel 1977, 688–730; Fiema 1987, 25–35; Freeman 1996, 91–118. Bowersock (1983, 80–1) was the first to suggest that the annexation of Nabatea was achieved without a real military campaign, and that the term 'annexation' would describe what really happened much better than 'conquer'. The main point put forward by the scholar is that Trajan did not take for himself the epithet of *Arabicus Maximus*, as he did after conquering Dacia (when he actually took the epithet of *Dacicus Maximus*). Even more significantly, on the celebrative coins minted after the annexation of Nabatea the legend *Arabia aquisita* appears, instead of *Arabia capta*, which would be the obvious choice in the case of military conquest.

34 Quotation from Spijkerman 1978, 20, n. 54. Similar opinions were expressed by Raschke 1978, 647–648; Bowersock 1983, 82; Parker 1986, 123; Strobel 1988, 256; Isaac 1992, 119.

35 Starcky 1955a, 103; Graf 1978, 5–6; Parker 1986, 124.

36 Bowersock 1983, 84; Strobel 1988, 256.

37 Rey-Coquais 1978, 54; Parker 1986, 123; Eadie (1986), 243–5. Kirkbride (1990, 256) suggested that the real aim was to conquer the port of Aila, because of its importance in international trade. Such a hypothesis does not appear sound, though, when one considers that in this period Aila was not yet a very important port of trade. See Parker 2009, 79–84.

38 Very interesting on this topic is the opinion expressed, very matter-of-factly, by Strabo 6.4.2, that client kingdoms are *de facto* part of the empire and the emperor could decide to incorporate them at any time, using any official reason he wanted. See also Brunt 1978, 159–191.

built connecting Bostra in the far north of the *provincia* with the Red Sea. The work most likely began in 106 CE, ending between 111 and 114.[39]

Trajan's activity in the area was not limited to Arabia; in Egypt, he restored what Romans called 'Trajan's Canal', between the Nile and the Red Sea, near Clysma (modern Suez).[40] The precise date of the inauguration of the canal is unknown, but an ostracon dated to 112 CE provides a *terminus ante quem*.[41] There is no agreement among scholars as to the reasons why Trajan built it, nor as to its utility. Some have postulated that the channel was to be used for the forthcoming war against the Parthians, while others suggest that it was meant to foster trade in the northern Red Sea area.[42] Equally unclear is whether or not the canal was actually navigable, or if it was only meant for irrigation in north-eastern Egypt.[43] Often quoted against such a reductive interpretation is a passage of Lucianus, who in one of his works tells the story of a young man who sailed from Alexandria to Clysma, and then on from there to India:[44]

> τοιοῦτον δέ τι ἐγεγένητο· ἀναπλεύσας ὁ νεανίσκος εἰς Αἴγυπτον ἄχρι τοῦ Κλύσματος, πλοίου ἀναγομένου ἐπείσθη καὶ αὐτὸς εἰς Ἰνδίαν πλεῦσαι.
>
> What had happened was this: The young man cruised up the Nile as far as Clysma, and as a vessel was just putting to sea, was induced to join others in a voyage to India.[45]

Such a text is not enough to prove that the channel was regularly used for trade, but what we can be sure of is that it was in use until the twelfth century,[46] and that it was regularly maintained to avoid its silting up. For this purpose, a λειτουργία was instituted, funded by ἐπιμεληταί. A number of papyri dated between the second and the sixth century CE attest the regular recruitment of

39 Pekáry 1968, 140–142; Isaac 1992, 120.

40 Ptol., *Geog*. 4.5. See Aubert's article in this volume for a complete overview of the history of the previous attempts by pharaohs and Hellenistic rulers to build a channel.

41 *SB* VI, 9545 (32).

42 The scholarship on Trajan's canal is now vast. See Faville 1902–1903, 66–75; Calderini 1920, 43–44; Bourdon 1925; Posener 1938, 25–26; Sijpesteijn 1963, 70–83; Oertel 1964, 18–52; De Romanis 1996, 71–95; Aubert 2004, 219–252; Cooper 2009, 195–209.

43 Hypothesis put forward by Mayerson 1996, 119–126. Similarly also Aubert 2004a, 219–252; Cooper 2009, 195–209.

44 Lucian, *Alex* 44, 16–18; also addressed by Aubert in this volume, p. 37.

45 Trans. by A.M. Harmon, LCL, 1921.

46 Cooper 2009, 198.

seasonal workers to clean the canal.[47] In none of these texts, however, is there any clear reference either to its use for trading purposes, or to a commercial fleet at Clysma ready to set sail to India.

Nevertheless, even if we accept the minimalistic view of a channel open only a few months of the year, and mainly to provide irrigation, we cannot fail to recognise the evident increase in activity at Clysma after the second century.[48] It is safe to assume that the canal played a role in economic development, at least through the provision of drinkable water to an otherwise poorly supplied region, as well as the opening of a channel of communication between the port and the hinterland.[49]

From all we have discussed so far in this section, it should be obvious that Trajan planned to better integrate the Red Sea region into the economic system of the Roman Empire by annexing a key area for trade (Nabatea), later providing it with roads to improve its communication system, and constructing a canal in Egypt that ended the isolation of the port of Clysma. These enterprises, along with the Parthian wars, should be enough to explain why the Spanish emperor Trajan was associated with a plan to conquer India. Festus, Eutropius, and Jordanes, however, do not talk only of a vague plan to conquer India—instead, they all precisely point to the establishment of a fleet in the Red Sea, connected to some plan to 'lay waste the coasts of India', though none of them has provided enough detail for us to understand the circumstances involved.

Two recently discovered inscriptions might shed some light on this issue. Beginning in 2003, a team of archaeologists working in the archipelago of Farasan (Saudi Arabia) made two extremely interesting discoveries. The archipelago, which is located close to the southern end of the Red Sea on the Saudi Arabian side, just 500 km north of the Strait of Bâb el-Mandeb, consists of some 200 islands, of which two stand out for their size. The closest part of the Roman Empire to the archipelago was the southern border of the province of Egypt, some 1,000 km distant,[50] which explains why the recent Farasan finds

47 *SB* VI 9545 (32): 112 CE; *P.Oxy.* LX 4070: *c.*208 CE; *P.Bub.* 4.69: 221 CE; *SB* V 7676 (= *P.Cair. Isidor.* 81): 297 CE; *P.Oxy.* LV 3814: end of third/beginning of fourth century CE; *P.Oxy.* XII 1426: 332 CE; *SB* V 7756 (= *P.Lond.* inv. 2574): 358/9 CE; *PSI* 689: 420/21 CE; *PSI* 87: 423 CE; *P.Wash.* 7: fifth or sixth century CE.

48 The first information on Clysma was available through the reports published by Bruyère 1966, although the quality of the archaeological investigation was very poor. A good analysis of the role of Clysma after the second century CE can be found in Ward 2007, 161–171.

49 Cooper 2009, 197.

50 For a complete discussion of the geographical context of the Farasan archipelago, see Villeneuve et al. 2004b, 143–149.

are so astonishing; these two inscriptions, both in Latin, attest for the first time the regular presence of the Roman army in the islands.

The first inscription to be discovered reads as follows:[51]

Imp(eratori) Caes(ari) Tito Ael(io) Hadr(iano)
Antonino Aug(usto) Pio Pont(ifici)
Maxim(o) trib(unicia) pot(estate) VII *co(n)s(uli)* III,
P(atri) P(atriae), vexill(atio) Leg(ionis) II *Tr(aianae) Fortis*
et auxil(ia) eius cạstrẹṇṣẹṣ-
q(ue) ṣụḅ praef(ecto) Ferresani pọṛṭụṣ
et Pont(i ?) Hercul(is) fec(erunt) ẹṭ ḍ[ed(icaverunt)]

The first four lines of the inscription are a dedication to the emperor Antoninus Pius, whose titles allow us to safely date the inscription between 10 December 143 and 9 December 144 CE.[52] The following lines of the inscription list the people engaged in building the statue to which the inscription was linked: a *vexillatio* of the *legio* II *Traiana Fortis*, its *auxilia*, and finally some other people possibly defined as *castrenses* (the text is not clear at this point). In its final lines, the inscription seems to attest for the first time the existence of an officer named *praefectus Ferresani portus* (?), whose name is not reported. This anonymous officer is *praefectus* of a district called *Ferresani portus*, though it is worth pointing out that only the toponym can safely be read, since only the *p* of the word *portus* is clearly readable. The word *Ferresani* makes it obvious that the stone was carved locally, and therefore the inscription has been found *in loco*. Finally, the toponym *Pontus Herculis* is, once again, a *hapax*—a previously unknown geographical location, whose interpretation is unclear.[53]

For the purposes of our analysis, the most important information provided by the inscription is the dating to 143–144 CE, under the reign of Antoninus Pius, and the mention of the presence of a *vexillatio* of the *Legio* II *Traiana Fortis* on the island. This legion was created by Trajan around 100 CE, and was eventually located in Egypt no later than 128 CE. From the reign of Antoninus Pius, it was the only legion located in this province.[54] This implies that the soldiers stationed at the Farasan Islands would necessarily have come from Egypt,

51 AE 2005, 1638; 1639 = 2010, 1761. The text was first edited in Villeneuve et al. 2004b, 143–190 and 2004b, 239–250. Later on, the editor suggested some corrections in Villeneuve 2004a, 419–429, and it is to this edition that I refer in this work.

52 Villeneuve 2004a, 422.

53 See the possible interpretations provided by Villeneuve 2004a, 426–428.

54 Devijver 1974, 452–492; Daris 2000, 359–363.

and realistically they would have been in touch with the province through Berenice, the Roman Empire's southernmost Egyptian Red Sea port.[55] Despite the fact that the inscription refers only to a *vexillatio* and not to a fleet, it seems plausible that a fleet would have been present in the Red Sea to provide a stable connection between the *vexillatio* and the empire.

A few years after the discovery of this first inscription, another one was found on the same island. Unfortunately this second inscription is very fragmentary, and it is possible to read only a few letters on its surface, from the lower right corner of the original block. It reads as follows:[56]

> ...] VIFERR
> ...] PRPR

Meagre as it is, this second inscription does not offer much for interpretation, nevertheless, the editor has tried. He started from the second fragmentary line of the document, (the abbreviation PR PR), which he interpreted as *pr*(*o*) *pr*(*aetore*). This interpretation is sound, and it implies that a *legatus Augusti pro praetore* was mentioned in the inscription. Given that the closest provinces to the Farasan archipelago are Arabia and Egypt, this *legatus* who was in some way in charge of the islands should have come from one of them. But in Egypt the officer in charge of the province was a *praefectus*, not a *legatus*, therefore the possibility of connecting this inscription to Egypt is ruled out. The only logical location would then be Arabia, which in fact was administered by a *legatus Augusti pro praetore*. This interpretation led the editor to interpret the abbreviation of the previous line as [... *legio*] *VI Ferr*(*ata*). The history of this legion is rather difficult to trace; it was originally located in Syria, then it took part in Trajan's eastern campaigns, it moved subsequently to Arabia for a short period, and from there it finally moved to Judea.[57] All these movements took place during an undefined time between the reigns of Trajan and Hadrian. Nevertheless, we do have two key dates: the *terminus ante quem* for the movement from Syria to Arabia is 119 CE,[58] while the final move into Judea took

55 On Berenice and its location, see Sidebotham and Wendrich 1995; Sidebotham and Wendrich 1996; Sidebotham and Wendrich 1998; Sidebotham and Wendrich 1999; Sidebotham and Wendrich 2000; Sidebotham and Wendrich 2007; Sidebotham 2002b.

56 Villeneuve 2007, 13–27.

57 On the *legio VI Ferrata*, see Kennedy 1980, 283–309; Isaac 1992, 349–352; Keppie 1986; Cotton 2000, 351–357.

58 Cotton 2000, 354–356.

place before 139 CE. The final reconstruction suggested by Villeneuve would therefore be:

> [..... vexill(atio) leg(ionis)] VI Ferr(atae)
> [sub .... leg(ato) Aug(usti)] pr(o) pr(aetore)

Given the very fragmentary status of the inscription, we must remember that other reconstructions are possible, though the one suggested by Villeneuve seems reasonable.[59]

We can safely assume that a *vexillatio* of the *legio II Traiana Fortis* was operating on the islands in 143–144 CE as a detachment of the main legion, which was based in Egypt. Much less certain is the information we can infer from the second inscription, since it requires corroboration from some more solid evidence. According to Villeneuve's hypothesis (which has necessarily to be taken as a working hypothesis), the second inscription might perhaps attest the presence of a detachment of the *legio VI Ferrata* in the archipelago in a year at some point before 139 CE. The presence of this legion in Arabia is attested with certainty in 119 CE, but it might well have been there earlier, perhaps having been moved by Trajan to defend the recently created province, or by Hadrian when he was reorganizing the whole region. If indeed the second inscription referred to the *legio VI Ferrata*, it would make sense to postulate that the legion in charge of the newly created province was also sent to occupy the far archipelago in the aftermath of Trajan's campaigns, and subsequently a further reorganization of the area made it more convenient to have a *vexillatio* from Egypt rather than from Arabia (since the latter was farther from the Farasan Islands). This would mean that the presence of a Roman military detachment on the Farasan archipelago might stretch from the last years of Trajan (or the first of Hadrian) at least to the reign of Antoninus Pius.

Defining the Roman Policy in the Red Sea in the Second Century CE

The evidence discussed in the previous section grants us a new perspective from which to reconsider the passages in Eutropius, Festus, and Jordanes that mention Trajan's new fleet in the Red Sea. As mentioned before, their manner misleads the reader into assuming that Trajan was the first ruler to station a regular fleet in the Red Sea, but this is definitely not true, as seen above.

59 AE 2005, 1640. Other possible reconstructions are also listed by Villeneuve 2007, 24–27, although the one discussed above seems the most convincing.

Nevertheless, there is in their reports an echo of something that actually happened at the beginning of the second century CE.

In order to draw appropriate conclusions, it is necessary to examine all of Trajan's activities in order to provide a context. The annexation of the Nabataean Kingdom and its subsequent connection to the Roman road system, the restoration of the canal on the Nile, and the occupation of the Farasan Islands are not separate actions, but rather distinct components of a larger master plan. All aspects of Trajan's policy in the East make much more sense when considered from this perspective: tighter control of the two ends of the Red Sea was the best way to secure control of the whole region.

If there was a master plan to control the Red Sea, what led Trajan to adopt such a plan? Along with military and administrative considerations, clearly his decision was motivated by the potential for economic gain. The Red Sea was a key area in the international trade route between the Roman Empire and the Far East (generally referred to by the Romans as 'India').[60] The importance of the contribution of eastern trade to the economy of the empire could hardly be overestimated;[61] this would be reason enough for the imperial interest in encouraging it.[62] Control of the Red Sea provided the best possible environment for trade.

This policy was first pursued by Trajan and then carried on by his successors, as demonstrated by some of the evidence presented in this work—most importantly, the permanence of the Roman army on the Farasan Islands at least until 144 CE, and possibly even longer. Other hints that commerce with India escalated from the reign of Trajan onwards are provided through a variety of different sources of evidence. Literary sources from the second century

60 See Mayerson 1993, 169–174; Schneider 2004.

61 Although the importance has been played down by some recent works such as Young 2001, most scholars agree. See, for instance, Sidebotham 1986a; De Romanis 1998; Tomber 2008.

62 On this subject, the most important evidence is still the 'Muziris papyrus', a twofold document containing two incomplete texts, one on its *recto* and the other on its *verso*, written in separate hands, both dateable to the mid second century CE. On the *recto* is one column, missing its left edge, with the end of a contract relating to a maritime loan for a trading voyage from Alexandria to Muziris. On the *verso* are the end of a line and the last column of an account of the value of a shipload of goods imported from India. It was first edited by Harrauer and Sijpesteijn 1985, 124–155. See also Thür 1987; 1988; Casson 1986; 1990; Foraboschi and Gara 1989, 280–2; Purpura 1996, 368–75; De Romanis 1996, 183–96; Id. 1998; Rathbone, 2000; Id. 2002, 179–98; Morelli 2011; De Romanis (2010/1) [2012]. Other aspects of the papyrus are referred to in the chapters of Wilson, Schörle, Aubert, and De Romanis.

CE reveal a very specific interest in the people living beyond the limits of the empire, especially on its eastern side. Works such as Arrian's *Indica, Parthica,* and the *Anabasis Alexandri* testify to the interest of Romans in the East. Authors such as Juvenal and Lucian exhibit considerable knowledge of India, including its products, culture, and religion.

The author who provides the best proof of an increased link between the Mediterranean World and India is Claudius Ptolemy (*fl.* 139–61 CE). In his *Geography*, he exhibits knowledge of the Far East well beyond that of earlier periods. He is not just more precise than his predecessors (Strabo, Pliny, and even sometimes the *Periplus Maris Erythraei*), he also describes regions which these earlier authors never mentioned in their works (e.g., East Asia). Ptolemy clearly obtained part of his information from travellers or merchants with an interest in the East, providing more proof of a strengthening of commercial relations between the Roman Empire and India during this period.[63]

It is within the context of this expansion into the East that we find the first evidence for direct Roman contact with China; in 166 CE a Roman 'embassy' reached China, hoping to open a direct commercial link between the two empires. This is recorded in the *Hou-han-shu*, the *Chronicles of the Han Dynasty*, ch. 88:

> They [i.e., the Romans] traffic by sea with An-hsi [= Parthia] and T'ien-chu [=India], the profit of which trade is ten-fold. They are honest in their transactions, and there are no double prices. Cereals are always cheap. The budget is based on a well-filled treasury. When the embassies of neighbouring countries come to their frontier, they are driven by post to the capital, and, on arrival, are presented with golden money. Their kings always desired to send embassies to China, but the An-hsi [= Parthians] wished to carry on trade with them in Chinese silks, and it is for this reason that they were cut off from communication. This lasted till the ninth year of the Yen-hsi period during the emperor Huan-ti's reign [= A.D. 166] when the king of Ta-ts'in [= 'Big China', i.e., the Roman Empire], An-tun [= Marcus Aurelius Antoninus], sent an embassy who, from the frontier of Jih-nan [= Annam] offered ivory, rhinoceros horns, and tortoise shell. From that time dates the [direct] intercourse with this country.[64]

For the purposes of this work it does not make any difference whether this expedition was an official embassy sent by the emperor Marcus Aurelius

63 Sidebotham 1986a, 142–3; Sidebotham 2011, 14–16.

64 Translation by Hirth 1975, 41; See also Hill 2009.

himself, or a group of private traders operating on their own. Two important points emerge from this story: first, whether official or private, the embassy certainly benefited from the favourable conditions for eastern trade created by Trajan's policy; second, the Chinese writer's assertion that the Roman traders wanted to establish a direct commercial connection with China but had always been blocked by the Parthians is significant. It makes perfect sense that the Roman traders would want to establish a direct commercial connection with China in order to increase their profits.

An attempt to cut the Parthians out of the trade would undoubtedly have been noticed by the Parthian rulers. It is perhaps not a mere coincidence that in the troubled-for-centuries relationship between Parthians and Romans the Arsacids attacked the Romans first only once—in 161 CE—[65] in a period when the Roman presence in the Red Sea and the Indian Ocean had reached its peak and trade with India was flourishing again.[66] I am not here suggesting that the main reason for this war was commercial (it is well known that the *casus belli* was the situation in Armenia),[67] but I do believe that the trade situation made the Arsacids more aggressive toward the Romans than they had ever been.

Conclusions

In conclusion, all the evidence collected here should prove that Trajan initiated a period of Roman expansion in the Red Sea that had important commercial consequences. This policy was also consistently pursued by his successors, probably reaching its peak under Marcus Aurelius; it provided the right context for Roman commercial expansion in the East, which culminated with the Roman embassy to China.

If what is proposed in this paper is sound, I believe that it is safe to affirm that the policy inaugurated by Trajan was designed to make the Red Sea a *mare internum* in some way—a sea completely controlled (though not completely ruled) by the Romans. I am aware that the possibility of government interference in the eastern trade, or of commercial considerations determining Roman policy in the east, has been ruled out by several scholars.[68] Still, other scholars have already opened to this possibility,[69] and I believe that the amount of

65 SHA *Marc.* 8.6; Birley 2000, 121; for the date, Flinterman 1997, 281.
66 Nappo, forthcoming.
67 Sicker 2000, 169.
68 See Isaac 1992, 101–218; Young 2001, 216–217.
69 Most notably Sidebotham 1986a, 48–77.

evidence made available by archaeology over the last few years should lead to a reconsideration of the matter.

I also believe that the 'military-economic' approach identified in this paper during the time of Trajan and his successors was far from being a *unicum* in the history of the empire, since parallels in other periods can be found (for example between the reigns of Anastasius and Justinian in the sixth century CE, when the empire again tried to control all of the Red Sea region).[70] I hope that these considerations will encourage a general rethinking of the imperial policy in this region and in particular concerning trade with the East, since they better reveal the real role of the emperor in such matters, and help us to more accurately assess the importance, in terms of international policy, held by this region.[71]

70 Nappo 2009.

71 The first example of such an approach can be found in Sidebotham 1986a, 48–77.

CHAPTER 5

Roman Trade with the Far East: Evidence for Nabataean Middlemen in Puteoli

Taco Terpstra

Puteoli, a major Italian harbour town serving Rome, was an important port for trade with the East. It was a hub for the Alexandrian grain fleet, but high-value goods such as Tyrian purple dye must have arrived there too.[1] The town probably also saw the movement of luxury products from distant lands outside the empire: spices, silk, and frankincense from Arabia, China, and India.

While Puteoli has not yielded archaeological evidence for eastern trade of the rare kind unearthed in Pompeii (where an Indian ivory statuette representing a voluptuous nude female figure was found), epigraphic evidence does exist.[2] A small but significant body of inscriptions from the Greek world and from Italy shows Nabataean activity in the Mediterranean. In this paper I will investigate this activity, concentrating most of all on Puteoli, the site where more than half of the known epigraphic evidence was discovered. I will argue, first, that Puteoli housed the only permanent Nabataean community in the Mediterranean and, second, that this community established a mercantile connection between the Nabataeans and their Roman buyers, securing a flow of information and establishing mutual trust for purposes of trade.

The Nabataean Kingdom, located about halfway between the Persian Gulf and the Mediterranean, was well positioned to play a major role in East–West exchange. The heyday of its commercial activity seems to have been from roughly the mid second century BCE to the late first century CE—the time from its rise as a regional power to the time just preceding its annexation by Rome in 106 CE.[3] From the silence in the historic record it would seem that with the Roman takeover, the Nabataeans 'softly and suddenly vanished away'. Still, a few references linger in the written sources. In a passage referring to India, Apuleius writes: 'Far away it lies, beyond the learned Egyptians, beyond

1 A Tyrian trading colony existed in Puteoli; Terpstra 2013, 70–79. On the Puteolan Annii family and their likely involvement in the eastern luxury trade, see Schörle this volume.

2 First published in Maiuri 1938/1939, there identified as the Indian goddess Lakshmi.

3 Wenning 2007; Graf 2007; Young 2001, 90–117; Bowersock 1983, 12–27, 59–75. On the Roman annexation of the Nabataean Kindom, see also Nappo this volume.

 | DOI 10.1163/9789004289536_007

the superstitious Jews and the merchants of Nabataea, beyond the children of Arsaces in their long flowing robes, the Ityreans, to whom earth gives but scanty harvest, and the Arabs, whose perfumes are their wealth.'[4] These ethnic stereotypes are poetic stock images of distant peoples, meant to evoke the exotic. Apuleius' description, in other words, should not necessarily be taken to mean that the 'merchants of Nabataea' were still a significant presence in his day; they may have already been a fading memory by the 160s CE.

Roman literary sources say expressly that it was the trade in aromatics from Arabia that formed the main source of wealth for the Nabataeans. Diodorus of Sicily makes this explicit, stating that they were the richest Arab tribe, 'for not a few of them are accustomed to bring down to the sea frankincense and myrrh and the most valuable kinds of spices, which they procure from those who convey them from what is called Arabia Eudaemon.'[5] From this remark, as well as from the writings of Strabo and Pliny the Elder, it appears that the Nabataeans acted first and foremost as transporters and middlemen. They did not produce goods or cultivate aromatic crops themselves, but instead took over merchandise entering their realm from the South and East, carried it over their territory, and brought it to the West. Although they must have taken goods back to the East as well, there can be little doubt that it was the westward movement of goods that formed the backbone of their commercial activity and the wellspring of their prosperity.

Two cardinal overland supply lines brought products to the Nabataean realm. Both of these routes as well as their sources are well attested. The most important reference is made by Strabo, who tells us that the incense the Nabataeans traded in was provided by the Minaeans and the Gerrhaeans.[6] The first were a south-Arabian tribe living in what is now principally Yemen. The route by which goods travelled from there to Petra ran more or less parallel to the eastern coast of the Red Sea. Another literary source, Pliny the Elder, tells us that to reach the Mediterranean, goods had to move through the territory of yet another Arabian tribe, the Gebbanitae, who thus had a chokehold on all northbound traffic and charged a tax for crossing their land.[7]

4 Apul., *Flor.* 6.1: 'ultimis terris, super Aegyptios eruditos et Iudaeos superstitiosos et Nabathaeos mercatores et fluxos vestium Arsacidas et frugum pauperes Ityraeos et odorum divites Arabas' (trans. H.E. Butler):, 165. See Graf 2007, 175.

5 Diod. Sic. 19.94.5: 'εἰώθασι γὰρ αὐτῶν οὐκ ὀλίγοι κατάγειν ἐπὶ θάλασσαν λιβανωτόν τε καὶ σμύρναν καὶ τὰ πολυτελέστατα τῶν ἀρωμάτων, διαδεχόμενοι παρὰ τῶν κομιζόντων ἐκ τῆς Εὐδαίμονος καλουμένης Ἀραβίας' (trans. by R.M. Geer, LCL 1962). See Young 2001, 90–91, 113–115.

6 Strabo 16.4.18.

7 Plin., *HN* 12.63. On the Yemenite Kingdoms and their role in the incense trade, see Singer 2007.

The Gerrhaeans, the second supplying tribe, lived east of Petra instead of south; they inhabited the city of Gerrha close to the Persian Gulf, a place mentioned by both Strabo and Pliny.[8] Strabo relates that the Gerrhaeans 'and all the neighbouring peoples' ('καὶ πάντες οἱ πλησιόχωροι') sent shipments of aromatics to Palestine via Petra. However, the route over which goods reached the Mediterranean from Gerrha is not as well known as the one running north from the Minaean territory. Caravan trains likely travelled more or less straight through the Arabian desert, probably with some variation in the exact itinerary, going over either Teima or Dumata. An alternate route may have conveyed goods overland from Gerrha to the Euphrates River first, then upriver to Babylon, and then onward through the desert to Dumata and Petra.[9]

Goods also reached Petra via Leukê Kômê, a harbour town on the Red Sea. There is still some uncertainty about its exact whereabouts, but the most likely location is either on the mouth of the Gulf of 'Aqaba roughly at modern-day 'Aynunah or further south at al-Wajh.[10] The existence of this harbour should perhaps be attributed to Egyptian competition. The *Periplus Maris Erythraei*, a mid first century CE handbook containing information on trade routes to India, says that goods moved to Egypt from the south-Arabian sea ports of Muza, Kanê, and Moscha Limen. Leukê Kômê, which on first consideration seems to offer only a maritime alternative to an important Nabataean land route, was perhaps constructed to capture part of the Egypt-bound seaborne trade that would otherwise have been lost to the Nabataeans. If so, the attempt seems to have been largely successful. The *Periplus* says that from Leukê Kômê 'there is a way inland up to Petra, to Malichus, King of the Nabataeans', and Strabo remarks that camel caravans as great as armies regularly moved between Leukê Kômê and Petra.[11] Though many goods arriving in the Red Sea must have gone to Egyptian ports like Berenice and Myos Hormos, apparently a sizable portion found its way up to the Nabataean capital.

Undoubtedly, aromatics grown and cultivated in Arabia formed the major trading commodity for the Nabataeans. However, products from further afield also arrived at Petra via south Arabia, Gerrha, and Leukê Kômê. The *Periplus* lists two Indian ports where goods could be picked up: Barbarikon

8 Strabo 16.3.3; 16.4.18. Plin., *HN* 6.147.

9 Both Strabo 16.3.3 and Plin., *HN* 6.148 mention overland and riverine transport, but both accounts lack clarity. See Young 2001, 92–94.

10 Nappo 2010; Eadie 1989.

11 *Peripl. M. Rubr.* 19: 'δι' ἧς ἐστὶν εἰς Πέτραν πρὸς Μαλίχαν, βασιλέα Ναβαταίων, <ἀνάβασις>'; the passage, by the way, provides the key to dating the *Periplus*; the king alluded to must be Malichus II, who ruled from 40–70 CE; Casson 1989, 6–7. Strabo 16.4.23. See Young 2001, 94–96.

and Barygaza, both located on India's north-west coast. Among the products available for purchase there was *bdellium*, an aromatic resin from trees common in the drier parts of India and Pakistan.[12] A surprisingly late source shows that this aromatic gum was conveyed at least partly through Petra; Diocletian's *Price Edict* mentions Petran *bdellium*. If this information reflects current trading conditions then this tells us that trade with India ran partly through Nabataea and continued into late Antiquity, despite a remark by Strabo implying that the Nabataeans were losing ground in the competition for Indian Ocean commerce.[13]

Silk was also for sale in Barbarikon and Barygaza. No archaeological traces of it have been discovered in Petra, but given the importance of Nabataean trade with Gerrha, where Chinese silk arrived via India, Nabataean involvement in the silk trade seems likely nonetheless. It has even been suggested that Petra appears in Chinese historical writings. According to the *Hou Han shu* and the *Wei lüeh* (histories of the later Han and Wei dynasties, 23–220 CE and 220–265 CE respectively) the region in the far West—from the Chinese perspective—was formerly known as 'Li-chien' or 'Li-kan'. This geographical knowledge seems to date back to a Chinese embassy to the Scythians in 126 BCE that failed in its diplomatic purpose but gathered much information about the lands in the West. 'Li-kan' does not resemble 'Petra', but it seems likely that in the East the city was known not by its Greek but by its ancient Semitic name, 'Reqem'. With a change from 'R' to 'L', common in renditions of western names in Chinese, equating 'Li-kan' with 'Reqem' becomes plausible.[14]

Goods going west through Petra reached the Mediterranean mainly at the port city of Gaza, travelling along an important road, mentioned by Pliny, that was the shortest route to the sea from the Nabataean capital. From there, they were likely shipped straight to destinations in the Roman Empire. Not all goods were conveyed westward in this way, though. Some stayed in the area, where they were sold for local consumption in places like Philadelphia, Gerasa, and Damascus; at least a portion, now unquantifiable, was also carried overland from Petra through the Sinai to Egypt and Alexandria.[15] Nonetheless, it seems clear that Gaza was the principal maritime jumping-off point for Nabataean

12 *Peripl. M. Rubr.* 39, 49. On *bdellium*, see Casson 1989, 185.

13 *Price Edict* 36,54 (see Lauffer 1971, 197). Strabo comments (16.4.24) that sea trade from the Indian Ocean was increasingly diverted to Egyptian ports. It is often assumed that Nabataean commerce declined sharply after the Augustan era; see Graf 2007, 175–176.

14 Graf 1996, 207–210; Zayadine 2007, 212.

15 On the importance for the Roman State of Alexandria as a place where taxes on eastern luxury goods were levied, see Wilson this volume.

merchandise.[16] It is therefore remarkable that to date not a single Nabataean inscription has come to light in Gaza, although Nabataean coins and ceramic fragments have been found there.[17] However, this situation might well change someday; it could be the result of ongoing political instability and military conflict in the region. This troubled present has left the ancient city less extensively explored than neighbouring archaeological sites in more politically stable areas.[18]

For the next two sections of this paper I will focus on the body of epigraphic evidence for Nabataeans in the Mediterranean that I have compiled for this study (see Table 5.1 appended to this chapter).[19] Excluded from this list are inscriptions mentioning Arabs who could, but need not, have come from Nabataea.[20] Also excluded are inscriptions from the Red Sea and Egypt, and the epigraphic material from the area immediately surrounding Nabataea. The reason for this limitation is that I wanted to investigate specifically the Mediterranean leg of Nabataean commerce, and not the overland legs discussed above which have been extensively studied. The body of inscriptions I have collected—twenty-one in total—reveals much about Nabataean activity in the West. One glance at the list is enough to see its most striking aspect: out of twenty-one inscriptions no fewer than twelve are from Puteoli. Before I discuss these twelve, though, let us first have a look at the other nine.

Nabataeans in the Greek World

So far, six inscriptions related to Nabataeans are known from the Greek world, all of them discovered in the Aegean. The oldest one dates to the second half of the second century BCE and contains evidence for a man from Nabataea, Salamenes, son of Edemon, who was honoured on the Greek island of Tenos

16 Young 2001, 97–99, 106–107, 111. See also: Erickson-Gini 2006; Jones, Hammond, Johnson, and Fiema 1988, 52–55; Cohen 1982. The Pliny passage is *HN* 6.144.

17 Bowersock 1983, 22–23; Roche 1996, 75; Sachet 2000.

18 Which is not to say no work has been done there. See the wonderful, diachronic publication by Humbert (ed.) 2000.

19 For similar lists, see Roche 1996, 75–95 and Wenning 1987, 22–24. Unlike Roche's and Wenning's, my list includes only Nabataean inscriptions, not coins or architectural fragments. I have also excluded *CISem* 2.1.160 (Nabataean *strategos* in Sidon) because it is not necessarily providing evidence for Nabataeans sailing the Mediterranean.

20 To my knowledge, this excludes only two instances. First, Theudotos the Arab (*SEG* III [1927], 674), member of a *koinon* on Rhodes; see Roche 1996, 78; Wenning 1987, 23. Second, the Arab Chauan on Delos (*I.Délos* 2321); see Wenning 1987, 23; Roche 1996, 84/85.

by the Tean city-council and people's assembly (*no. 21*). Salamenes had acted as a benefactor to the Teans, receiving a crown and *proxenia* (guest friendship) for his trouble.[21] What largesse won him these honours is unfortunately not made explicit.

An altar found on the island of Chalce (*no. 20*), close to Rhodes, provides more tentative evidence for Nabataeans in the Greek world. Inscribed on the altar is an honorary decree: two crowns were awarded to a now-anonymous man by the 'Ἡρακλεωτᾶν' and the 'Ξουσαριαστᾶν'. That last word is rather mysterious. Reading 'Ξουσ-' as a mistake for 'Θουσ-' or 'Δουσ-' is a possibility.[22] If so, the inscription could refer to a group of people worshipping the Nabataean chief deity Dushara, who figures as 'Δουσάρης' in inscriptions and on Arabian coinage, and whose name is spelled as 'Θεὺς Ἄρης' in the *Suda* (a tenth-century CE lexicographical compilation).[23]

A more straightforward instance of Nabataean religious activity is presented by a bilingual inscription in Aramaic and Greek, datable to either 68 BCE or 9 CE, discovered on Cos (*no. 19*). It was set up by the Nabataean Aswallah to the goddess al-ʿUzzā, whose name in the Greek text is rendered as 'Aphrodite'. This equation is not surprising; we know that al-ʿUzzā was a planetary deity representing the morning star Venus.[24] The dedication was found close to an Aphrodite temple situated in the Coan harbour, and it seems almost certain that the dedication was originally placed there. That idea finds support in another Coan inscription. It contains a law compelling traders and shipmasters to sacrifice to Aphrodite on sailing out, stipulating that, on failure to do so, they should pay a fine.[25] Because of this law and because of the archaeological context of the dedication, it would seem that Aswallah was a merchant travelling through. If he was obeying the Coan law, he was in effect paying his dues more to Aphrodite than to al-ʿUzzā.

A grave stele contemporary with or slightly younger than the Tean inscription lists the names of nineteen slaves owned by a certain Protarchus (*no. 18*).

---

21 *I.Priene* no. 108 (line 168) also deserves mention in the context of possible political connections between the Aegean and Nabataea. It contains evidence for a diplomatic mission undertaken by a certain Moschion from Priene to Petra, shortly after 129 BCE. See Bowersock 1983, 22.

22 Wilamowitz's suggestion in *IG* 12.1.963.

23 Healey 2001, 85–107; Graf 2007, 184; Roche 1996, 78.

24 On al-ʿUzzā, see Healey 2001, 114–119. See also Levi Della Vida 1938, esp. 144–146.

25 For information on the find-location of the inscription, see the note by Mario Segre (pp. 147/148) to the edition by Levi Della Vida 1938. The inscription containing the Coan law which Segre lists as still unpublished in 1938 is *I.Cos* ED 178 (late 3rd c. BCE); see section a(A) lines 21–26.

All died on the island of Delos, presumably all together in a tragedy like a fire or a building collapse. These slaves had come from an astoundingly wide geographical area: from the Black Sea via Caria, Pamphylia, Cappadocia, Syria-Palestine, to Cyrene; among the group of slaves was also one Nabataean named Zaidos.

The Dushara dedications from Miletus and Delos (*nos. 16* and *17*) relate to a colourful story we also happen to know about through the writings of Josephus. They were set up during the journey to Rome that Syllaeus, the ambitious and unscrupulous vizier of the Nabataean King Obodas, undertook in 9 BCE. Nabataea was at that time involved in a skirmish with its arch-rival (and Rome's client kingdom) Judaea, under Herod the Great. To secure the support of Augustus, Syllaeus decided to travel to Rome personally and plead before the Emperor. But while his diplomatic offensive was underway, King Obodas suddenly died. This event increased the stakes for Syllaeus; he may have seen it as an opportunity to further his own ambitions of becoming the new—Rome-endorsed—Nabataean ruler. However, before the new situation was fully digested at the imperial court, back in Nabataea a new King (Aretas IV, probably not a blood relative of the deceased monarch) filled the power vacuum and ascended to the throne. Syllaeus, dismayed, tried to persuade Augustus to reject the new ruler and instate him instead, but his attempts were ultimately thwarted by the diplomatic cunning of Nicolaus of Damascus, the Jewish advocate before Augustus.[26]

None of the inscriptions so far discussed necessarily indicate the existence of Nabataean communities anywhere in the Aegean. Tenos may have counted one Nabataean inhabitant among its denizens around 150–100 BCE. But although Salamenes received *proxenia* there, which might suggest more regular contact between Tenos and Nabataea, there is no sign that he formed part of a larger resident community; indeed, it is not even certain he lived on the island himself. The two Nabataean inscriptions from Delos constitute the largest body of such evidence in the Mediterranean outside Italy. It could perhaps be argued that a Nabataean community must therefore have existed on the island. This is not unimaginable since second- and first-century BCE Delos is known to have housed many 'international' trading communities. However, the only Nabataean inhabitant we know of for certain was of slave status. Syllaeus' stopover on the island might be interpreted as a visit to a community from his home country, but this event occurred a century or so after the grave stele was set up, at a time when Delos had long been in decline as a commercial

26 Joseph, *AJ* 16.286–299; 16.335–355. See Bowersock 1983, 50–53. See also Roche 1996, 80–85. On Syllaeus and his scheming ways, see also Nappo this volume.

centre. On close inspection, the story told by the Delian inscriptions is not as coherent as it seems at first sight.

Syllaeus also visited Miletus on the same trip and, as with Delos, it could perhaps be argued that a Nabataean colony must have been present there. However, as with Delos, Syllaeus' stay in Miletus was probably simply the result of sea routes and prevailing winds.[27] It is also important to note that his dedication to Dushara was set up not in a Nabataean temple but in the Milesian Delphinium.[28] Had there been a structure devoted exclusively to the gods of his native country, Syllaeus would surely have turned there, and the apparent absence of such a structure seems to belie the presence of Nabataean settlers. As we have seen, the votive offering from Cos made by Aswallah to the goddess al-ʿUzzā is similar to the Milesian dedication in the sense that it was attached to a local Aphrodite temple, not a Nabataean sanctuary. It should almost certainly be seen as an act by a single travelling merchant. The Chalcian altar may provide evidence for a Nabataean religious community, but unfortunately the meaning of the text on the altar is obscure. In short, although the cluster of inscriptions from a relatively confined geographical area in the Aegean can surely be taken to show Nabataean interest in the region, both political and economic, as evidence for Nabataean communities it is tenuous at best.

Nabataeans in Italy

Things are different in Rome, though only marginally. The one dedicatory inscription (*no. 15*) to an unidentifiable male deity (Dushara is logical but not certain) is too fragmentary for us to know if it was attached to a Nabataean religious structure. In fact, its bilingual nature in Aramaic and Latin rather suggests it was attached to the temple of a Graeco-Roman god just like the Dushara dedications from Miletus and Cos (both bilingual, both in Aramaic and Greek). The inscription set up by the Nabataean envoys Rabeibelus, son of Thaemus, and —(?), son of Thaemoobdadallus (*no. 14*), was self-evidently a marker left behind by two men who were only visiting the imperial capital.[29]

27 Clermont-Ganneau 1906, 323–327.

28 The dedication by Syllaeus is the only evidence for Nabataeans in Miletus. The *Petraioi* we see as co-signers in a 3rd c. BCE treaty between Miletus and a number of Cretan cities (*I. Delphinion* no. 140) were not people from Nabataean Petra but from a city on Crete with the same name; Robert 1940, 123–126. Cf. Wenning 2007, 29.

29 See Roche 1996, 90–93 for a discussion on the political events that may have occasioned the embassy.

On the other hand, the grave stele erected by Abgarus from Petra for his relative Abdaretas (*no. 13*) seems to tell a different story, a story of Petran settlers in the city.[30] However, apart from this single instance no further evidence for the presence of a Nabataean community in Rome exists. To find strong evidence for such a community we need to turn south to Puteoli.

A Nabataean grave inscription has come to light in Puteoli as well (*no. 12*); together with the Roman and Delian epitaphs the third of only three so far found in the Mediterranean. The stele, written in Greek, marked the final resting place of Tholomaios son of Thaimallos from Petra, who died age thirty-three. A precious bit of added information makes it almost certain that he was a Nabataean who had moved permanently to Puteoli. The inscription records that Tholomaios was 'also known as Maximus' ('ὁ καὶ Μάξιμος'). The Roman nickname of this very foreign individual strongly suggests ties to the local Puteolan community.

Unlike Rome and unlike the places in the Aegean so far discussed, Puteoli provides unequivocal evidence for a Nabataean temple maintained by a religious community. A marble plaque tells us in Aramaic that around 50/49 BCE a sanctuary was constructed by Banhobal, a structure that in 5 CE was enlarged by a group of men, also with Semitic names (*no. 2*). The deity to whom this sanctuary was dedicated can no longer be identified in the mutilated text, but the Nabataean context is not in doubt; the inscription, written in the Nabataean version of Aramaic, wishes well-being on the Nabataean King and Queen, Aretas and Huldu. A second commemorative plaque, also in Aramaic, records a votive offering made in 11 CE: in that year, Zaidu and Abdelge presented Dushara with two camels (whether this meant live animals or votive images is unclear) (*no. 1*). Almost certainly, this plaque was attached to the Nabataean sanctuary, providing the first indication that it was a Dushara temple. Both Aramaic inscriptions were carved on pieces of Italian Carrara marble, showing that these objects were not imports but were produced locally. Nabataean craftsmen must have been available in Puteoli to carve them.[31]

---

30 Even here, one could argue that both men were envoys or otherwise visitors, with one of them dying while on the road. Roche 1996, 94 points out that the word used for 'grave marker' ('*nefesh*') was particularly apt for graves of merchants, ambassadors, or caravaneers—people exposed to the dangers of travel.

31 Lacerenza 1988/1989, 140. A similar reasoning could, of course, be adopted for nos. 13, 15, 16, 17, and 19 (all containing Aramaic writing), but unfortunately the publications do not list the type of marble used for any of these. No. 13 is, because of its nature, the only one for certain carved locally.

Much more evidence for a Dushara cult in Puteoli exists. One altar and three marble bases were found bearing the words 'Dusari' or 'Dusari sacrum' (*nos. 3–6*). The altar has a more or less traditional Graeco-Roman shape, but the bases are different. Their flat top surfaces contain slots (either seven or three) intended to hold plain limestone steles, four of which were also found. This design is well known from traditional Nabataean religious practices in which gods were revered in the shape of steles or pillars (*betyls*), usually without any facial markings. The representation of deities as plain stone blocks reflects a reluctance by the Nabataeans to make images of gods in human form, a reluctance shared by the Jews and, later, Muslim Arabs.[32]

In addition to the altar and bases, the words 'Dusari' or 'Dusari sacrum' appear on four marble revetments (*nos. 7–10*) and one possible *ex voto* (*no. 11*). The two largest blocks (*nos. 8 and 9*) show unmistakably that they are architectural fragments; they have a layer of mortar on their un-inscribed reverse side, and show in one case a groove for a dovetail clamp, in the other, traces of rust produced by an oxidising metal pivot. The palaeography in the Latin inscriptions, including the ones on the altar and bases, is remarkably similar, suggesting that they all came from the same building. This combined evidence renders it all but certain that the Nabataean sanctuary built in 50/49 BCE was indeed dedicated to the Nabataean god Dushara.

The Latin inscriptions seem to have come from the same find-location—a patch of seabed off the Pozzuoli coast—indicating that the remains of the temple lie underwater.[33] The Aramaic dedication commemorating the temple's renovation, on the other hand, was discovered on dry soil near the Pozzuolan *macellum*. However, it seems not to have been *in situ* there. Its find-location is close to where the Latin inscriptions were found,[34] and the logical conclusion seems therefore to be that the Nabataean temple stood in a city quarter that now lies submerged due to 'bradyseism', the slow volcanic activity in the Phlegrean fields that makes the whole area periodically rise and sink. Based

32 Healy 2001, 155–158. See also Lacerenza 1988/1989, 132–136.

33 Nos. 3, 4, 5, 6, 10, 11 were all dragged out of the sea (the oldest finds were made in the 18th c., see Ruggiero 1888, 152). Nos. 8 and 9 were robbed from a building at an unknown date, and then hidden near the *Portus Iulius*. Both Lacerenza 1994 and Camodeca 2001 seem to be certain that these objects were originally attached to the now subaquatic Nabataean temple. The find-location of no. 7 is unknown. When Dubois published his monograph, the fragment was set up in the subterranean chambers of the Pozzuolan amphitheater (p. 162), but it seems no longer to have been there at the time Tran tam Tinh wrote. I have not been able to locate it.

34 Ruggiero 1888, 146. It is unknown where the plaque commemorating the offer of two camels (no. 1) was found. Lacerenza 1988/1989, 140.

on another inscription dragged out of the sea, there is general consensus that this vanished part of Puteoli was called the *vicus Lartidianus*.[35] The temple site must be located there somewhere, but unfortunately underwater archaeology has so far not been able to pinpoint it.

Because the words 'sacred to Dushara' were inscribed not only on the movable parts of the temple but also on its fixed architectural elements, the whole complex as such was apparently deemed holy. Semitic temples were more often consecrated to a god in all their constituent parts in order to render them ritually pure. A story dating to 402 CE illustrates this aspect of ancient Semitic religion. In that year Porphyrius, the bishop of Gaza, ordered the temple to the ancestral city-god Marnas demolished and burnt. Attempting to stamp out the pagan cult thoroughly, he shrewdly decided to reuse the marble from the old building in a plaza in front of the temple site 'so that it might be trodden upon not only by men, but also by women, and dogs, and swine, and beasts'.[36] The result was that the people of Gaza, who thought this a worse injury even than the temple's razing, refused to set foot on the marble.

Returning to the Dushara temple in Puteoli, it is unfortunate that we have no clear idea of what it looked like. A sense of its architectural features might have explained a puzzling aspect of the inscriptions, namely the separate use of two languages. The temple dedication and votive offering of camels are in Aramaic only, yet all the other inscriptions—repeating the same one or two words—are exclusively in Latin. In the epigraphic record from Petra and environs, Latin inscriptions are not particularly numerous; to the extent that they do appear they all postdate the Roman annexation of 106 CE.[37] By implication, Latin seems an unlikely language for Nabataean emigrants to have carried with them overseas. Furthermore, in the material I have collected from the Mediterranean, Latin is used only in the inscriptions from Italy.[38]

35 The identification of this area as the *vicus Lartidianus* is based on a pedestal dedicated to Hadrian by the 'inquilini vici Lartidiani', first published by Sogliano 1890, 17–18. See Camodeca 1977, 75–80. See also Camodeca 2001, 95–98; Steuernagel 2004, 46, 50, 247.

36 Marcus Diaconus *Vita Porphyrii episcopi Gazensis* 76: 'ἵνα καταπατῶνται οὐ μόνον ὑπὸ ἀνδρῶν, ἀλλὰ καὶ γυναικῶν καὶ κυνῶν καὶ χοίρων καὶ κνωδάλων' (trans., with modifications, by G.F. Hill 1913). See Bauzou 2000, 58–60; Lacerenza 1994, 16/17.

37 *IGLS* 21.4. 1–8, 40, 41, 44, 45, 47, 51–53, 71, 146, 150, 151. Most of these are late, dating to Severan times or later. Even Greek was apparently not extensively used before the Roman annexation; no. 54 is the only Greek text for certain predating that event.

38 Mommsen, in his commentary to *CIL* 10.1556, proposed to interpret an inscription from *Germania Inferior*, dating to 223 CE, as a Dushara dedication: 'DEO [APO]LLINI DYS PRO. LU. S[O]L(I)Q. DE. . . .', but without being able to explain 'PRO. LU.' However, later editors read *Dyspro* (see *CIL* 13.8607; *CIMRM* no. 1008); the meaning of this word remains unclear.

It seems obvious, in other words, that the appearance of the Latin dedications in Puteoli should be attributed to the Italian location of the Nabataean temple. But what does that signify? We could postulate that worshippers from the local community had joined the Dushara cult, similar to what happened with the Roman Isis cult.[39] But although this hypothesis cannot be ruled out, I do not find it particularly attractive; the proper names we read in the inscriptions are all suggestive of the community's Semitic origin.

An alternative explanation is imaginable: perhaps the dedications were meant to be seen by the Puteolan public. Weighing against that idea is that the inscriptions sanctified the objects on which they were written. These objects, then, were not merely ornamental and are unlikely to have graced a publicly accessible part of the temple complex. However, Nabataean temple structures were typically surrounded by a marked-off piece of land, a *temenos*.[40] Maybe the Aramaic inscriptions were set up in the temple's inner sanctum with the Latin inscriptions in the area around it, visible even from certain points outside the open sacred space.[41] If so, this could perhaps be interpreted as an attempt by the Nabataean community to maintain a distinct religious identity while at the same time displaying a degree of 'Romanness'. Unfortunately, without any notion of the temple's architectural design, this suggestion will have to remain conjecture. It is to be hoped that a more thorough exploration of the ancient shoreline and the now subaquatic structures off the Pozzuoli coast will one day provide us with more data in this respect.

The Nabataean Trading Community in Puteoli

As we have seen, the Nabataeans were most of all transporters and middlemen. They purchased goods from suppliers in the East and transported them to the Mediterranean. As we have also seen, they specialised in overland traffic. Although they did business in the Red Sea, and although the harbour of Leukê Kômê formed part of their supply system, they dealt mostly with desert caravans that traversed the Arabian Peninsula. In that light it is surprising to

39 Lacerenza 1988/1989, 148 toys with this idea.

40 No explicit reference to a *temenos* is made in the Puteolan inscriptions. The word *mḥrmt'* in dedication no. 2 (which can mean 'enclosure') here refers to the building itself; Healey 2001, 71–79, 101–102. The word *wḥgr'* too can mean 'enclosure', but the reading is uncertain; Lacerenza 1988/1989, 125. See also Roche 1996, 86–89.

41 See Dessau's comment to *ILS* 4350: 'lapides N. 4350b and 4350c [= my nos. 4 and 5], qui sunt paullo longiores, fortasse pro terminis erant quibus area Dusari sacrata distinguebatur'.

see them involved in what looks like maritime shipping, west of the harbour of Gaza, far outside their native land. The evidence for Nabataean activity in Puteoli leads to two separate though related questions. First: why did the Nabataeans apparently not content themselves with selling their wares to merchants at Gaza, unloading their goods and taking their profit there? Second: why did they choose to maintain trade relations with Puteoli through a resident community?

Put in the context of the Nabataean trade network as a whole, the community in Puteoli—though definitely a literal outlier—is not altogether unique. In fact, the existence of this group fits a larger pattern of Nabataean occupation along trade routes that seems to betray a desire for control over traffic. There is, first of all, the oasis of Dumata far out in the Eastern Desert at the entrance to the Wādi Sirhān, where there is evidence of a Nabataean military presence. The forces patrolling the desert in this area were in all likelihood expected to protect trans-Arabian caravans against raids by nomadic tribes.[42] Nabataean garrison stations also existed in the West along the road between Petra and Gaza. These stations were clearly set up to secure the passage between Nabataea and its principal trade outlet on the Mediterranean.[43]

Perhaps a better parallel, because civilian in nature, is provided by the traces of a Nabataean presence in the Eastern Desert, consisting of graffiti and some ostraca, many of them found in the Myos Hormos–Coptos–Berenice triangle. Some of the people who left these graffiti were cameleers, although one text mentions a plasterer and another a patcher (of clothes?).[44] However, this epigraphic evidence seems to date mostly to the second century CE or later (the only legible date is 266 CE), and it is not entirely clear how to interpret the presence of Nabataeans in this part of Egypt at this relatively late date.[45] Perhaps Nabataean camel drivers moved goods between the Red Sea and the Nile because of their expertise in desert transport, but it is uncertain whether they came over of their own accord or whether they were brought there.

---

42 Young 2001, 94, 115. The Nabataean desert defence system was continued by the Romans; Bowersock 1983, 154–159.

43 Cohen 1982; Young 2001, 97.

44 Littmann and Meredith 1953 nos. 34(?), 37, 46a: cameleers; Littmann and Meredith 1954 no. 61: patcher; no. 75: plasterer. Inscriptions discovered later: Hammond 1979. Nabataean ostraca: Toll 1994. See also Wenning 1983, 126–128 (with map 10); Young 2001, 65.

45 Littmann and Meredith 1953 no. 46a dates to 266 CE; it was found 'likely … on the direct road from Abu Darag to the Nile, i.e. at Bīr Dakhal' (Littmann and Meredith 1953, 1). On the date, cf. Starcky 1955b, 154/155. Littmann and Meredith 1954 nos. 75, 77, and 78 may date to the 1st c. CE, though (or maybe even the 1st c. BCE).

Without a doubt the best parallel to the community in Puteoli is provided by the Nabataean trading stations in the Sinai. The impressive remains of one such station were discovered at Qasrawet (north-western Sinai) in 1909. Archaeological data show that it was in use roughly from the mid second century BCE until the late second century CE, after which date it was peacefully abandoned. This station was probably a stopping-point for Nabataean caravans either travelling from Petra through the Sinai to Pelusium or travelling between the Mediterranean coast and the Gulf of Suez. Unlike the station in Dumata and the stations along the Petra–Gaza road, it seems not to have had a military component; it shows no sign of defensive walls or towers. It did, however, comprise a large necropolis and two monumental temples surrounded by a *temenos*.[46] In the oldest temple, dated to the first century BCE, an inscribed alabaster altar base was found, revealing that the structure was dedicated to the Nabataean deity al-Kutbā.[47]

From another dedicatory inscription we know that a sanctuary to the same deity existed also in the eastern Nile Delta, probably at or near modern-day Tell esh-Shuqafiya where the inscription was found. The text, dated to around 77 BCE, mentions a priest, which seems to suggest a permanently maintained building. Unfortunately, the structure it alludes to remains undiscovered and unexcavated.[48] Another Nabataean inscription found more recently reveals that a shrine, dedicated to Dushara in this case, also existed in the Nile Delta, in all likelihood at the town of Daphne (present Tell ed-Defenna). The text refers to both the current Egyptian and the Nabataean rulers, which gives us a firm date of construction: 37/36 BCE. These two places of worship, combined with the one at Qasrawet, trace the line of important trade routes to Palestine and Syria. They probably all formed part of a system of Nabataean trading settlements, linked throughout the eastern Delta.[49]

In sum, a study of the Nabataean trade network shows that the Nabataean community in Puteoli had parallels elsewhere. But all the same, there seems to have been something peculiar about it. After all, it was a community in a large urban centre which could only be reached from Nabataea by sea. The lone

---

46 Clédat 1912; Oren 1982; Gawlikowski 2003.

47 Clédat 1912, 157. Confusion about the provenance of the inscription led to a double entry in Littmann and Meredith 1954, nos. 82/83. Strugnell 1959, 34/35 with n. 23 both clarifies the confusion and provides the correct reading.

48 Clermont-Ganneau 1924, 229–257; Littmann and Meredith 1954, no. 81 with corrected reading by Strugnell 1959, 31–34. See also Jones, Hammond, Johnson, and Fiema. 1988, 48/49. There is uncertainty about the gender of al-Kutbā; Healey 2001, 120–124.

49 Jones, Hammond, Johnson, and Fiema 1988, 53/54; Zayadine 1985.

stations in the Sinai may have been intended to provide weary caravaneers with repose, food and drink, and a place to worship the Nabataean national gods. The colony in Puteoli may have provided similar services to sea voyagers, but in the trading system of a desert people that is unlikely to explain its incipience or its main function.

Of course Rome (and Italy in general) is likely to have been the terminus point of much of the goods the Nabataeans traded in; these were high-value products that the Roman elite would have had the money to pay for. At the time the Nabataeans seem to have been most active in Puteoli—the late Republican and Augustan era—the city was still the uncontested principal harbour serving Rome. Furthermore, Puteoli is known to have been a major centre for the lucrative trade in incense and perfume.[50] It would therefore seem that the focus of the Nabataean community there was not primarily on seagoing Nabataeans but rather on Puteoli itself. It would seem, phrased differently, that the main purpose was to maintain contact with the Puteolans.

One important motive for a desire to establish a direct link can easily be imagined, namely access to information. Under preindustrial conditions, such as obviously existed under the Roman Empire, communication was dreadfully slow—information could only travel as fast as sails and legs would allow. For traders it was therefore difficult to learn about commercial opportunities and market conditions from anywhere outside of their immediate vicinity. This limitation must have presented a serious problem for the Nabataeans; Italy, an important market for their products, was far away from their homeland. They could have turned to shippers and merchants at Gaza to gain knowledge about demand, prices, and competition overseas, but relying on middlemen for such crucial trading information bore grave risks. Middlemen could misrepresent the situation over the horizon, exaggerating the level of competition or stating lower prices for Nabataean products than they were actually fetching. It is imaginable that the Nabataeans intended to circumvent that problem by maintaining a link to Italy themselves. If true, this would explain why they traded not just at Gaza, but travelled beyond what would seem to be a natural halting point.

But that still does not explain why they chose to maintain commercial relations with Puteoli through permanent settlers. To answer that question we should take into account that by making Puteoli their home, emigrating Nabataeans effectively became part of their newly adopted social environment; they became part of the local face-to-face community that traded, socialised,

50 Camodeca 1977, 65/66; Camodeca 1979, 24. See also De Romanis 1996, 247–250; De Romanis 1993; Dubois 1907, 129/130.

and exchanged gossip. They thus gained access to information that would have been impossible for occasional visitors to obtain. In addition, they established trust with the Puteolan trading community, which furnishes another reason why the Nabataeans maintained a resident colony. Living permanently in Puteoli effectively enabled them to establish long-term commercial relationships with their buyers, to negotiate contracts, and to have the assurance that they could resolve any trade conflicts that might arise. In this respect, it is crucial to realise that the Roman government did not use its coercive powers to enforce private contracts. A merchant could draw up a formal legal contract with another merchant, but if something went wrong—unsatisfactory delivery, non-payment, or outright fraud—he was on his own. Even if he managed to take a defaulting business partner to court and was vindicated *in iure*, the Roman authorities would not provide physical assistance in enforcing the court's decision. Given these conditions, long-distance contractual exchange must have relied on personal contacts, trust, and reputation.

As permanent residents, Nabataean settlers in Puteoli would have had every incentive to cooperate with the local merchants and to refrain from bad behaviour; they thus became trustworthy contractual partners. At the same time, they remained recognisable as a foreign element—they did not assimilate to the extent that they became indistinguishable within their new social environment. The existence of the Nabataean temple I discussed above is relevant in this regard; it is a sure sign of the colonists' collective separateness from their adopted host community. This collective separateness must have had a number of effects stemming from their group's reputation. Because the actions of individuals would be at least partly attributed to the group, the collective would have had an incentive to monitor the behaviour of its individual members. Equally important, it had the effect that the newcomers, though domiciled in Puteoli, continued to be 'the other'. This, in turn, meant that their membership of and allegiance to the foreign trade network was never called into question.

Because geographical provenance and religious identity formed the defining elements of this group, it was effectively a closed network with fixed membership. Non-Nabataeans would not have been able to join, nor would Nabataeans, if expelled, have been able to join another network. The members making up the network as a collective therefore had a large amount of coercive power over individual members; they possessed the power to include and exclude, and they thus controlled access to Nabataean business in Puteoli.[51]

51 A similar network seems to have been maintained by a group of Jewish merchants, known from the famous medieval 'Genizah archive', who conducted long-distance trade in the Mediterranean and the Levant. Their mercantile coalition was founded upon a sense of shared origin, religion, ethnicity, and history. Their system of internal monitoring,

As members of a foreign trade network centred on geographical provenance, they would have had more occasion for monitoring and punishment than their native business partners. They could, for example, ostracise members from the collective or spread negative reports about them, thereby ensuring that misbehaving members could no longer get any business. The result of all this would have been that trust was established between Nabataeans and Puteolans, and that both sides could feel secure that trade conflicts could be resolved through the proper legal channels, even in the absence of government enforcement.

I can illustrate this last point with a set of two wax tablets from the so-called Sulpicii archive, found in Pompeii but mostly drawn up in Puteoli. Both documents are private contracts in which two parties agreed to appear in court at a mutually agreed-upon future date. The first was made by a Puteolan banker and a man from the Syrian city of Tyre. It was drafted in Puteoli on 9 June 52 CE and reads:

> Commitment to appear made by Zenon the Tyrian, freedman of Zenobus, for the third day before the Ides of next June (= June 11th) at Puteoli in the forum in front of the Hordionian altar of Augustus at the third hour. Gaius Sulpicius Cinnamus asked to be paid in good faith HS 1,200; Zenon the Tyrian, freedman of Zenobus, promised in good faith . . .[52]

The second document, similar to the first, is a contract between the same Puteolan banker and an Egyptian from Alexandria. It cannot be precisely dated, but must have been drafted between the years 44 CE and 79 CE:

> Commitment to appear made by Trypho the Alexandrian, son of Potamon, for the ?sixteenth? day before the Kalends of next April at Rome in the Forum Augustum in front of the triumphal statue of Gnaeus Sentius Saturninus at the fifth hour. Gaius Sulpicius Cinnamus asked to be paid in good faith HS 3,000; Trypho the Alexandrian, son of Potamon, promised in good faith . . .[53]

---

social control, and ostracism as a form of punishment is, I propose, comparable to the Nabataean network. See Terpstra 2013, 95–100; Greif 2006, 58–90.

52 *TPSulp*.4: '[Vadimoniu]m fac[tu]m [Zenoni] Zenobi l(iberto) [T]yri[o] [in] III idus Iunias primas, [P]uteolis in foro [an]te ara[m] A[u]gusti Hordionianam hora tertia; [H]S ∞ CC da[r]i fide r[o]gavit C(aius) Sul[picius] Cinnamus f[ide promi]sit Zenon Zenob[i] l(ibertus) Tyrius . . .'

53 *TPSulp*.13: 'Vadimonium factum Truphoni Potamonis f(ilio) Alex(andrino) in X[. .]I k(alendas) Apriles primas Romae in foro Augusto ante statuam Cn(aei) Senti Saturnini triumpha[l]em hora quinta; HS ∞ ∞ ∞ [dari] fide rogavit C(aius) Sulpicius [Cinnamu]s fide promisit [Trupho Potamonis f(ilius) Alex(andrinus)] . . .' The same two parties appear

A Puteolan banker in two separate instances entered into contracts with men from overseas. In both cases the banker and the stranger agreed to go to court, in the one case in Puteoli itself and in the other (for unknown reasons) in Rome. This course of action might seem unremarkable but is actually quite significant. Litigating is a long-term investment; an investment in the trial itself—possibly a long, drawn-out, and costly affair—and ultimately also an investment in a business relationship. Such voluntary cooperation in conflict resolution would simply not have occurred without a social incentive. The Puteolan financier would have had to know that his debtor would not one day decide that the affair was becoming more trouble than it was worth, and that it was more beneficial for him just to sail off. Apparently Cinnamus could trust both the Tyrian and the Alexandrian to have an incentive to cooperate. Because the Roman authorities did not provide for an enforcement mechanism, that incentive must have been social in nature: it must have stemmed from the relationship of the foreign men to a group they formed a part of, and that they wanted to continue forming a part of. From an important inscription found in Puteoli we know for a fact that there was a club of permanent settlers from Tyre living in the city;[54] a group of settlers from Alexandria seems highly probable too: the oldest Italian Serapeum that we know of was already standing in Puteoli in at least 105 BCE.[55]

The evidence from the Sulpicii archive in combination with the Puteolan epigraphic record suggests that the system of overseas exchange through foreign settlers was adopted more widely in Puteoli than just in Nabataean–Italian trade. The Nabataeans may therefore have been conforming to a general way of doing business in Puteoli.[56] But in any case, although the Sulpicii archive does not contain a litigation contract in which a Puteolan banker and a Nabataean appear (which, given the scarcity of our data, would perhaps be a bit much to ask for), the same constraints on business applied to Nabataean–Italian trade as applied to Tyrian–Italian and Alexandrian–Italian trade. There is, therefore, no reason to think that for Nabataeans operating in Puteoli things were any different.[57]

again in the archive in yet another *vadimonium* (*TPSulp.*14). It is not clear if that document is connected to the same dispute.

54 *IG* 14.830. See Terpstra 2013, 70–84.

55 *CIL* 10.1781. See Tran tam Tinh 1972, 3–11; De Romanis 1993, 62.

56 This argument I have made elsewhere. See Terpstra 2013, 84–92.

57 A difference between these situations was, of course, that Syria and Egypt were Roman provinces at the time the contracts were drawn up, while Nabataea was not. That differ-

A passage from Strabo is also relevant in this regard. It describes the mirrored situation of Nabataeans living in Puteoli, namely Romans living in Petra. Strabo's friend, the philosopher Athenodorus of Tarsus, had visited the city and 'said that he found both many Romans and many other foreigners living there ('ἐπιδημοῦντας'), and that he saw that the foreigners often engaged in lawsuits, both with one another and with the natives...'[58] The real point of Athenodorus' story was to express amazement that the Nabataeans lived peacefully together and did not prosecute each other. However, this amazement probably reflects Athenodorus' ignorance about the role of Nabataean tribal organisations and tribal assemblies in administering justice.[59] But however that may be, the most interesting aspect of this passage, at least for my purposes, is the resident Romans' involvement in litigation with the native population. Apparently, the Nabataeans could trust the Romans in their midst to honour judicial outcomes. I propose that this trust was based on the knowledge that individual Romans could not pack up their bags and leave from one moment to the next if it suited their interests, because this would have eliminated them from their ethnic trading community.

But to confine my conclusions to Puteoli: the Nabataean colony in the city helped the Nabataeans maintain a commercial network that spanned a vast area. In this commercial network, much was at stake for both sellers and buyers. The Nabataeans dealt in high-value goods: frankincense, myrrh, spices, and likely silk. Sending such goods or sending payment for such goods over long distances under conditions of limited information and limited government support was a high-risk business. The system of merchants from one community living in another, functioning as agents, reduced those risks to an acceptable level.[60]

---

ence does not affect the problems of pre-industrial long-distance exchange and imperfect government enforcement, though, nor does it influence the proposed solution.

58 Strabo 16.4.21: εὑρεῖν γὰρ ἐπιδημοῦντας ἔφη πολλοὺς μὲν Ῥωμαίων, πολλοὺς δὲ καὶ τῶν ἄλλων ξένων· τοὺς μὲν οὖν ξένους ὁρᾶν κρινομένους πολλάκις καὶ πρὸς ἀλλήλους καὶ πρὸς τοὺς ἐπιχωρίους,...' (trans., with small alteration, by H.L. Jones, LCL 1930). See Bowersock 1983, 61; De Romanis 1993, 65; 1996, 165–166.

59 Wenning 2007, 34.

60 I would like to thank Marco Maiuro for inviting me to the conference. I would further like to thank Roger Bagnall, David Ratzan, and Federico De Romanis for their comments and help with this paper. Any mistakes are, of course, wholly mine.

TABLE 5.1 *Epigraphic evidence for Nabataeans in the Mediterranean.*

	Location	Date	Language	Description	Publication
1	Puteoli	11 CE	Aramaic	Plaque commemorating offer of two camels (votive statues?) to Dushara by Zaidu and Abdelge	*CISem* 2.1.157 (= Tran tam Tinh, no. S.2 = Lacerenza 1988/1989, 140–142)
2		5 CE	Aramaic	Plaque commemorating enlargement of Nabataean sanctuary, originally built 50/49 BCE	*CISem* 2.1.158 (= Tran tam Tinh, no. S.1 = Lacerenza 1988/1989, 123–128)
3		Early 1st c. CE?	Latin	Base with 7 slots for *betyls* consecrated to Dushara	Tran tam Tinh, no. S.3
4		Early 1st c. CE?	Latin	Base with 3 slots for *betyls* consecrated to Dushara	*ILS* 4350b (= Tran tam Tinh, no. S.4)
5		Early 1st c. CE?	Latin	Base with 3 slots for *betyls* consecrated to Dushara	*ILS* 4350c (= Tran tam Tinh, no. S.5)
6		Early 1st c. CE?	Latin	Altar consecrated to Dushara	*CIL* 10.1556 (= *ILS* 4350b = Tran tam Tinh, no. S.6)
7		Early 1st c. CE?	Latin	Broken piece of marble (revetment?), carrying the word 'Dus[ari?]'	Tran tam Tinh, no. S.7
8		Early 1st c. CE?	Latin	Marble revetment, carrying words 'Dusari sacrum'	Lacerenza 1994[61] (= AE 1994, 422)
9		Early 1st c. CE?	Latin	Marble revetment, carrying words 'Dusari sacrum'	Lacerenza 1994 (= AE 1994, 423)

61 Note that the pictures in Lacerenza 1994 are reversed by mistake: A should be B and vice versa.

	Location	Date	Language	Description	Publication
10		Early 1st c. CE?	Latin	Marble revetment, carrying words '[Dusari s]acrum'	Camodeca 2001, 97–99 (=AE 2001, 843)
11		Early 1st c. CE?	Latin	*Ex voto*(?): '[Du] sar[i sacrum?] [C.?] *I*ul(ius) T[---]'[62]	Camodeca 2001, 97–99 (=AE 2001, 844)
12		1st c. BCE–1st c. CE?	Greek	Grave stele of Tholomaios, son of Thaimallos, from Petra; died age 33	IG XIV *add. et corrig.* 842a
13	Rome	1st c. CE	Aramaic/ Latin	Abgarus from Petra set up a grave stele for his relative Abdaretas, died age 30	*CISem 2.1.159* (= CIL 6.34196 = Vaglieri *N.d.Sc.* 1892, 411/412)
14		9 BCE–40 CE	Latin/ Greek	Rabeibelus son of Thaemus and —(?) son of Thaemoobdadallus, Nabataean envoys in Rome	*IGUR* 1.16
15		?–mid-first c. CE[63]	Aramaic/ Latin	Dedicatory inscription to Dushara(?)	Amadasi Guzzo 1988
16	Miletus	9/8 BCE	Aramaic/ Greek	Dedication to Zeus Dushara by Syllaeus, minister of Nabataean King Obodas, for King's health	*I. Delphinion* no. 165

62 I am not as convinced as Camodeca that this is actually a Dushara inscription. The palaeography is clearly different from the revetments. If it is a Latin *ex voto* instead, it would be unique in the corpus; in my view, too little of the text survives to warrant that conclusion. The text may (by Camodeca's own admission) well have read '[Cae]sar' instead of '[Du]sar[i]'.

63 Roche 1996, 90 proposes a date of 58-30 BCE (reign of Malichos I rather than Malichos II).

TABLE 5.1 *Epigraphic evidence for Nabataeans in the Mediterranean* (cont.)

	Location	Date	Language	Description	Publication
17	Delos	9/8 BCE	Aramaic/ Greek	Dedication to Zeus Dushara by Syllaeus, minister of Nabataean King Obodas, for King's health	*I.Délos* 2315 with Bruneau p. 244
18		Late 2nd–early 1st c. BCE	Greek	Grave stele for 19 slaves, owned by Protarchus; among them Zaidos, a Nabataean	Marie-Thérèse Couilloud *Délos* vol. 30 (1974), no. 418
19	Cos	68 BCE or 9/10 CE[64]	Aramaic/ Greek	Dedication by Aswallah to the goddess al-ʿUzzā ('Aphrodite' in Greek) for the health of Aretas, King of the Nabataeans	*I.Cos* EV 259 (= Levi Della Vida 1938)
20	Chalce	?	Greek	Honorary decree on altar by groups worshiping Heracles and Dushara(?)	*IG* 12.1.963
21	Tenos	150–100 BCE	Greek	Crown and *proxenia* granted to Nabataean Salamenes by the city of Tenos	*IG* 12 Suppl. 307

64 For a discussion on the date, see Levi Della Vida 1938, 142/143 with n. 2; Roche 1996, 79.

PART 2

Comparative Perspectives on the India Trade

CHAPTER 6

Indian Gold Crossing the Indian Ocean Through the Millennia

Harry Falk

The north-western part of ancient India is the land of gold, at least if we believe the classical authors. Herodotus tells us in the sixth century BCE that India is immensely rich in gold, partly sifted from the river sands, partly dug up from the earth, and partly stolen from gold-digging ants.[1] River-sourced gold, however, certainly has a background in reality and accords with the tributes the Indians had to deliver year after year to the court of Achaemenid Iran, from Darius I onwards. According to the same book of Herodotus,[2] the Indians had to deliver 360 talents of gold every year, more than any other single country. With Megasthenes as an additional reference, Strabo corroborates Herodotus with regard to gold gleaned from rivers and tribute paid to the king.[3]

In the second century CE Dionysios Periegetes mentions Taxilans and then moves farther to the east 'where, swiftest of streams, the Hypanis and the divine Margarsos carry down the shining seeds of gold.'[4] According to Strabo,[5] 'Hypanis' can only be the Sutlej. The 'divine Margarsos' is impossible to locate; a likely river was the Son/Swan in Himachal Pradesh, flowing into the Beas, which flows into the Sutlej; its name probably derived from Sanskrit *suvarṇa*, 'gold'. At least the Hoshiarpur District Gazeteer states that 'gold is washed in insignificant quantities in the bed of [the] Swan and other streams.'[6] The quantities may well have been considerably more 4000 years ago. The Chinese monk Xuanzang visited a place in northern Pakistan in the seventh century CE, either the Darel valley on the upper Indus or the Swat valley, and reports that 'this country produces much gold'.[7] When and for how long did the Indians

1 Hdt. 3.106. The latter method is locally fixed by Herodotus to Paktia, eastern Afghanistan, and is the topic of an amusing story in 3.102–105.

2 Hdt. 3.94.

3 Strabo 15.1.57; 69.

4 Dionys. Per. 1143–1146.

5 Strabo 15.1.32.

6 Hoshiarpur District Gazeteer 1884, 9.

7 Xuanzang 134.

 | DOI 10.1163/9789004289536_008

produce so much gold? Prior to Herodotus two cultures are worth examining: the Harappan or Indus Valley Culture, rich in archaeological vestiges, but no literary heritage, and the Vedic culture, rich in literary evidence, but almost entirely lacking in material remnants.

The Harappan Weights

There are a few gold ornaments found at the Harappan sites, even a few elaborate ones, but on the whole, gold does not play a significant role in the households at any of the city sites, if we are to rely on the actual finds. Did the Harappans not care much about gold? We know that Gudea of Lagash (2141–2122 BCE) imported gold dust from the mountains of Meluḫḫa.[8] After the dissolution of the Harappan civilisation, gold was imported by Gungunum of Larsa (1932–1906 BCE) from Dilmun (Bahrain),[9] which acted as a conduit for a series of South Asian regional suppliers. A simultaneous import of gold into India, as occasionally assumed,[10] seems very unlikely.

The field of information gets wider once we look at the Harappan weight system. Skinner[11] was of the opinion that weights as such were first introduced to weigh gold, and that their use only later expanded to include commerce. He credited the Harappan civilisation with introducing weighing in the service of commerce. Why not then credit the Harappans with the use of weights for trading gold on a widespread commercial basis? The Harappan system of weights has been described and explained several times and presents a basic weight, variously defined as 13.71 g,[12] or, at Chanhu Daro, 13.63 g,[13] with variations of less than 2 per cent over seven centuries. The multiples are decimal, that is 2, 3, 4, 5, and 10, and more units are found in nicely polished cubes of chert or agate, both substances hard enough to withstand wear and tear. The lower units are subdivided on a binary system, that is 13.63 g, 13.71 g, or similar are divided by two, again and again, down to the smallest cube of less than 1 g. This system appeared spontaneously complete and unchanging over the centuries.

---

8 Hansman 1973, 556, 560.

9 Ibid. 556.

10 Asthana 1984, 276.

11 Skinner 1954, 779.

12 Hemmy 1938: 603; Skinner 1967: 11.

13 Petruso 1981: 50.

What are these weights used for? The excavations do not provide a simple answer but point towards jewellers as the main users. On the other hand it has long been known[14] that this basic weight as well as its decimal multiplication and binary subdivision finds an exact match in Egypt in a weight unit called *beqa*. Early forms differ, but the later ones are flat cuboids of mostly black stone, inscribed with the hieroglyph for gold (*nub*), together with a number indicating its place in the scale of a weight unit called *beqa*. Its unit was defined by Skinner,[15] who showed that the *beqa* had three important substandards, of 12.42 g, 13.35 g, and 13.67 g, the latter being in the range of the Harappan standard.

The western connections through weights are also obvious in the barrel-shaped weights introduced in Sumer around 2000 BCE,[16] with a standard of 8.36 g. In the Harappan cities such a shape is also found, but centring around a base of slightly larger than 8 g at Harappa[17] and Lothal.[18] It is the shape that matters: cuboid and barrel-shaped weights at the same time in all cultures from Egypt to late Sumer to late Harappa could not originate in the absence of a common idea behind them.

Where did the trade go? The Egyptians obviously had enough of their own gold resources. Imports would presuppose a rather low buying price. Or did Egypt and Harappa both export to a common customer? There is Dilmun, which includes the island of Bahrain, trading with Mesopotamia as well as with the Harappan culture. Within the common ranges, their weight system is absolutely identical with the Indian one. Cuboid stones found there weigh 1.8, 13.5, and 27 g, which is ⅛, 1, and 2 times the basic unit, and hemispherical weights were found weighing 13.9, 171, 670, and 1370 g, which are 1, 12.5, 50, and 100 units.[19] In Ur this weight was called the 'standard of Dilmun'. The exchange formula was that 1 Ur *mina* of *c*.500 g divided by three was equivalent to 1 Dilmun *mina* divided by 8, a system that nicely took advantage of the

14 Hemmy 1938: 604.

15 Skinner 1967: 11.

16 Ibid. 17.

17 Vats 1940: 362, Type b, where no. 7597 with 128.15 g would contain 16 units, no. A333 with 80.65 g 10 units. The specimens show a sequence of 1, 3, 5, 8, 10, and 16 units, with 3 and 5 deviating significantly.

18 Rao 1985: 561 has two with 203.6 and 54.0 g, which he regards as imports. The first one would contain 25 units of 8.14 g. Table XX on p. 565 seems to show another barrel of 33.1 g, which could represent a unit of 4.

19 Roaf 1982: 140.

sexagesimal system in Mesopotamia and the decimal and binary system of the Dilmun-Harappa.[20]

In summary, I assume that in the third millennium BCE gold from the Indus valley went west, probably to Dilmun, from where it was sold to Mesopotamia, where gold was in high demand, while the Indus valley produced gold and did not use it for much except barter. The mass of the Harappan stone weights range between 1 to 100 g, certainly useful for measuring gold. The heavier stones of more than one kilogram could be used for copper, as attested on a tablet from Ur which documents the import of an incredible 18,000 kg.[21]

The Vedic Times

After the downfall of the empire of Akkad in Mesopotamia the Indian trade westward likewise came to a close. The Harappan civilization declined and finally dissolved. In the following centuries of the second millennium a series of texts were produced by people variously regarded as invaders, intruders, or native populations. The origin of the creators of the vast Vedic literature does not concern us here. We only state that the Vedic poets and the civil society around them had a certain taste for gold. From the Brāhmaṇa literature we learn that gold was taken from rivers,[22] as well as from mountains. It was melted, refined with salt,[23] and turned into a variety of ornaments. The Vedic Indians measured it and prescribed how much of it should be given as a fee to priests performing their ritual sacrifices. An early unit seems to be the 'drop', *pṛḍ*/*pruḍ*. Gold measuring 8 drops is given as a present to the priest, symbolizing by its number the eight feet of a pregnant cow and thus fecundity and growth.[24] The idea of a 'drop' is not confined to Vedic India; it is also found in Egypt.[25]

The measure most often mentioned is the *śatamāna*, literally a 'measure of one hundred'. It was not a single piece of metal, like a coin,[26] but could be

20 Ibid. 141.

21 Ibid. 137.

22 Rau 1973: 30.

23 Falk 1997.

24 Taittirīyasaṃhitā 3.4.1: *dákṣiṇā aṣṭā́padī hy èṣā́ ātmā́ navamáḥ paśór ā́ptyai*; cf. Kāṭhakam 13.10 (*aṣṭāpṛḍaṃ hiraṇyaṃ*) and 11.1 (*upacāyyapṛdaṃ hiraṇyam*) and the discourse on *pṛḍ*/*pruḍ* in von Schroeder 1895: 164.

25 *LÄ* III s.v. Maße und Gewichte → Werte → Tropfen.

26 For older theories cf. Ganguly 1989, who again takes it as an ingot and who stresses the change in meaning towards a silver measure by the time of the Manusmṛti.

subdivided in twice thirty and once forty,[27] to enhance the fee with symbolic numbers. At other occasions a *śatamāna* of precious metal was divided twenty-five or twenty-six times into units of four,[28] which indicates that the metal was not solid, but probably gold dust, easy to separate. In the Sūtra period the term *śatamāna* was used simply to denote a weight, irrespective of the material used.[29]

An object of this weight can be a breast ornament (*rukma*)[30] or a neck ornament (*niṣka*). It could be gold and silver (Āpastambaśrautasūtra *suvarṇa* & *rajata* 15.5,16; *harita* & *rajata* Āpastambaśrautasūtra 19.2,6).[31] And from phrases like Āpastambaśrautasūtra 19.21,1 (*prājāpatyāṃ śatakṛṣṇalāṃ nirvaped āyuṣkāmaḥ*) it looks as if the unit behind the 'hundred' was the *guñja* seed, also called *raktika* or *kṛṣṇala*, because it is black with a bright red spot. Its weight, on average, is 0.114 g[32]—one hundred would add up to 11.4 g. But the weight as such is less important than the symbolic value of 100, which denotes the full span of life, hopefully conferred upon the donor through everything counting

27 Maitrāyaṇisaṃhitā 1.6.4 [93: 3ff.]: *'śatámānaṃ bhavati (…) púrvayor havíṣayor dvé triṁśánmāne déye úttarasmiṁś catvāriṃśánmânaṃ'*; cf. Kāṭhakam 8.5 [89: 6ff.], 'A measure of hundred is used. At the two earlier offerings two measures of thirty are to be given, a measure of forty at the later.'

28 Baudhāyanaśrautasūtra 13.23 [134, 3–4]: *'atha vai bhavati "catvāricatvāri kṛṣṇalāny avadyati caturavattasyāptyai" iti aṣṭau devatāyā avadyati catvāri sviṣṭakṛte 'ṣṭāv iḍāyai catvāry avāntareḍḍyā ekaṃ prāśitrāyaikaṃ yajamānāya'*, 'Now we deal with the saying of the Veda (e.g. Kāṭhakam 11.4): "He separates [gold of the weight of 100 *kṛṣṇalas*] in groups of four guñjas one by one, to achieve the division by four." This in mind he separates eight (times four) for the deity, four for (Agni) Sviṣṭakṛt, eight for Iḍā, four for the intermediate Iḍā, one for the Brahman's portion, one for the sacrificer.' There is one group too many, explained in Baudhāyanaśrautasūtra 23.3 [152,4]. The division as such follows the idea of the Vedic game of dice, that a given number fully divided by four means success.

29 Baudhāyanaśrautasūtra 18.37: 386,10: *'duraśena yakṣyamāṇo bhavati sa upakalpayate ṣaṣṭiṃ śatamānāni hiraṇyāni triṃśataṃ suvarṇāni triṃśataṃ rajatāni bahv anyad dhiraṇyam'*; 'He wants to sacrifice with the Duraśa. He prepares 60 śatamānas of precious metal, 30 of gold, 30 of silver, and lots of other stuff made from precious metal.'

30 Vārāhaśrautasūtra 3.3.2,28: *'śatakṛṣṇalaṃ rukmaṃ śatātṛṇṇam'*, 'a breast ornament, weighing hundred Kṛṣṇalas, having hundred holes.'

31 See n. 29.

32 This is my own measurement of 20 seeds received in Kathmandu from a jeweller. There are many slightly differing and higher measurements listed in Thomas (1874, 65): 0.117 (Elliot), 0.118 (Laidlay, Cunningham), 0.124 (Jervis, Sykes) and 0.125 (Mirat trials), possibly taken from freshly picked seeds in Bengal. Mainkar (1984, 144) after 'many experiments' saw a range from 105 to 125 g, 'with a general average around 110 milligrammes'.

one hundred. This explains why the gold used could be counted in *guñjas* or in another unit, like one called *kṣara*,[33] or the 'drop' of gold mentioned above.

The Vedic period can thus be summarized: after an initial phase when a 'drop' was a certain unit, the *guñja* seeds occur as a dominating unit of weight; however, it is not mentioned as the absolute basis of the *śatamāna* or any other (number)-*māna* in the oldest literature. The *guñja* seed occurs from the Mantra-period onwards, roughly somewhere in the first part of the first millennium BCE. The early Kāṭhakam [11.4] still measures an oblation of boiled barley against a standard of a hundred *kṛṣṇalas*, while the later Sūtra-texts seem to use the measure only for metals.

The Arthaśāstra

The Arthaśāstra presents a very similar system. Unfortunately, this fourth century BCE text has a limited informative value, since it was adulterated by the incorporation in the second/third century CE of parts of several of its own commentaries. If we take the single lines for what they say we get a basic weight of 9.12 g for gold, and possibly another one of 11.14 g for silver. One line tells us that there is a sequence of ½, 1, 2, 4, 8, and 16 units, which is binary, another one of 2, 4, 8, and 10, which is probably decimal, and a subsequent sequence of 20, 30, 40, and 100, which is definitely decimal. This means that we again encounter the twofold division into a binary subdivision and a decimal sequence upwards. The basic weights seem to be 9.12 and 11.14 g. These can be easily explained as being 80 and 100 times the weight of the *guñja* seeds. When we compare the Harappan weight of 13.68 g, we see that it continues the series and consists of 120 such seeds.

How to explain the differences? It is clear on the one hand that 80, 100, and 120 follow the same idea. Eighty can be subdivided in a binary way four times, one hundred only two times, and 120 takes middle position with three times. From a practical point of view, eighty looks like the most useful ground weight. This is the weight called *suvarṇa*, 'gold', in late Vedic and early historic texts.

---

33 Āpastambaśrautasūtra 18.15,5 '(*a*)*mṛtam asīti tasmiñ chatamānaṃ hiraṇyaṃ nidhāya didyon mā pāhi_iti sauvarṇena śatamānena śatakṣareṇa śatakṛṣṇalena vā yajamānasya śīrṣann adhi nidhatte*', 'With the stanza beginning with *amṛtam asi* he lays a measure of hundred in precious metal down; with the stanza beginning with *didyon mā pāhi* he places (it) together with a golden measure of hundred on the head of the sacrificer, be it (of the measure of) hundred *kṣara* or hundred guñjas.' The term *śatakṣara* occurs only in the Taittirīyabrāhmaṇa 1.8.9.1, ĀpŚS 20.20,2 (without *vā*), and seems to escape definition so far; in any case *kṣara* is different from *kṛṣṇala*.

Seen this way the development follows the evolution of usefulness. The reverse process looks rather unlikely. But how did the basic weight of 120 originate? This should be connected with the question of why the *guñja* seed was chosen; why not another fruit or grain? The texts tell us that one *guñja* seed is equal in weight to three barley grains, barley being the staple food of Vedic Indians. If we multiply the standard numbers, then the standard Harappan weight is not 120 *guñja* seeds, but 360 barley grains. This rings a whole series of bells: 360 symbolizes the days of the year, the absolute unit in Vedic thinking. The year is 'everything' in that it symbolizes cyclical regeneration. The 360 barley grains equalling 120 *guñja* seeds as the basic unit of the Harappan weight system does not necessarily presuppose a Harappan origin of the Vedic society; rather it shows that there is a continuum, either solely of ideas, or of people, or of both.

The Akṣa Weight

Once we imagine that the Harappan system could have a continuation in standard 'Sanskritic' India, we encounter another strange coincidence. The classical sources present several sequences of weights. They seem to copy diverse older texts, not fully understanding all of them, thus producing quite a number of contradictions. There is one weight defined only in the Viṣṇusmṛti, which states, as we already know, that three barley grains weigh as much as one *guñja* seed.[34] Then we learn that five *guñjas* make one *māṣaka*, as found in most other texts as well. Then we learn that twelve of these *māṣaka*s make half an *akṣa*.[35] The eponymous Viṣṇu could have said as well that twenty-four *māṣakas* make one *akṣa*. The weight of an *akṣa* thus is five *guñjas* times twenty-four, 120 in all. As we already know, 120 *guñjas* define the weight unit of the Harappans, 13.68 g. The weight stones of the Harappans were cubes, and the Sanskrit term for cube is *akṣa*. Whether we like it or not, the historic term *akṣa* at the same time complies with the weight as defined by Viṣṇu, and it also describes the shape of the pre-historic cubes. This can be a coincidence; I for one would rather think it speaks of some sort of continuation.

A change was mentioned before: the *guñja* seed could have replaced an older barley grain, 360 of which would as well define the Harappan weight. Did the *śatamāna* describe one hundred barley grains or one hundred *guñja* seeds? We only know that the more recent Vedic literature takes the *guñja* seeds for granted.[36] For the older time, evidence is missing.

---

34 KA 4.6.

35 KA 4.8: *taddvādaśakam akṣārdham.*

36 ŚB 13.4.1.6; ĀpŚS 5.21,8.

Subsequent Weights

If we consider a sort of continuation of the Harappan weight for 2000 years we might ask if we can find it, or some of its derivatives of eighty and one hundred *guñjas*, in more recent times as well.

Gold Darics

Coinage starts late in India, compared to the Near East. Gold was used by the Achaemenid kings, who also ruled western India, and it was used by the first so-called Indo-Greek kings. From Darius onwards, gold coins were issued, showing a king with a bow or lance, one knee touching the ground. The weight of these so-called Darics was 8.34 g.[37] This weight was ultimately derived from the Sumerian (later Babylonian) shekel of 8.36 g, which itself had been defined 2000 years earlier as the weight of 180 wheat grains, 'from the middest of the spike', meaning the largest grains from the middle of the ear of wheat.[38] Amazingly, the same description can also be found in India, when Yājñavalkya 1,363 and Manu 8,134 speak of 'middle barley grains', *yavo madhyaḥ*, to define a weight relationship.[39] It seems that an idea about how to define grain weights is common to ancient Mesopotamia and India.

Hellenistic Gold Standards

The weight of the Achaemenid Daric gold coin is around 8.4 g, with variants up to 8.8 g. It must be compared to the golden Philippeios of Philipp II of Macedonia (8.6 g), based on the Attic silver standard. Because of the proximity of the measurements and the weight variations it seems possible that the two standards were mixed or mutually approached, but on the whole it seems safe to say that the Hellenistic kings in Mesopotamia and Bactria maintained the Iranian rather than the Attic standard with regard to gold. This applies to coins of Antiochus (280–261 BCE), to the first independent kings of Bactria, to Diodotus I and II (*c.*250–230; 230–225 BCE), to Euthydemus I (*c.*225–200 BCE), and to Eucratides I (*c.*170–155 BCE). The latter issued a unique coin of 169.2 g,

37 Skinner 1967, 52.

38 Ibid. 18; Salonen 1965, 290.

39 The Arthaśāstra 2.20, 5–6 speaks of *yavamadhya* in a compound, possibly mixing it with a certain atonement ritual.

equal to twenty staters, each of 8.46 g. After Eucratides, gold coinage went out of common use. Single issues by Menander or Zoilos (145–130 BCE) do not seem to represent a wide-spread system of gold coinage. On the whole it seems as if the Hellenistic kings of Bactria used the Daric gold standard, or simply heated and re-struck Achaemenid gold coins.

Kuṣāṇa Gold Standard

Vima Kadphises revived gold coinage in the early decades of the second century CE. His first issues are known for only a couple of years, from a treasure find in Peshawar city.[40] It seems as if the royal family had collected pieces of coinage of the standard series, and also some early types later withdrawn from circulation. The oldest pieces are made notable by the king naming his father by name, Vema Takhtu, meant to read OOEMO TAKTOO in Greek letters. Amongst them is one gold coin of 8.62 g on which the king's bust is seen on the obverse, and a composite god on the reverse.[41] It is the only one with text arranged in rectangular outline, and it is the only one with such a high weight. Possibly, judging by its mint state, this type was never given into circulation. It shows at least that Vima Kadphises initially considered the Attic standard for his new gold coinage.

The next pieces of very early type are based on a standard of 8.1 g. However, all following issues centre much lower, around 7.9 g. Very rarely the staters weigh exactly 8 g, and weights above that appear to be absent. Apart from sporadic exceptions much above 8 g, the same applies to the gold coinage of Kaniṣka I, Huviṣka, and Vasudeva. With Kaniṣka II and all following kings the weight never exceeds 7.9, and falls slowly down to 7.8 g.

The following Gupta dynasty cuts the weight further, down to around 7.5 g;[42] some, like Candragupta II, return to the old 7.9 g standard of the Kuṣāṇas, only to replace it by a new heavier standard rising up to 9.2 g and even higher,[43] obviously expecting more prestige from higher standards, irrespective of the mess created for traders who have to inspect every single coin to estimate its mercantile value. For our concerns, here it is only important to restate how

40 Bopearachchi 2006; 2008.

41 Bopearachchi 2008, 8, no. 1.

42 At the risk of ending in her n. 29, I refuse to follow the idea of Raven (2006, 214) that the weights of the Roman *aureus*, the Kuṣāṇa stater, and the early Gupta gold coins are not related to each other.

43 Raven 2006, 214f.

Vima Kadphises proceeded: he first thought of the Attic gold weight of 8.6 g, then shortly tried 8.1 g, and after a very short time ended with 7.9 to 8 g. Why? Apart from monetary reasons, we need always look for symbolic values when it comes to the early Kuṣāṇa kings.

The Roman Aureus

The Roman gold coins are easy to describe. Julius Caesar defined the aureus as one-fortieth of a Roman pound of 327.17 g, leading to a weight around 8.18 g. The surviving coins of Julius Caesar, who lived 100–44 BCE, rarely surpass 8.10 g, while most of them are just slightly lighter than 8 g. Something similar applies to the aurei of Augustus, who reigned as emperor from 27 BCE until his demise in 14 CE. They rarely surpass 8.01 g and are often in the range of 7.80 to 7.95 g. The aurei of Tiberius (14–37 CE) do not exceed 8 g and centre around 7.80 g. Caligula (37–41 CE) comes down to an average of 7.75 g, as does Claudius (41–54 CE). Nero, ruling 54 to 68 CE, then officially changed the old ratio of one-fortieth to one-forty-fifth of a pound, so that the aureus came down to 7.27 g. If we compare these to Vima Kadphises' weights, we see that after the initially adopted classical Attic standard, his next weight of 8.1 g roughly coincided with the theoretical weight as defined by Julius Caesar, whereas the final resolution of 7.9 to 8.0 g coincides with what Augustus actually used.

The Base of the Kuṣāṇa Standard

We know that Vima Kadphises dealt with Rome through middlemen. The impact of Roman coin design and metrology has early and often been described.[44] Through the Kṣatrapas of Broach and other middleman channels, Vima Kadphises sold silk to merchants sailing from Egypt around Arabia. His gold standard of exactly or slightly less than 8 g has no antecedents in India, Iran, Bactria, or anywhere in the Near East, but it was more or less identical with the gold standard in practice during the time of Augustus. Even before the Kuṣāṇas, Augustus was well known in India—at least, he was visited by an ambassador from one king, Porus, according to Strabo.[45] There is an interval of about one century between Augustus and Vima Kadphises. Why should Vima Kadphises copy such a high standard, when after Augustus all emperors in Rome had purposefully downplayed any connection to Julius Caesar?

---

44 Göbl 1960; MacDowall 1960, 1997.

45 Strabo 15.1.73.

The similarity of the early Roman and the Kuṣāṇa gold standards have led some scholars to believe that the Kuṣāṇas bought Roman denarii and re-struck them into their own coinage.[46] However, isotope analysis has shown that this is not the case.[47] The gold from Rome and the one used by the Kuṣāṇas produce rather different isotope profiles. Is there any interrelationship at all? I would venture to say yes, there is a relationship on a higher level. The Kuṣāṇas cannot be understood as mere successful soldiers and merchants. They strove to be as elevated above ordinary men as were the emperors of China and Rome. Starting from Vema Takhtu, alias Sōtēr megas, we can tell from their coins that they insisted on their heavenly nature. Of greatest import was the veneration of Augustus by the first imperial Kuṣāṇa, Kujula Kadphises. His coinage was well-known, and the head of Augustus was copied on his main copper type, issued in large numbers. There are only about forty years between the demise of Augustus and Kujula Kadphises' full success over an array of kings between Bactria and Taxila. The reason for, and understanding of, the success of Augustus must have spread like fire: the elimination of some co-rulers and aggressive acquisitions at the periphery. Kujula did just that—he eliminated four of his co-rulers and went where commerce would be most promising, down to the Indus, which would allow him to circumvent the Parthians who blocked the way from Bactria to the Romans in Mesopotamia. The Romans were the most consistent customers for Chinese silk, and they likewise had lots to offer which could be used in turn for exchange with China.

Augustus had called himself *divi filius* on his coinage, 'son of a god', viz. Julius Caesar. I have expressed the idea[48] that this was one of the reasons why the Kuṣāṇas, from Kujula onwards, called themselves *devaputra*, 'son of god'. Like Augustus, Kujula also managed to build a large and stable kingdom, which profited greatly from overseas trade and a new role among the inter-linked great cities. Seen in this light, we can assume that the adoption of the Roman weight standard was not primarily motivated by reflections on how to facilitate commerce. When introduced in India, the actual Roman standard was already decidedly lighter. Adopting the standard of Julius Caesar, and particularly of Augustus, produced a link to that great figure for Vima Kadphises. He revived the standard of Augustus, in line with the fact that his family copied Augustus in producing prosperity for a vast country by the elimination of republican forms of rule.

---

46 Suresh 2004, 35.

47 Sachs & Blet-Lemarquand 2005; Blet-Lemarquand 2006.

48 Falk 2010, 77.

The Import of Roman Aurei

Though initially restricted to denarii, lots of Roman aurei were ultimately brought to India as a result of this trade.[49] Krishnamurthy postulated that this influx started as early as the second century BCE.[50] We find aurei predominantly in the south of the subcontinent.[51] Western research would place it much later, e.g. Adams and Berghaus,[52] who date the imports towards the end of the first century CE, thus following in the lines of MacDowall.[53] We find aurei predominantly in the south of the subcontinent. Why so? It seems that the Kuṣāṇas, as in the case with their predecessors in northern India, did not buy Roman money, probably because they had a cheaper source for the metal in their own confines, or up in Sogdiana. South India always had the Kolar gold fields, but exploiting them was not easy until the British introduced new technologies. According to Adams[54] the import of Roman gold primarily served the need of Indian merchants to concentrate and secure wealth between transactions, necessitated by the lack of an effective banking system.

Roman aurei were not only imported from Augustan times onwards, but also copied in south India, including the cut, which invalidated the coins as a means of exchange in the Roman Empire.[55] Adams reports that there are two forms of copies.[56] One he terms 'Indian imitations'; these are in good gold, minted from nicely engraved dies. They are usually lighter than their Roman exemplars and their legends are often purposefully distorted, according to Adams, to produce something that is as good as Roman money in terms of metal value, but which is demonstrably not a counterfeit piece in a legal sense.[57] They were made in South India from dies,[58] by and for the predominantly Greek sea-merchants as a trading good. The second form Adams labels 'Indian copies'. Their gold

49 Berghaus 1998.

50 Krishnamurthy 2005.

51 The latest list aiming at comprehensiveness is found in Suresh 2004, 160–177.

52 Adams 1989, 70a and Berghaus 1998.

53 MacDowall 1991.

54 Adams 1989, 72a.

55 MacDowall Hellings 1998; Suresh 2004, 40ff.

56 Adams 1989, 72a, 74b.

57 According to Metcalf 1979, 127 the reason is found in the transfer process from a genuine piece through a sand casting mould to the final copy, more in favour of the deeper verticals in letters, leaving connecting horizontal or slanting lines out. Several factors may have been at work at different workshops.

58 So far one original die was found (Krishnamurthy 2000) in India, producing one side of a coin in the name of Hadrian.

content is not optimal, their sides may be copied through dies or moulds from two different originals,[59] and they do not follow a strict metrology. They were produced in India by Indian jewellers for nothing but ornamental purposes.[60]

If there was a trade in aurei in southern India, as Adams assumes with good reasons, where traders, and not kings, used Roman coins in their bullion value as a means for capital exchange and storage, then we can dismiss this business as completely irrelevant for an understanding of the conditions in the north-west, where Vima Kadphises as a royal authority introduced a gold system under his own regulation. In the south it made no difference to the merchants if the gold coin was original, if it was original but defaced, or if it was imitation. Being simply bullion, every form served the same purpose, and it never interfered with local royal issues. In the north-west, however, Roman coinage would have monetarily represented a second power present in the country, an idea certainly not favoured by the Kuṣāṇa kings. However, keeping foreign pieces as curios was not forbidden. Deposits of single Roman gold coin types in Buddhist stūpas are well documented,[61] while discovered hoards of Kuṣāṇa coins never include a Roman aureus.

With regard to the time frames, Sewell's[62] seminal analysis still holds good: there was a major phase of economic exchange from Augustus to Nero, concentrating on luxury goods. The subsequent phase of decline lasted into the time of Caracalla, who died in 217 CE. Then trade came almost to a standstill, starting again only when Rome had settled herself around the middle of the fourth century. In India, 217 CE falls in the final years of Vasudeva, the last of the 'Great Kushans'. Whether trade with Rome came to a close because of inner changes in Roman society, as Sewell would have it, or because the Sasanians started to control and block the trade routes, is a matter of dispute. The result for northern India was the same; the economic base and the military strength of the Kuṣāṇas dwindled away.

The Export of Kuṣāṇa Gold Coins

While Roman gold went to South India via Egypt, Kuṣāṇa gold seems to have travelled west toward Africa. Mordini reports about his tracing a treasure of Kuṣāṇa gold coins from Dabra Dāmmo, a monastery in the Enticcio region

59 Berghaus 2006.

60 Cf. Metcalf 1979, 123, n. 1: 'Pierced gold coins are far more common in India than elsewhere.'

61 Errington 1998.

62 Sewell 1904.

of northern Ethiopia, roughly 120 km west of the lower western shore of the Red Sea.[63] It consisted of five double dinars of Vima Kadphises, five dinars of Kaniṣka, eighty-eight dinars of Huviṣka, and six dinars of Vasudeva. One single Kuṣāṇa coin is reported from Zimbabwe.[64] All of which points to close contact with Indian sea merchants around 230 CE between the coast of northern India and the lower region of the Red Sea. It remains unclear if these gold coins were the 'spending money' of Indians, or the imports of local merchants.

Gold Coins in Indian Literature

Adams was of the impression that 'the entire history of India seems to be a protest against the use of money.'[65] In a way this continues what Onesikritos reported about the land at the lower Indus in the time of Alexander, that 'people do not make use of silver or gold, although these metals are found (in their country).'[66] Although exaggerated, there is a certain truth to both statements, at least when we look at the extant Sanskrit and Prakrit literature of the period.

Gold coins as a means of exchange rarely occur in the literature of Northern India. One notable exception could be the coin called *nāṇaka*, found just once in the law book of Yājñavalkya. It may have gotten its name from the goddess NANAIA, NANA, or NANAÞAO, written in Bactrian script on coins of Kaniṣka and Huviṣka. With Kaniṣka it is certainly the most frequently found type. The law text deals with faked coins and the fine a coin expert has to pay when calling a faked one genuine, or a genuine one faked. Since the NANA coins of both kings are found as gold and as copper issues, counterfeiters could have copied gold or bronze issues.

There are more gold-coin names. One is spelled *sadera* in Kharoṣṭhī and one *suvarṇa-satera-* in Brāhmī script, derived from the Greek *statēr*, made unambiguous by *suvarṇa*, 'golden', in a donation grant from the Kashmir Smast.[67] This term seems to be confined to the north-west and was in use at least until the fourth or fifth century. Five coins of this sort were enough to establish an 'eternal' donation, of which only the yearly interest was meant for spending.

In land grants gold coins are mentioned more often, always called *dīnāra*, adding just another example of the split 'cultural ancestry'—the north-west

63 Mordini 1967; cf. Chatterjee 1997.
64 Horton 1996a, 448.
65 Adams 1989, 71f.
66 *FGrH* 134 F 24 (= Strabo 15.1.34).
67 Falk 2003, 10.

uses *sadera/satera*, a term derived from Greek, whereas the rest of India is oriented towards Rome, naming *dīnāra* for *denarius*. The *dīnāras* are used in transactions for acquiring irrigable land called *kulyāvāpa*, two pieces for one stretch of land. Examples are found in Bandyopadhyay for Gupta contexts.[68] Raven,[69] dealing with the same time, presents cases in which *dīnāras* were donated as an 'eternal' religious endowment, amounting to six, twelve, or twenty-five.

We have textual evidence relating to *dīnāras* in the Nāradasmṛti, which tells us in 2,34 that a *dīnāra* is made from gold (*hiraṇmayam*). In line 19,68[70] we hear that twelve *dhānakas* of gold make one *dīnāra*, which is *citraka*, 'showing a picture'. The term *dhānaka* is not found in Sanskrit literature apart from a few texts, but it occurs on inscribed metal objects of a definite weight. These objects in silver and gold come from Gandhara, but also from Uzbekistan and Turkmenistan. Their inscriptions contain abbreviated weight names, where *sa* stands for *sadera, dra* for *drachma*, and *dha* for *dhānaka*. Since a statēr contains twenty-four *dhānakas*, and since according to Nārada twelve *dhānakas* make one *dīnāra*, we know that a *dīnāra* weighs half a *statēr*. Such a *statēr* or tetradrachm in the Attic system can be as heavy as 18 g; however, most weigh 17.1 to 17.5 g. Our gold *dīnāra* would come down to 8.5 to 8.7 g. Some completely preserved and inscribed pieces[71] from Gandhāra are based on a *dhānaka* of 0.61 up to 0.67 g, leading to *dīnāras* of 7.32 and 8.04 g, the latter weight well in the range of the gold pieces of Kaniṣka and successors.

In short, one golden *dīnāra* weighs half a *sadera*, which is around 8 g, more or less. The 'more' cases would also apply for the gold issues of the two Diodotoi (*c.*250–225 BCE, average 8.35 g) of Euthydemos (*c.*225–200 BCE, average 8.25 g) and Eucratides (*c.*170–155 BCE, average 8.48 g). This rather precisely fits the solitary first gold coin of Vima Kadphises, and the 'less' cases would still apply to the latest pseudo-Kuṣāṇas and many Gupta issues.

Conclusion

All evidence adduced above leads to some basic statements: north-western India was rich in exploitable gold sources while the south was not. The northwest exported gold from the time of Harappa to the West, or had to deliver it

68 Bandyopadhyay 2007–08.

69 Raven 2006, 201f. with fns.

70 Nārada 19.68c *taddvādaśa suvarṇasya dīnāraś citrakaḥ smṛtaḥ*. For a parallel or quotation cf. Kātyāyanasmṛti (Kane) 494.

71 Salomon 1990, 152b.

as tribute to the Achaemenids. The same area was also productive in Kuṣāṇa times for currency needs. The north-west also developed all sorts of gold weighing standards, which, however, show that there was some sort of exchange with standards in the Mediterranean world. As the earliest example we found the Harappan weights to have a parallel in Egyptian *beqa* weights, both probably used for gold, and both following a similar system of binary subdivision and decimal multiplication. How and why these similar weights were used in actual business transactions we do not know, but a close connection of the Harappan and the Mediterranean world seems obvious.

In Vedic times we find a unit named *śatamāna*, which was used in rituals mainly for its symbolic value, since the number one hundred is used in various forms to bestow a full life-span of a hundred years on the donor. At least in Middle Vedic times the basic weight behind the *śatamāna* is the *guñja* seed, which seems to have supplanted an original barley grain weight in the ratio of one to three. The standard Harappan weight, which can be defined on the basis of the *guñja* weight, may then be regarded as equalling 360 barley grains instead of 120 *guñja* seeds. In Vedic thinking, 360 denotes the days of the full year, and as such it symbolizes regeneration. So, a Harappan weight seems to follow the very same system of symbolic numbers as are used a short time later in Vedic rituals. The method of defining the barley grains used as the 'middle' ones from the ear in classical India (Manu) has a parallel in a much older Mesopotamian definition. Again, we see similarities between India and Mesopotamia in technical matters, which are hardly accidental. The parallelism touches some significant details, but not the whole standard. Such a partial relationship with Mesopotamia has also been observed regarding a method of time calculation.[72]

In CE times, dynasties in the south did not use gold as royal coinage, but traders there needed it to build up a more flexible economy. For this reason they imported aurei from the West, most likely from the end of the first century CE onwards. Roman aurei are too rarely found in the North to assume commercial importation there as well. However, the idea that an economy greatly profits from the ability to store wealth for a while in gold may have been the incentive for Vima Kadphises too.[73] If he was led to the idea through his contacts with Rome directly, or through intelligence from the South, where Roman imports had brought about the change, or through both channels, we do not

72 Falk 2000.

73 Recent evidence has shown that 'measured gold' was used in donations already in the times of his father Kujula. Vima Kadphises only turned this into a state monopoly: Falk 2014.

know. We only see that initially he experiments with weights and soon decides to use one standard which is also the one used earlier by Augustus.

We should envision a fast flow of information between the Roman parts of the Orient and India. Vima Kadphises certainly knew about the devaluation brought about by Nero in 64 CE; he may even have been aware of the short-timed rise of coin weight under Domitian in 82 CE, back to something near the Augustan standard. I interpret Vima's choice to use the standard of Augustus as inspired by thoughts on prestige, as yet another means to stand on a par with the greatest ruler in the West.

Through all the millennia concerned, India is not living a life in seclusion, but continually interacts with the West. The two parallels of the *beqa* weight and the barley grains do not disclose who was borrowing from whom. But in the third case of the Kuṣāṇa gold weight it is clear that the Roman world was the prototype; regarding political behaviour, regarding expressions of self-esteem, and regarding monetary standards as well.

CHAPTER 7

'Regions that Look Seaward': Changing Fortunes, Submerged Histories, and the Slow Capitalism of the Sea

Jairus Banaji

All scholars are familiar with the fascinating passage in Procopius where he tells us that 'it was impossible for the Ethiopians to buy silk from the Indians, because Persian merchants would always locate themselves at the very harbours (*hormoi*) where the Indian ships first put in and were used to buying up whole cargoes'.[1] By suggesting that 'the Iranians' near-monopoly in the markets of South India and Ceylon'[2] was a drastic limitation on Byzantine access to South Asian ports, the least it implies is that by late Antiquity trade networks in the Indian Ocean had been radically reconfigured to eliminate any significant Roman/Byzantine presence. Sasanian dominance of the sea lanes in the western Indian Ocean, which was firmly established by the late sixth century, is a major part of why Islam was able to expand in the Indian Ocean in the way it did, by extending and consolidating links established in the Sasanian centuries.[3] Moreover, Procopius also documents the commercial strategies used by Sasanian traders in buying up whole cargoes, a fascinating allusion to the way merchants worked in the maritime trade. But there are two other features of this passage that have gone largely unnoticed. Procopius tells us that it was *Indian* ships that imported the cargoes that were subsequently bought by Iranian merchants, and he implies that the harbours where these transactions took place were South Asian.

Among classical sources and leaving Ptolemy aside, the most informative accounts of South Asian ports are certainly those in the *Periplus* and in Cosmas. If we disregard Barbarikon (which was in Sind) and start south of the Gulf of Barake (Dwarka?), the following local and major ports are listed: Barygaza, Akabaru, Suppara, Kalliena, Sêmylla, Mandagora, Palaipatmai, Melizeigara, Byzantion, Toparon (?), Tyrannosboas (?), Naura, Tyndis, Muziris,

1 Procop., *Pers.* 1.20.12.
2 Whitehouse and Williamson 1973, 44.
3 E.g., Williamson 1972.

 | DOI 10.1163/9789004289536_009

Nelkynda, Bakarê, Balita, Komar, Kolchoi, Kamara, Podukê, and Sôpatma.[4] Of the twenty-two ports listed here, roughly half are either known to us or susceptible to identification, while two of the place names are clearly corrupt. In Cosmas (again disregarding 'Sindou') the crucial passage in Book XI mentions eleven place names: Orrothâ, Kalliana, Sibôr, Malé, Parti, Mangarouth, Salopatana, Nalopatana, Poudapatana, Marallo, and Kaber (with an epsilon).[5] Of these, two are the names of regions: Orrothâ is Saurashtra, i.e. Kathiawar, and Malé is the Malabar coast. Excluding these, Cosmas seems to list a total of nine ports (five of these in Malé/Malabar), of which five are known or can be found. Since Kalliana occurs in both lists, we have a net total of fifteen Indian ports whose locations are either well established or can be surmised with some certainty or probability.

I'd like to start this paper by considering some of these uncertain-looking place names whose locations can be mapped with more confidence. In the Cosmas/*Periplus* lists there are six in particular that are worth sorting out. These are Mandagora (*Periplus*), Mangarouth (Cosmas), Sibôr (Cosmas), Poudapatana (Cosmas), Bakarê (*Periplus*), and Kaber (Cosmas). Mandagora was either Mandwa, 18 km north of Alibag in Raigad district, near its northern tip, or, as Vasant Shinde has suggested, Kuda-Mandad at the head of the Janjira creek, a short distance south of Chaul.[6] Since it is listed after Sêmylla in both the *Periplus* and Ptolemy, and Sêmylla was medieval Saimur, that is, Chaul in Raigad (today Revdanda), Shinde's suggestion preserves the sequence of both sources. Mangarouth in Cosmas was almost certainly Mangalore.[7] In Cosmas it is the second Malé (Malabar) location after Parti (unknown but possibly Barçelore), and before Salopatana and Nalopatana (both unknown). This gives us some idea of how far *up* the west coast Malé/Malabar was thought to extend, at least in the circles Cosmas moved in.

In Cosmas, Sibôr is sandwiched between Kalliana and Malé and was almost certainly his name for Sindābūr of the Arabic sources, namely, Goa.[8] In other words, Cosmas' description of the west coast of India divided it into four major segments: Saurashtra or Kathiawar in Gujarat, Kalyan just north of Bombay, Sindābūr or Goa, and the Malabar ports ending with Poudapatana. This last location can be identified with 'Budfattan' in Ibn Baṭṭūṭa[9] or modern

4 *Peripl. M. Rubr.* 49, 52–60.

5 Cosmas Indicopleustes 11.16.

6 Shinde, Gupta, Rajgor 2002, 78.

7 Yule 1915, I 228, n. 1; IV 73.

8 Ibid. IV 65: Sindabur 'substantially identical with the port of Goa'; Tibbetts 1971, 455.

9 Ibn Baṭṭūṭa, *Travels* IV 811.

Puthupatanam/Puthupanam at Vadakara Beach, south of Thalassery. In late medieval times Puthupatanam was a satellite port of Calicut, like Pantalāyini, described by Tomé Pires as one of several 'small ports' that the Zamorin or ruler of Calicut depended on because, as he said, 'The port of Calicut is not good because the land slopes up from the sea.'[10] (In the Lisbon manuscript of the *Suma* the name appears as 'pudy patanam'.)

Bakarê in the *Periplus* was Pliny's Becare (*HN*, 6.105), described by him as a 'more useful port' than Muziris, though further south in the Pandyan territory. It has usually been identified as Purakkad,[11] but the decisive clue to its true identity is the statement in the *Periplus* that 'After Bakarê comes Red Mountain, as it is called, and another region extends ….'[12] From this it is certain Bakarê/Becare was Varkala 20 km south-east of Kollam, which the *Rough Guide* describes as backed by 'sheer red laterite cliffs', a unique geological feature of the otherwise flat Kerala coastline and the 'Red Mountain' of the *Periplus*.[13] Pliny tells us that pepper was transported to Becare (Varkala) in country boats from 'Cottonara'. This has to be Kuttanad, the Kottanarikê of the *Periplus*, which the latter wrongly describes as the pepper-growing region par excellence, whereas Pliny simply says it was 'the region from which pepper is conveyed to Becare', implying it may just have been a transhipment hub.[14] In that case, Nelkynda would have been somewhere in this vicinity, not far from Varkala, since the *Periplus* reports that 'vessels' (*ta ploia*), the country boats described by Pliny, came downriver from there to Becare on the outbound voyage.[15] That a port so far south was 'active' when the *Periplus* was written

10 Pires I 78.

11 E.g., Dames 1989, II 95 n. 2.

12 *Peripl. M. Rubr.* 58.

13 Abram, et al. 1999, 300f.

14 I borrow the expression from James Michael who notes that Kuttanad itself, as a flat, low-lying, largely coastal region 'does not have the right kind of climate to grow pepper' (James Michael, pers. comm. dated 14 December 2012). Also see De Romanis, this volume, but locating Becare-Nelkynda in the southern part of the Vembanad Lake, which would mean that the Pandyas of Madurai had substantially more territory on the west coast than they are likely to have done, since the Pandyas had control of Becare which lay in the territory of the 'Neacyndi'. As Michael pointed out to me, Kollam would be a more natural southern extension of the Vembanad pepper system than Kochi-Thrissur (e-mail, 7 January 2014). In his edition of the *Periplus* Schoff had already remarked that Varkala '*was formerly the southern end of the long line of backwaters*, and a place of considerable commercial importance' (Schoff 1912, 234).

15 No one has identified Nelkynda so far, but in Ptolemy's sequence of place-names (*Geog.* 7.1.9) it lies south of Bakare (Pliny's Becare), in Āy territory, and the river connecting Nelkynda with Becare is called the 'Barios'.

shows that by the first century the *whole* of the Kerala coast had been drawn into the Red Sea trade orbit.

'Kaber' in Cosmas is clearly Ptolemy's Khaberis (*Geog.* 7.1.13), long identified with Kaveripattinam or Poompuhar in Nagai district of Tamil Nadu, a major Sangam-age Chola port,[16] which from all accounts seems to have had a quarter for foreign merchants.[17] It is also a rare example of a South Asian port with an actual harbour, judging by the remains of a wharf. Part of Kaveripattinam seems to have been washed away, possibly in the late fifth or early sixth centuries, according to its excavator K.V. Soundara Rajan.[18] But Rajan is cautious both about the scale of this incursion and its timing, and describes it as a temporary setback. That Cosmas listed Kaber among the major east coast ports is in itself interesting. It suggests that no dramatic incident had been witnessed by the merchant circles from which he gathered his information (in the second or third decades of the sixth century) for the purely geographical book he was writing.[19]

A final toponym worth examining in some detail is the mysterious BLBQ/B.-llin in various manuscripts of Ibn Khurradādhbih and al-Idrīsī. Idrīsī's manuscripts reflect complete uncertainty about this place name, with Jaubert vacillating between two main readings, بلنق (transliterated 'Balanc') and بلبق ('Balabac'; 'Balbak' in Elliot and Dowson),[20] and Maqbul Ahmad printing بليق (Balīq) in his extracts in *India and the Neighbouring Territories as described by the Sharīf al-Idrīsī* (1954).[21] Now it is clear that part of Idrīsī's information about this 'island', as he calls it, was drawn from a crucial passage in Ibn Khurradādhbih. This, coupled with the fact that the latter's manuscripts show a less dispersed

16 McCrindle 1885, 63ff.; Sastri 1939, 89.

17 Champakalakshmi 1996, 108, 127, 193. Since this chapter says nothing further about the place names in Ptolemy, it may be worth drawing attention to the following likely or possible identities (in the coastal stretch that runs from Maleo in *Geog.* 7.1.4 to Maliarpha in 7.1.14 in the catalogue of locations, Stückelberger and Graßhoff 2006, II 688–690). Nusaripa = Navsari; Balepatna = Kharepatan in Ratnagiri district (cf. Chakravarti 1998, 107–8); Bakare = Varkala; Sosikurei = Tuticorin; Cape Kory 'also called Kalligikon' = Valinokkam Point; Salour = Saliyur (the Sangam name of Alagankulam, cf. Champakalakshmi 1996, 133, 140); and Maliarpha = Mylapore (Raman 1988, 115). The remarkable feature of Ptolemy's list is how easy it is to identify east coast place names from it.

18 Soundara Rajan 1994, 130.

19 The claim that 'it is safe to assume that a major portion of Kavirippompattinam was lost (washed away) during the middle of the sixth century', Seshadri 2009, p. 107, is untenable.

20 Jaubert 1975, 73, 175, 178; Elliot and Dowson 1867, I 89.

21 Maqbul Ahmad 1954, 11 (§29): بليق in the Bodleian and BM manuscripts, بلبق in Paris A; p. 57 (§4): بليق in Paris A, بلبق in the BM manuscript; at p. 63 (§29) he prints بلبق, following Paris A and BM.

range of readings that fluctuate around the ones that de Goeje published in his edition of 1889, suggests that Ibn Khurradādhbih's manuscripts are our best guide to the name the 'Abbasid geographer must have used in the original mid-ninth century version of his work. De Goeje published بُلّين and بلّين in his text of Ibn Khurradādhbih (p. 63, lines 2; 3–4; p. 66, line 1), and noted بلين , بلىن, and بلىن as variants in the apparatus. Here the strong inference is that the uncertainty regarding where to put the diacritical marks involved not the last letter *nūn* but the first and the third, the *bā'* and the *yā'*. For the moment, let me retain de Goeje's name 'Ballīn' (with the *shadda* on the *lām*) as a rough reading of the port he was referring to.[22]

So where was Ballīn? The crucial fact about it is that this was where 'the maritime route for eastbound ships bifurcated.' As Minorsky says, paraphrasing Ibn Khurradādhbih, 'one branch followed the east coast of India while the other went to Ceylon and China.'[23] Minorsky realised that Ballīn would have to be on the east coast, since 'Generally speaking a place on the west coast of India is hardly suitable for bifurcation of roads leading further east.'[24] Ibn Khurradādhbih bases his account of the ports and distances in southern India on the testimony of sailors (*al-baḥriyyūn*) and states that Ballīn was roughly equidistant between Malabar (Mulay, مُلَى) and the 'Great Gulf' (*al-lujjat al-'uẓma*). Since the latter was clearly the Bay of Bengal, Maqbul Ahmad's suggestion that Ballīn was on the Tanjore coast—and may even have been Nagapattinam, or a port in its vicinity—seems quite impossible.[25] Ballīn was a day or a little more than a day's journey from Sri Lanka ('Sarandib'),[26] and clearly much further south than Nagapattinam, which Ibn Khurradādhbih called 'Bāpattan' (بَابَتَّن), if anything. All the indications are that Ballīn lay in the Palk Bay region or the Gulf of Mannar, not far north or south of Rameshwaram Island. Idrīsī's description of it as located in an estuary makes the Vaigai Delta the most likely candidate for a location.[27]

The key ancient port in this vicinity at the mouth of the Vaigai River was of course Alagankulam, which has thrown up both torpedo jar sherds and late Roman coinage and was without doubt a major international port.[28] If Champakalakshmi is right in suggesting that Nellin was one of the ancient

22 That was how Maqbul Ahmad rendered it in his translation of al-Idrīsī, Maqbul Ahmad 1960, 62.

23 Minorsky 1937, 243.

24 Ibid. 243–44, n. 4.

25 Maqbul Ahmad 1989, 24.

26 Ibn Khurradādhbih 64, ll. 5ff.; al-Idrīsī 73.

27 Al-Idrīsī 73.

28 E.g., Nagaswamy 1991, 252, 'profuse Roman contacts in the later period'.

names of Alagankulam,[29] then it is almost certainly this name that lurks behind the mysterious Ballīn of Ibn Khurradādhbih, with the first diacritical (the *nuqṭa* or dot) displaced from top to bottom to transform the *nūn* into a *bā'*. In short, if this reconstruction is at all plausible, Alagankulam's chronological span can be extended to the ninth century, when, according to Ibn Khurradādhbih, it formed the main east-coast port where the eastern shipping lanes bifurcated, with ships bound for China heading for the Nicobars from here. But of course ultimately it is the archaeologists who will have to give substance to this picture.[30]

Let me turn now to the chronological patterns of individual sites and their possible connections to each other. The maritime regions that made up the Indian Ocean and its historical life were of course always more stable than the fortunes of the individual ports within them, and the same could be said of the networks that linked those regions together across vast distances. Thus coastal regions scarcely ever disappeared completely as commercial entities. With our notions of late Antiquity radically overhauled in the past four decades, the Red Sea too has come back to life as a zone of more dynamism in the fourth to sixth centuries than formerly suspected. For example, 'The fourth century and later were periods of intense activity at Clysma and Aila', says one scholar.[31] Ayla in fact enjoyed a renewed lease of life with the founding of a new port in the seventh century, and flourished through the 'Abbāsi and Fatimid periods until it was abandoned in the twelfth century. Adulis, which appears in the *Periplus* as a thriving port, became even more vigorous in the late antique centuries till it declined or was destroyed in the seventh century.[32] Its termination was abrupt compared to 'Aqaba's slower demise. These are reasonably well-defined patterns but they are the exception.

Ports like Clysma (Suez) or Aden have more complex chronologies. Aden had been a major transhipment centre for ships from India to Egypt but was little used in the first century because, as the *Periplus* says, Caesar had sacked it. It reappears in the mid-fourth century *Arabica* of Uranius as Yemen's second city (*polis*) (*FGH* IV, p. 523ff., *Arabica* fr. 13). By the ninth century Ibn

29 Champakalakshmi 1996, 134.

30 The current view is roughly the one stated by Begley 1996–2004, vol. 1, 290: 'The site [Alagankulam] seems to have flourished from the third century B.C. to the fourth-fifth century A.D.'

31 Tomber 2008, 66. Power 2012 is now the best synthesis we have for the Red Sea (not seen by me when this paper was written).

32 Phillipson 2009, 357ff. argues that Aksum was a major source of the African ivory exported to Mediterranean markets in the Roman period.

Khurradādhbih could describe it as one of the 'greatest ports' of the Indian Ocean; it was a 'splendid, flourishing, populous town' in al-Muqaddasī's day,[33] and then of course it became a key base of the Indian Ocean shipping industry, as Margariti has shown,[34] still prosperous and rich in the early sixteenth century.[35] Here is an arc of some sixteen centuries, with a long spell of obscurity in between.

The Persian Gulf is another region where continuity was sustained by the reshuffling of ports. As Rougelle showed in an important paper, the rise of the Fatimids and the great change in the balance of the Islamic world that came about in the later tenth century did not mean the end of the gulf networks. Cairo and the Red Sea could now access markets in the Far East and did so on a substantial scale, but 'the gulf area never lost the part it played in the international trade of the Indian Ocean to the Red Sea merchants. Only the nature of the gulf trade changed, in the eleventh century, from a free economy handled by private traders... to a monopoly economy concentrated in the hands of some local rulers.'[36] Here the 'transfers' between ports were abrupt and often dramatic. Ubulla, the Apologos of the *Periplus* and the main international port of the Sasanid rulers,[37] declined to the level of a village, certainly by the tenth century replaced by Basra, which, founded in the late 630s, developed with astonishing speed. Barely two decades after its foundation it was described by Ananias of Širak as 'filled with merchants and ships coming from India and all parts of the East'.[38]

Sīrāf, a substantial Sasanian port, known apparently as 'Sūriyānj' (?), expanded rapidly in the 'Abbāsid commercial boom, reached a peak in the early tenth century, and was then dramatically hit, first by a succession of earthquakes in 978 and 1008 and then by the economic recession that spread through the gulf in the eleventh century. The author of the *Fārs Nāmah* claimed that merchants boycotted Sīrāf because the rulers of Kīsh finally gained control of it. Hamdollah Mostowfi, writing later, stated more simply, 'during the Buyid supremacy the sea trade was transferred from here to Kish'.[39] Sohar was closely linked with the Omani overseas community living in Basra,[40] flourished in tandem with Siraf and was a major international port in the ninth century—a thoroughly cosmopolitan centre, until it lost its status in the thir-

33 Al-Muqaddasī 76.
34 Margariti 2007.
35 Pires I 17.
36 Rougelle 1996, 175.
37 Dīnawarī 123, ll. 9ff.
38 Ananias of Širak 71A (short recension).
39 Ibn al-Balki 322 f.; Hamdollah Mostowfi 116.
40 Wilkinson 1979, 889.

teenth century.[41] Kīsh cornered the Persian Gulf trade in the second half of the eleventh century,[42] and was the leading entrepôt until its dominance was finally destroyed in the 1330s. The history of the struggle between Kish and Hormuz is conceivably the most dramatic instance of commercial rivalry in the Indian Ocean prior to the expansion of the Portuguese, and illustrates both the fluidity of ports and the mobility of merchant families within broadly integrated coastal regions. The growth of Hormuz was largely due to the migration of Sirafi merchant families,[43] and Hormuz itself was a port that moved from the mainland to Jarun Island in 1300.[44]

A rapid survey, it is true, but this exercise can of course be extended to *all* the main sectors and micro-regions of the Indian Ocean, in more detail no doubt, and with greater precision. For example, among the Tamil ports, Arikamedu fades after the second century but resurfaces in the Chola period.[45] Puhar/Kaveripattinam to its south was a thriving Coromandel port down to the fifth century, when part of it was washed away by a tidal wave, an event reflected in the legend that the goddess Manimekhalai had cursed this grand port to engulfment by the sea. In fact, Kaveripattinam retained its vitality down to the tenth and eleventh centuries, once the Imperial Cholas had wrested Thanjavur from the local chieftains who ruled it for the Pallavas of Tondaimandalam and made it their capital. There is a profusion of Rajaraja I's coinage.[46]

Nagapattinam emerged by the seventh century and was the main Chola port by 1000, still thriving in the thirteenth and fourteenth centuries.[47] Kayal further south replaced Korkai (the Kolchoi of the *Periplus*),[48] but seems to have flourished only in the thirteenth century,[49] when the waters around it silted up and 'traders had to seek new harbour sites large enough to accommodate ocean-going ships.'[50] New Kayal and Kayalpatnam emerged as replacements, demonstrating the essential resilience of the seaside villages. K. Rajan has pointed out

---

41 Ibid. 890, 899, 903.

42 Di Meglio 1970, 107.

43 Piacentini 1992, 170.

44 Morgan 1991; Aubin 1953, 94.

45 Begley 1996–2004, vol. 1, 31 ff. Nagaswamy 1995, 24–25 notes a substantial third-century hoard some forty miles west of Puducherry, 'A huge treasure of over 200 Roman gold coins found' in 1992 at Sorayapattu near Tirukoyyilur.

46 Soundara Rajan 1994.

47 John Carswell suggested that Nagapattinam 'probably supplanted Mantai as the chief South Asian trading centre' soon after the end of the tenth century, following the Chola conquest of Sri Lanka, cf. Carswell 1985, 58.

48 Hornell 1914, 45.

49 Karashima 2009, 240f.

50 Ptak 1993, 139 (my thanks to Sanjay Subrahmanyam for this reference).

that 'Ports like Kaveripattinam (Poompuhar), Alagankulam, and Korkai were affected either by sea-level variations or changes in river courses. The ports Korkai and Alagankulam are now located away from the present sea coast on the rivers Tambaraparni and Vaigai respectively. At Kaveripattinam too, the present river Kaveri flows about two kilometres south of the ancient port.'[51]

In Kerala it was K.P. Shajan's work on the geomorphology of the central coast that proved decisive to the identification of Muziris as Pattanam, some 3½ km east of the present coast.[52] Muziris (Murachipattanam) saw 'intense occupation' in the Roman period (the Tamil 'Early Historic'), extending down to the fourth century. It was obviously a thriving port when the substantial cargoes in *SB* XVIII 13167 were contracted by an Alexandrian firm in the late second century,[53] and saw continued occupation in the 'Early Medieval' period.[54] But since large-scale excavations at Pattanam have only just begun (in 2007), the chronological pattern is still fuzzy. What *doesn't* seem credible is Tomber's inference that since Cosmas fails to mention Muziris, it no longer functioned by the mid sixth century.[55]

Kollam (Quilon) may well have emerged by the ninth century to fill the void left by Pattanam's decline, battening on the gulf networks and attracting a cosmopolitan community of traders who were literate in Arabic, Hebrew, and Pahlavi[56]—Nestorians, Jews, Muslims, and Zoroastrians.[57] It was dominant down to the twelfth century when it was (momentarily) destroyed by the Chola armies[58] and its place taken by Calicut. Calicut, founded in 1042, became the 'great country of the Western Ocean', as the Chinese described it,[59] and reached its own apogee in the mid fifteenth century. Like Kollam, it was a late development—a port for which no late antique evidence exists, while Kochi of course emerged even later, becoming prosperous after the arrival of the Portuguese, as Pires said.[60]

The excavations at Pattanam may indicate a more vibrant 'Late Antique' phase, but until that happens Kerala is a perfect example of what I call a 'submerged' history—the gap between Cosmas' listing of five ports along the coast

51 Rajan 1996, 99.
52 Shajan Tomber, Selvakumar, Cherian 2004, 313–16.
53 Rathbone 2000, 43 ff., calculating the staggering value of the cargo.
54 Selvakumar Shahjan, Tomber 2010, 34.
55 Tomber 2008, 143.
56 Abraham 1988, 21 ff.
57 On the last see Cereti 2003, esp. 202.
58 Bouchon 1988, 50.
59 Ma Huan 137.
60 Pires I 79.

and the current state of the archaeology. In any case, the sheer density of ports along the Malabar coast that Tomé Pires documented for the early sixteenth century (he listed no fewer than twenty-nine)[61] was the more or less permanent background from which the cosmopolitan ports emerged. The reshuffling of ports that went on throughout the history of the Indian Ocean drew on a huge reservoir of informal harbours that moved back and forth between their stellar moments (if they were lucky) and their unrecorded or submerged histories.[62] And clearly the vast mass of these lesser ports survived on coastal trading.

Now Hermann Kulke has argued that the late tenth century ushered in a major break in the constellation of forces that had shaped the destinies of the Indian Ocean. The Fatimids, Cholas, and Northern Song emerged more or less simultaneously, and redrew the economic map of the Ocean for the next two or three centuries—indeed, in a sense down to the advent of the Portuguese.[63] A key upshot of this conjuncture was the further dramatic expansion of the trade with China, as well as the more aggressive role played by Indian merchants, both Hindus and Muslims, in contrast to the Omani and other gulf communities that had dominated long-distance voyages till then. All the major coastal regions of India now had substantial settlements of Muslim traders, both natives and foreigners—an expat elite, the *pardesis*, who dominated the trade of the western Indian Ocean, and indigenous groups like the Marakkar Muslims of the east coast, who controlled the coastal trade between Malabar and Coromandel.

That the Portuguese set out to break the power of Muslim-dominated commercial networks on both coasts of India and across the Indian Ocean shows the amazing tenacity and reach of networks that had first emerged in the eighth century, and evolved patiently and gradually through a pattern of migration that is best described by Mark Horton in his work on Shanga. This was, Horton writes, 'not a large-scale migration of Arabs to East Africa, but often single individuals who settled and established substantial lineages.'[64] Horton dates the 'beginnings' of Swahili Islam to *c.*780–850.[65] These were precisely the decades when the Rashtrakutas controlled much of Gujarat; Masʿūdī was especially struck by the Rashtrakuta reception of Arab traders—the respect and

61 Ibid. 74.
62 Braudel 1975, I 148.
63 Kulke 1999.
64 Horton 2003, 79.
65 Horton 1996b, 397 ff.

tolerance shown to 'Arabs and Muslims' in a kingdom that often seemed to roughly contemporary Arabic sources the only one worth mentioning![66]

Among the Hindu trading communities, the most important were the Gujarati *baniyas* and the Tamil-speaking Chettis. The Gujaratis were the most powerful expat community in Malacca on the eve of its capture by the Portuguese,[67] but so too were the Coromandel Chettis, described by Barbosa as 'men of great estates and owning many great ships which they call *juncos*'.[68] These groups controlled a substantial part of the trade between India and the Far East, especially the trade in textiles. Pires reported that 'There used to be a thousand Gujarat merchants in Malacca, besides four or five thousand Gujarat seamen, who came and went',[69] which gives us some sense of the scale of this business. He also claimed that the Gujaratis had 'larger ships and more men to man them'.[70] Indeed, Gujarat vessels were built to a thousand tons and upwards, according to one scholar,[71] and to me it seems certain that the 'massive' Indian ships that Egeria saw at Clysma in the 380s, over ten centuries earlier,[72] were Gujarati *baniya*-controlled vessels of substantial tonnages, possibly 300–600 tons.[73] The other classical reference to the sheer size of Gujarati vessels is of course the *Periplus*, with its statement that the merchants of Barygaza (Bharuch) would send out 'big vessels' (*ploia megala*) to Omana (ed-Dur?) and Apologos (Ubulla) with supplies of copper, teakwood, and beams. And of course Bharuch also exported textiles of all kinds, including silk from China.[74]

So, if Procopius was right, the import of silk into the Byzantine markets depended not just on the Sasanian merchants buying up whole cargoes in the South Asian ports, but on Indian merchants shipping those cargoes in vessels that they owned or chartered. The *sa-po* or *sārthavāha* who turn up in Fa Hsien (Fa Xian) owning 'stately and beautiful' homes in Anuradhapura in the early fifth century were surely neither Sabaeans, as Samuel Beals suggested, nor

---

66 Mas'ūdī I 382; Nizami 1994, 59.

67 Thomaz 1988, 36: 'la communauté la plus puissante de Malaka'.

68 Dames 1989, II 172.

69 Pires I 45.

70 Ibid.

71 Ray 2003, 73.

72 *Itinerarium Egeriae* 101 (Y6): 'Naves autem ibi et multe et ingentes sunt; quia portus famosus est pro advenientibus ibi mercatoribus de India'; trans. Wilkinson 1971, 206: 'the ships there are numerous and massive because the port is famous for the Indian merchants who come there'.

73 Cf. Pearson 2007, 68–69, on the size of Gujarati ships, 'on average 300 to 600 tons'.

74 *Peripl. M. Rubr.* 49.

Sogdians, as Paolo Daffina argued, but simply South Asian traders, possibly including big merchants from the Gujarat ports where *sārthavāha* was a generic term for merchants but referred especially to the wealthier merchant princes active in the long-distance trade.[75] But how do we characterise merchants at this level? The Alexandrian financier whose investment was secured by commodities worth well over seven million sesterces in the famous shipment from Muziris? Or Abu Bakr b. 'Umar as-Sirāfī, whom Ibn Hauqal was desperate to meet in 961, and who operated from Basra with a whole fleet of ships, agents (*wakīl*), business partners, warehouses, and so on, trading to India, China, and East Africa?[76] Or the 'merchant millionaire' Rāmisht of Siraf who came back from China with merchandise worth half a million dinars?[77] Rāmisht was a *nākhudā*, as he was described on his tombstone in Mecca, a ship-owning merchant of the kind that 'ran both shipping and trading enterprises'.[78] Margariti has suggested that he was based in Aden,[79] and, if so, he would certainly have interacted closely with the Jewish India traders who operated out of there.

Or, finally, how do we characterise the great business firms that dominated Chinese shipping in the Song–Yuan periods? Jung-Pang Lo tells us that the heads of these joint-stock companies 'employed factors (*kang-shou*) to take charge of the merchant fleets and to transact business abroad'.[80] In China, shipbuilding, like the silk, pottery, and iron industries, was based on industrial-scale production. Chuimei Ho has suggested that one reason why Quanzhou superseded Guanzhou as the busiest seaport in China was the spectacular growth of the ceramic industry in the Quanzhou area, starting in the late eleventh century when factories sprawled over entire valleys, churning out stoneware and porcelains for the South Seas trade.[81]

As we move into the early modern period, historians become progressively less reluctant to recognise the signs of a precocious capitalism in these various groups and the networks and practices bound up with them. In her excellent monograph on the Coromandel merchants, Kanakalatha Mukund has no hesitation describing the Chettis as 'merchant capitalists'.[82] In the seventeenth

75 Jain 1990, 221ff. (discussing Gujarat).

76 Ibn Hauqal 290–91 (= trans. Kramers and Wiet II 284 f).

77 Stern 1967.

78 Margariti 2007, 144–5.

79 Ibid. 148.

80 Lo 1970, 173.

81 Ho 2001, esp. 268ff., where she accepts the notion of 'some kind of quasi-capitalistic investment' for the early phase of Minnan's ceramic industry, viz., 1050–1150.

82 Mukund 1999, Chapter 5.

century, they were large-scale export merchants who owned their own ships and traded extensively with the Southeast Asian ports. 'The trade links of these merchants radiated from the ports to the hinterland, giving them a very large sphere of influence.'[83] Jeyaseela Stephen has used the same description of the Tamil-speaking Mudaliars of the early sixteenth century.[84] Braudel's pages on the Mediterranean are replete with references to this capitalism of the sea, of the big merchants and the financiers connected with them. In a classic study, Giorgio Cracco reduced this 'Mediterranean capitalism'[85] to an early microcosm, that of the Venetian *Duecento*, suggesting that by then the evolution of Venice's mercantile economy had generated a sharper demarcation between the capitalists and the merchants, that is, between the *big* merchants ('il grande imprenditore mercantile') and the mass of 'merchant-workers' (mercanti lavoratori), as he called them.[86] This, I suggest, was one strand of an ancient Mediterranean tradition, the distinction between the *nauklēroi* and the *daneistai* that runs through Justinian's attempt to regulate the system of maritime loans in the year 540.[87] The former were shipmasters and smaller-scale merchants (they are also called *emporoi*), the latter big financiers who had no intrinsic connection with the maritime means of production, even when they specialized in financing voyages across the Mediterranean, or possibly further afield. By contrast, the Indian Ocean networks typically seem to have involved merchant capitalists who owned their own ships, like the Aden merchants described by Ibn Baṭṭūṭa,[88] or the Tamil Naina Suryadeva, who was the richest merchant in Malacca around 1511.[89] In the Mediterranean this type, too, was well known. Indeed, when the fourth-century senator-cum-astrologer Firmicus Maternus refers to *potentes navicularii*,[90] he is clearly describing ship-owners who were also powerful merchants, on a pattern exemplified later by the *nākhudās* of a bigger and different kind of sea.

83 Ibid. 60.

84 Stephen 1997, 134.

85 Braudel 1975, vol. 1, 445.

86 Cracco 1967, esp. 38ff., 86, 189, 193ff.

87 *Nov. Justin.* 106 (540).

88 Ibn Baṭṭūṭa 251 (= *Travels* II 371–372). Cf. Goitein and Friedman 2007, 'Shipowners were wealthy merchants', about the Aden-based Jewish shipowners.

89 Thomaz 1988, 37.

90 Firm. Mat., *Mathesis* 8.20.10.

CHAPTER 8

Comparative Perspectives on the Pepper Trade

*Federico De Romanis**

This paper aims to elucidate three features related to the importation of South Indian pepper by the Romans in the first to the second centuries CE and by the Portuguese in the sixteenth century: first, the size of the ships required in each era; second, the quantitative dimensions of the import; and third, the dependence of the trade on the ecological and anthropological particularities of the Malabar region in south-western India. It will be shown that the huge pepper production of central Malabar encouraged the deployment of ships with considerable, albeit different, carrying capacities in both eras. Moreover, it will be argued that the remarkable Malabar productivity was largely based on the pepper grown and harvested by the local foraging communities in the foothills of the Western Ghats.

Pepper and Seagoing Ships at the Periyar Delta, in the Sixteenth Century CE ...

In a letter dated 24 December 1504, Álvaro Vaz, officer of the Portuguese garrison of Cochin, could describe to his king D. Manuel the commercial implications of Portuguese control over the small kingdom of Cochin and the nearby delta of the Periyar River.[1] With a patrol of just a few warships to deter

* This paper benefited enormously from the stimulating environment and facilities of the Italian Academy at Columbia University. I wish to thank Prof. D.A. Freedberg, Director of the Academy, for the invitation, as well as my co-Fellows and the Academy staff.

1 CA III 258: 'Se vosa Senhorja manda aquy amdar d armada as fustas e bragamtijns que lhe tenho scprito, que tolhan que nenhuuns çambuquos navegem, com este par de caravelas que qua estam, e, jsso mesmo, se nesta forteleza tem deposito XX ou XXX (mil) cruzados, aja por çerto que XXX (mil) quintaes de pimenta cad ano se podem rrecolher, d aquy tee coullam,— XX (mil) aquy, e d hy pera çima, e os mais lla [...] Ora veja vossa Senhorja quamto proueito se d isto segue, e quamto majs certa estara sempre a carregaçam e seguramça da partida das naaos, a tempo que nam pasem o rrisquo que passou o almjrante [...] e, em breue tempo, este rrio de coochy he pera ellas mjlhor do mumdo, nem majs seguro, e podem hir per ele açima b e bj leguoas, e meter tamto espamto aos senhores que jazem per ele açima, omde

 | DOI 10.1163/9789004289536_010

Muslim traders and funds of 20,000–30,000 *cruzados* to purchase the commodity, His Highness could secure for his ships as many as 30,000 *quintais* (more than 1,500 tons)[2] of pepper each year—20,000 from Cochin, and the rest from Quilon.[3]

Very soon, reality surpassed imagination. Tomé Pires, *feitor das drogarias* in Cannanore in 1511, estimated 20,000 *bahar* (*c.*3,200 tons) as the yearly production of Malabar, coming from the region between Chettuva (*c.*70 km north of Cochin) and Kayamkulam (*c.*90 km south of Cochin).[4] In a letter to D. Manuel dated 31 October 1520,[5] Nuno de Castro argued that from the region

---

a pimenta da sserra vem teer, que ajam em booa vemtura nam comsemtjr que nenhuum mouro a compre, senam nos, que, sem jsto, nam pode ser em nenhuũa maneira [...] Neste porto de coochy, Senhor, deve vosa Senhorja fazer todo seu fumdamento, porque, elle ssoo, abasta mais pera huũa carregaçam que todo outro rrestamte; e, despois, em coullam, que sempre ajudaraa com caecoulam muy bem, e asy pollos christãaos, que naquela terra ha majs, virem a perfeito conheçimento de nosa ssamta fee etc.'

2 In sixteenth century Portuguese documents, pepper is usually measured either in *bahar* of Cochin and Quilon (166.272 kg) or in *quintais do peso velho* (51.405 kg): Lima Felner 1868, 47; Bouchon 1977, IX.

3 Vaz's estimate is echoed by Leonardo da Ca' Masser and Vincenzo Quirini, each of whom, around 1506, foresaw a yearly import from Cochin to Lisbon of as much as 10,000 *bahar* or 30,000 to 35,000 *canatara* of pepper: Da Ca' Masser 33; Quirini 9–10. A similar amount of *espesiaria* is also mentioned by Pacheco Pereira 100.

4 Pires II 362 (fol. 129 v.): 'a pimenta avera no Malabar atee vimte mjll bahares E naçe de chatua athee o Reyno De caya coulam E alguuã pouca por coulam por cramganor E cochim he a escala Desta pimenta a mais perto E omde mais ganham a levam aJmda que seja com trabalho [...] a q̃ nacee no senhorio Do Reino De cochim e melhor.' Very close to Pires' amount are the 60,000 *cantera* (*c.*3,000 tons) estimated as the Malabar production by Francisco d'Albuquerque (Francesco dal Bocchier) in 1518: Aubin 1973, 194; maybe directly inspired by Pires is the estimate (20,000 *bahar* = 60,000 *quintais*) repeated in a 1569 text, on which see Thomaz 1998, 39.

5 CA VII 175–176: 'Senhor nesta terra do Malavar—a saber—de Belymjaom, que he acem de Coulã porto ate ij legoas alẽ de Cramganor pera Calequt, tenho sabido que se colhe cadano xb (mil) bares de pimenta ate xbj, nõ [*contando?*] a que lhe fica pera velha de hũ ano pera outro que se gasta per esta maneira—a saber—na mesma terra se gastarã ij (mil) ij (mil)b[c] bares dela em seus comeres, e se leva pera fora ẽ boys e nas cabeças ate iij (mil) bares que sã ja grãdes caminhos abertos pera Cale Care e outras partes do sertão e a hy hũ caminho que se chama Putura, e des Belĩjã a levam a cabeça pera Comorym e asy a mais tres caminhos outros que levam a pimenta ẽ boys e trazẽ nele arroz e o retorno ha pimenta dos paraos de Panane, Chatua, Cranganor levarã cadano pera Dio ate b[c] bj[c] bares dela que vã per longo a costa como ja dyse a V.A. e os nove myll que pode ficar guardã pera velha ij (mil) iij (mil) bares dela, e nesta velha fazẽ eles a royndade por que tem mais sostamçia que ha verde que logo cõ pouco

between Vizhinjam (*c.*200 km south of Cochin) and Cranganore (*c.*30 km north of Cochin), 25,000 or even 29,000 *bahar* (*c.*4,100 and *c.*4,800 tons, respectively) were produced.[6] As Portuguese awareness of Malabar's potential for pepper production deepened, their pepper import to Lisbon also increased: the *quintais* of spices, which in 1504 amounted to only 24,000 (of which 22,000 *quintais* were pepper), grew to 76,000 (of which 56,000 were pepper) in 1519.

---

se mostra a roŷdade nela, e posto que acima diga a V.A. xb (mil) ou xbj (mil) bares, eu tenho sabido per homẽs da terra que a bẽ sabem e tratam que me diserã que se colherã até xx (mil) bares e pareçeme que asy pode ser, por que nam crea V.A. que sam pequenas as sacas da pimenta, asy para Oromuz, como pera Dio, como pera o estreito de Meca aos mouros, como pera Choromãdell etc.'

6 Later data show de Castro's estimate to be fairly accurate. The most significant piece of evidence is in the margin of a page of Francisco da Costa's *Relatório sobre o trato da pimenta* (1607); cf. da Costa 315:

'Nos tecanqutes em Canharapely	4,000	bares;	(Kanjirappilly)
En Iratepely	1,000	»	(Erattupetta)
Erimamoly	3,000	»	(Erumely)
Zaruquly	5,000	»	(Chalakudy)
Corgeira	3,000	»	(Kodakara)
Paleacate Cheri	3,000	»	(Palakkad Churam)
	19,000		

São 61 mil 453 quintaes de pezo pequeno.'—The six villages listed are all in central Kerala, but none was inside the so-called 'Pepper Kingdom' (on which, see below). They are credited for a total production of 19,000 *bahar* or 61,453 *quintais* (*c.*3,158 tons). On the same order of magnitude of de Castro's estimate are the 11,752 *candies* (= *c.*3,400 tons) recalled by Buchanan II 457 to be collected by the king Marthanda Varma in 1757. Perhaps less reliable is the more general estimate made by *Malavares* and repeated by Francisco da Costa 350–351: 'Pois se sabe por estimação dos Malavares que de Onor atte Travancor nunqua ha hum anno por outro menos de cem mil bares de pimenta que são 258 mil quintaes, e destes se levão pera Portugal de vinte atte trinta mil, e a mais se consume nestas boiadas, e em naos de Meca, e outra muita que com castigo executado se pudera remediar.' A hundred thousand *bahar* (here more than 13,350 tons)—more or less ten times the amount yearly exported to Lisbon—would suggest a Malabar production considerably higher than the estimates and data quoted above. However, the round (one *lakh*) figure, already surfacing in a letter of Franz Cron (Fuggerarchiv, MSS Codex no. 46.1. fols. 50–51), and the wide geographic scope of the estimate may inspire scepticism.

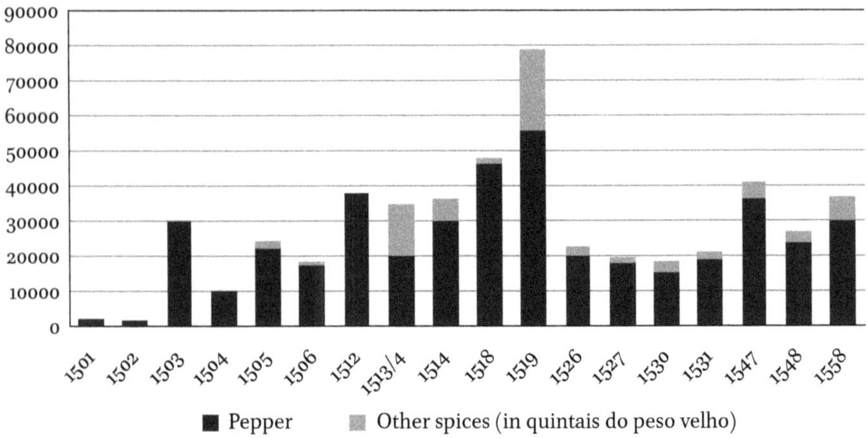

FIGURE 8.1 *Spices exported to Lisbon in some years of the 16th century.*[7]

In a period during which both accomplishments and expectations multiplied every year, it is not surprising to see constant upgrades in the Portuguese transportation system. In a letter to D. Manuel written from Cannanore on 9 October 1512, Afonso de Albuquerque announced his decision to send to Lisbon 38,000 *quintais* (*c.*1,950 tons) of *pimenta e drogoarias* with only five 'new ships', whose carrying capacity—between 7,500 and 8,000 *quintais*—would be enough to accommodate the projected amount. The *Nazaré*, an 'old' ship which

7 Sources: 1501: da Ca' Masser 15; 1502: da Ca' Masser 16; 1503: da Ca' Masser 17; 1504: da Ca' Masser 19 (Aubin 1987, 46–53); 1505: da Ca' Masser 20; Bouchon 1976; 1506: da Ca' Masser 23; 1512: CA I 83 (no distinction is made between pepper and other spices); 1513/4: Sanuto XVII 191; XVIII 143; 1514: Sanuto XVIII 409 (I use the aggregate data reported at the beginning, leaving aside the subsequent analytical lists); 1518: Bouchon 1977; Sanuto XXV 594–595 (which I follow for the cargo of the *Madanela*); 1519: Correia II² 561; Sanuto XXVII 641; 1526: Sanuto XLII 453–454; 1527: ANTT CVR 16; 1530: Sanuto LIV 131; 1531: Sanuto LIV 599; LV 63; 1547: Livro das mercês que fez D. João de Castro ff. 59–60v; ANTT Colecção São Lourenço IV ff. 329–330; 1548: Livro das mercês que fez D. João de Castro ff. 62–64v; 1558: Seure 71. I take unspecified *quintais* (as well as Sanuto's *canteri*) to be *quintais do peso velho* (51.405 kg) when related to pepper and *quintais do peso novo* (58.752 kg) when related to other spices; here and elsewhere in this chapter all the data have been recalculated in *quintais do peso velho*. Most of these documents were already published and/or analyzed by Bouchon 1976; Bouchon 1977; Godinho 1981/1983² III 73–74. As for ANTT CVR 16 and ANTT Colecção São Lourenço IV ff. 329–330, my thanks go to Prof. L.F. Thomaz, who brought them to my attention, and to P. Pinto, who made his transcription of ANTT CVR 16 available to me.

could not carry more than 6,000 to 6,500 *quintais*,[8] was to be used for other purposes.[9]

Although the convenience of the larger capacities did not result in the abrupt discontinuance of the smaller ships,[10] the trend towards greater tonnages continued. In Andrea Corsali's opinion, of the six ships that arrived at Lisbon in 1518, two had a capacity of 2,000 *botte* and four had capacities of 800, 900, or 1,000 *botte*.[11] If the quantities of goods recorded in the *Caderno dos ofiçiaes da India da carreguaçam das naos* do not show a similar disproportion, they make clear that the *Santa Catarina do Monte Sinai* and the *Nazaré*[12]—apparently the two ships whose capacity was evaluated at 2,000 *botte* by Corsali—carried more than 460 tons of pepper each.[13] It is not known when this *Nazaré* was built; the *Santa Catarina de Monte Synay* was built in Cochin in 1513,[14] and carried at least 1,000 to 1,500 *bahar* more than the 'new' ships of 1512.

---

8 Fonseca 1989², 232–236.

9 CA I 83: 'acerqua das naos da carga que est ano vieram de portugall, e asy as de dom Garcia, eu tomey por fumdamento de irem est ano a vosa alteza xxxbiij (mil) quintaes de pimenta e drogoarias, que poderiam alojar as cimqo naos novas; e porque a nazaré estava hum pouco duvidosa, se poderia a carga seguramente tornar nela, eu mandey a iso mestres, pilotos e carpinteiros ajuramemtados, e polo que neles achey, me pareceo voso serviço nam se avemturar a carga nela e que seria milhor ir em hũa nao nova, pois que a nazaré era nao que de necesidade avia de levar mill e quinhemtos quintaees de carga menos que a primeira, de maneira que ficava em sete mill e quinhemtos até oito mill quintaes, que pouco mais ou menos carregam as naos novas.'

10 On 25 June 1511, D. Manuel ordered the construction of four other ships, again for the Cape Route, of only 460 *toneladas*, which makes them more similar to the old *Nazaré* than to the new ships: ANTT, C.C., P. I, M. 10, D. 53. A *tonel* is a cask 1.54 m high and 1.027 m wide at its maximum diameter. A *tonel* of pepper weighs approximately 13.5 *quintais*: Costa 1997, 79.

11 Corsali 188: 'Dopo la tornata del Capitan maggiore, non si attende ad altro, che a mettere in ordine naui sei per Portogallo, le quali si partiranno per tutto questo mese di Gennaio, & di già tre vanno alla vela, & questa sarà la quarta. due d'esse sono ciascuna di dua mila botte, & tutte l'altre di 800. 900. & 1000. & leuano per il Re, 50000. quintali di pepe, & molto giengiouo, cannella, & garofani, gomma, lacca, & seta della Cina, Sandalo vermiglio, oltre a infinite ricchezze d'huomini particolari.'

12 There were several homonymous ships active in those years: Fonseca 1989², 236–237. This *Nazaré* is not the same ship referred to by Albuquerque in the letter quoted above in n. 9: Bouchon 1977, VI–VII.

13 Bouchon 1977.

14 Cf. CA I 121.

FIGURE 8.2 *Tons of spices per ship in some years of the 16th century.*

The chart above represents the average cargo per ship, in tons, of the spices imported by the Portuguese in some years of the sixteenth century, obtained by dividing the weight of the total cargo by the number of ships.

The low values for the years 1519 and 1526 have different explanations. The quantity of spices imported in 1519—56,000 *quintais* of pepper and 20,000 of other spices—is the highest amount ever achieved by the Portuguese in a single year.[15] The relatively high number of ships involved (fourteen) suggests that in order to transfer that exceptional (and perhaps unexpected) cargo size, several ships of lower tonnage had to be loaded in addition to the 'new' ships of quite high tonnage. On the contrary, the relatively modest quantity (22,700 *quintais*)[16] of spices carried by the five ships of the 1526 fleet reflects the supply problems of those years more than the limited capacity of the ships of that fleet: the only ship whose cargo Sanuto accurately describes carried a little more than 7,000 *quintais* (6,210 of which were pepper). An even smaller cargo (*c.*19,300) was sent in 1527, but the ships of that fleet (probably three) were very big and two of them did not sail fully loaded.[17] Only three ships came back in 1530, and their total cargo was a little more than 18,000 *quintais*. The four ships of 1531, whose loading capacity was 500 *tonéis* each (= 6,750 *quintais* of

15 Correia II[2] 561: 'cincoenta e seis mil quintaes de pimenta, e vinte mil de drogas; a mór carga que se nunqua fez'.

16 Assuming that pepper was only 20,000 *quintais*, but Sanuto XLII 453 writes: 'Per quel che si pò comprendere, il cargo di queste navi serà in tutto più di vintimila cantara de piper boni'.

17 ANTT CVR 16: 'as naaos qu estauam a caRega serem muy grandes e aviam mester mujta pimemta [...] [a naao] burgalesa e a naao Samta Cateryna [nam estauan de] todo carregadas nem lhe dey majs pimemta'.

pepper), had a total cargo of *c.*20,800 *quintais*. The fleet that returned in 1547 comprised six ships and carried 40,657 *quintais* (averaging 6,776 per ship), with two of them, the *Burgalesa* and the *São Filipe*, carrying 7,488 and 9,069 *quintais* respectively.[18]

The chart does not take into account the exceptional capacity of two galleons, the *São Bento* and the *São João*, which could be loaded (and in 1551 the former seems to have actually been loaded), with as many as 12,000 *quintais* of pepper.[19] The 1552 misfortune of the latter vessel, which after a late departure from India ended up wrecking off the South African coast, may have recommended a more cautious approach towards the size of the *Carreira da Índia* ships. A 1558 *Relatório* shows that by then it had become customary to send five ships, two of which held 750 to 800 *tonéis*, two that held 500, and one that held 600.[20] In 1570, D. Sebastião required a more drastic downscaling, prescribing tonnages between 450 and 300 *tonéis*, in India as well as in Portugal.[21] For the Cape route, however, that upper limit was unrealistically low and the injunction was simply overlooked.[22] In the eighties, the ships still numbered five and their tonnage remained approximately 600 *tonéis*.[23] Further proposals to reduce the tonnage and increase the number of ships remained on paper.[24]

... And in the First–Second Centuries CE

The different commodities that complement Roman and Portuguese pepper cargoes make the changes in the Indian Ocean from Roman to Portuguese

18 De Caminha 85.

19 ANTT C.C. P. I, M. 86, D. 94; Gomes de Brito I 5.

20 ANTT C.C. P. I, M. 103, D. 31: 'Hus anos per outros comúmente pera huã caregua se estimão çimqo naos Duas de VII^cL e VIII^c tonés et duas de V^c pouco mais ou menos e ahuã meaã—Amtre e huã grãde e huã piquena q(ue) sera de VI^c tonés.' In terms of pepper cargoes, these loading capacities correspond to 10,125, 10,800, 6,750, and 8,100 *quintais* respectively. As a matter of fact, the 1558 fleet comprised five ships for a total cargo that included 30,000 *quintais* of pepper and 6,000 *quintais* of other spices.

21 Leis, e Provisões, que Dom Sebastião fez 81.

22 Godinho 1981/1983² III 51: 'A ordenação de 1570 não foi respeitada; era de prever—o máximo admitido parece demasiado baixo.'

23 Santa Cruz 53: 'cinco viages' made by ships of '600 toneladas de Portugal que hacen mas que 1200 de Castilla'. The 1585 contract (Mathew 1997, 256–257) foresees an import of 30,000 *quintais* of pepper by six ships, five from India and one from Malaca.

24 Santa Cruz 54: 'Todas estas cosas se evitarian, y mejorarian, siendo las naos de a 600 toneladas de Castilla, porque las de a 1200 que aora navegan, traen los inconvenientes que he dicho.'

times obvious. While Portuguese pepper cargoes were supplemented with other spices such as ginger, clove, cinnamon, and mace, the heaviest and/or most voluminous commodity after pepper carried by Roman ships was malabathron—leaves of *tamāla*—which was imported from the Ganges valley. The implications of these differences will not be investigated here; instead I shall focus on the common features that Roman and Portuguese trade with South India shared in certain periods. Among them are the deployment of big ships, the pivotal role of pepper, and the harbourage in the Periyar valley and Vembanad Lake regions.[25]

Although evidence for a history of the Roman Indiamen is meagre,[26] the assumption that unusually big ships remained a typical long-time feature of this branch of Roman trade with India is justified by the fact that already by the mid first century CE the author of the *Periplus Maris Erythraei* states that 'very big ships' were used to sail to the emporia of the Limyrike[27] and that Philostratus (at the beginning of the third century CE) in his albeit largely fictional *Life of Apollonius of Tyana* still vividly describes a gigantic Indiaman that could only have been the successor of the 'very big ships' that conveyed pepper in the mid first century CE:

> Let us imagine a ship such as the Egyptians construct and launch on our waters, giving Egyptian exports in exchange for Indian ones. There is an old rule of the Red Sea, which king Erythras once laid down when he ruled that sea, that Egyptians may not enter in a warship, but instead must use a single round-bottomed vessel. So the Egyptians construct a ship equivalent to many of those used by others. They seal it with all the joints that hold a ship together, and over these they build hulls and a mast, and make numerous cabins such as those over the benches. There are many captains of this ship, sailing under the command of the eldest and most skilful among them, and many steersmen at the stern, and excellent, nimble sailors who eagerly tend the sails. This ship also carries

25 By contrast, pre-Portuguese trade between Malabar and Arabia was centred on Calicut and conducted with ships of more modest tonnage (1,000 to 1,200 *bahar*: Barbosa 160–161), whose cargoes included a less overwhelming preponderance of pepper. For more on Muslim trade with Malabar, see Prange 2010 and Banaji in this volume.

26 A profile of one of those 'very big ships' has been recognized in a two- (or three-) masted Roman vessel portrayed in a potsherd graffito from Alagankulam (Tamil Nadu): Tchernia 2011a.

27 *Peripl. M. Rubr.* 56: πλεῖ δὲ εἰς τὰ ἐμπόρια ταῦτα [sc. τῆς Λιμυρικῆς] μέ<γι>στα πλοῖα. For the correction μέ<γι>στα, cf. De Romanis 1996, 178–180. Limyrike is the Greek choronym for Malabar: De Romanis 2012.

> armed men, since the barbarians of the gulf live on the right side of its entrance, and the ship must do battle with them when they attack and try to plunder it.[28]

Philostratus blends realistic and mythical elements: the description of the ship, modelled on the 'very big ships' that sailed to the Limyrike, is real, while King Erythras' eccentric laws are Philostratus' personal inventions to account for the actual features of the South India trade in his time.

It is now possible to argue that the Roman pepper carriers were really substantial and that Philostratus' emphasis on the size of 'Egyptian' Indiamen ('equivalent to several ships at once') must be taken seriously. The tonnage of a South India-bound ship can be inferred from the data of the fragmentary text on the verso side of the Papyrus Vindobonensis G 40,822 (= SB XVIII 13,167), widely known as the 'Muziris' papyrus,[29] which gives the monetary evaluation of three-quarters of the cargo of the *Hermapollon*, a ship that was most likely returning from Muziris (the celebrated ancient pepper emporium of South India) sometime around the mid second century CE. The Muziris papyrus, furthermore, gives an example of how the relative weights of pepper and malabathron, the two major commodities imported from the Limyrike emporia,[30] could balance each other within the cargo of a Roman Indiaman.

A crucial correction to an earlier misreading by the first editors of the Muziris papyrus led to the identification of the 771 money talents and 4,632

---

28 Philostr., *VA* 3.35: 'ὑποκείσθω δὲ ναῦς, οἵαν Αἰγύπτιοι ξυντιθέντες ἐς τὴν θάλατταν τὴν ἡμεδαπὴν ἀφιᾶσιν ἀγωγίμων Ἰνδικῶν ἀντιδιδόντες Αἰγύπτια, θεσμοῦ γὰρ παλαιοῦ περὶ τὴν Ἐρυθρὰν ὄντος, ὃν βασιλεὺς Ἐρύθρας ἐνόμισεν, ὅτε τῆς θαλάττης ἐκείνης ἦρχε, μακρῷ μὲν πλοίῳ μὴ ἐσπλεῖν ἐς αὐτὴν Αἰγυπτίους, στρογγύλῃ δ' αὖ μιᾷ νηὶ χρῆσθαι, σοφίζονται πλοῖον Αἰγύπτιοι πρὸς πολλὰ τῶν παρ' ἑτέροις καὶ παραπλευρώσαντες αὐτὸ ἁρμονίαις, ὁπόσαι ναῦν ξυνιστᾶσι, τοίχοις τε ὑπεράραντες καὶ ἱστῷ καὶ πηξάμενοι πλείους οἰκίας, οἵας ἐπὶ τῶν σελμάτων, πολλοὶ μὲν κυβερνῆται τῆς νεὼς ταύτης ὑπὸ τῷ πρεσβυτάτῳ τε καὶ σοφωτάτῳ πλέουσι, πολλοὶ δὲ κατὰ πρῷραν ἄρχοντες ἄριστοί τε καὶ δεξιοὶ ναῦται καὶ πρὸς ἱστία πηδῶντες, ἔστι δέ τι τῆς νεὼς ταύτης καὶ ὁπλιτεῦον, πρὸς γὰρ τοὺς κολπίτας βαρβάρους, οἳ ἐν δεξιᾷ τοῦ ἔσπλου κεῖνται, παρατάττεσθαι δεῖ τὴν ναῦν, ὅτε ληίζοιντο αὐτὴν ἐπιπλέοντες' (trans. C.P. Jones LCL, 2005).

29 Besides Harrauer/Sijpesteijn 1985, cf. especially Thür 1987; 1988; Casson 1986; 1990; De Romanis 1998; Rathbone 2000; Morelli 2011; De Romanis 2010/2011 [2012]; and, in this volume, the essays of Wilson, Schörle, Nappo, and Aubert.

30 Indeed, the bulk import of these two commodities was the reason for using 'very big ships', cf. *Peripl. M. Rubr.* 56: 'πλεῖ δὲ εἰς τὰ ἐμπόρια ταῦτα μέ<γι>στα πλοῖα διὰ τὸν ὄγκον καὶ τὸ πλῆθος τοῦ πιπέρεως καὶ τοῦ μαλαβάθρου.' The wording of the author is explained by the fact that compared to pepper, dried malabathron leaves were a bulkier but lighter commodity.

drachmas, recorded at col. i, ll. 25–26, as the value of (almost) three-quarters of the pepper imported by the ship.[31] Federico Morelli argued that this value results from a price of 24 drachmas per mina, and a total cargo of less than 140 tons of pepper; I have suggested instead that only a price of 6 drachmas per mina is compatible with the structure of the text and with other numerical data in the papyrus.

As a matter of fact, if the price of pepper were 24 drachmas per mina, we would not be able to answer the following questions:

1) Why the monetary evaluation of three-quarters of the pepper (col. i, ll. 25–26) comes three lines after the weight number on which it is supposedly based (col. i, l. 21).
2) Why the malabathron, to be identified with the item evaluated at col. i, ll. 17–19,[32] would have a price lower than that of the pepper.[33]
3) Why, at col. i, ll. 1–3, the weight number minae 58 (l. 2) is inserted between minae 59 (l. 1) and minae 14 ¾ (l. 3); if the evaluation of pepper ended with col. i, l. 25, that sequence makes no sense.
4) Where to find the other addend ending with three obols. The total of the evaluation (col. ii, l. 29) is an amount of money with no obols attached, but the subtotal of the items evaluated at col. ii is an amount of money ending with three obols. Therefore, the subtotal of the evaluations calculated in col. i must be an amount of money ending with three obols as well. The only addend which can end with three obols is the one in the lost lines at the end of the column, as an evaluation of the quantity specified at col. i, l. 27. As the latter ends with 44¼ minae, its price per mina cannot be a number of drachmas that is a multiple of four.

Therefore, it seems certain to me that:

1) The pepper was evaluated with the same complex procedure followed for tusks and fragments of ivory.
2) Both col. i, ll. 1–3 and col. i, ll. 20–29 (and the missing lines below) refer to the evaluation of pepper.

---

31 Morelli 2011; De Romanis 2010/2011 [2012].

32 At col. i, l. 18 I consider certain the reading of 1,800, which implies, for the malabathron, a price of 12 drachmas per mina.

33 Pliny (*HN* 12.129) gives 60 *denarii* per pound as the price of the *malabathrum* leaves. In fourth century CE documents, the malabathron price either equals (*P.Oxy.* LIV 3731) or far surpasses (*P.Oxy.* LIV 3733; 3766) that of pepper.

3) The value for pepper was 6 drachmas per mina.
4) At col. i, l. 21 the reading weight talents 1]3,223 minae 2̣ (*c.*405 tons) must be restored.

A monetary evaluation based on a price of 6 drachmas per mina implies a total quantity of more than 544 tons of pepper, an amount worth comparing both with the estimated pepper production of the Malabar region and with the Portuguese pepper import in the first part of the sixteenth century.

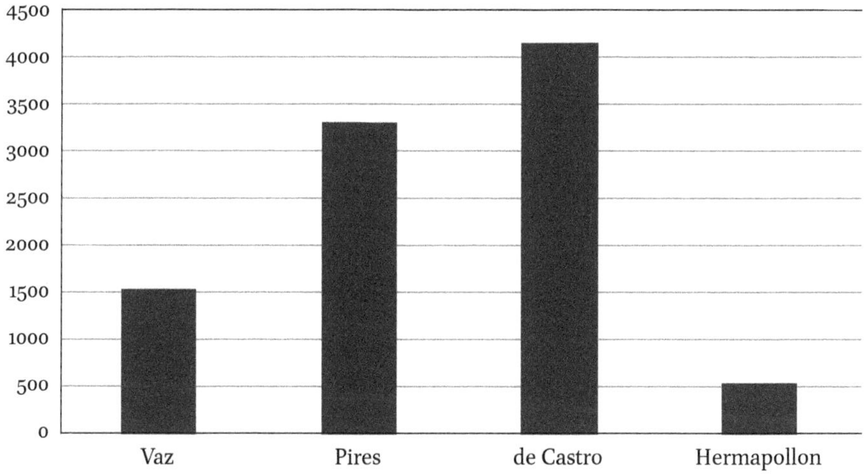

FIGURE 8.3 *Estimated production of Malabar pepper and* Hermapollon *pepper cargo (in tons).*

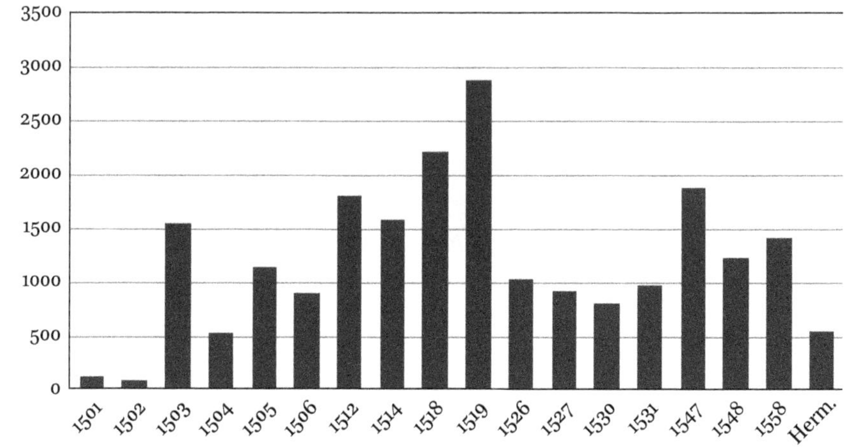

FIGURE 8.4 *Portuguese import of pepper and* Hermapollon *pepper cargo (in tons).*

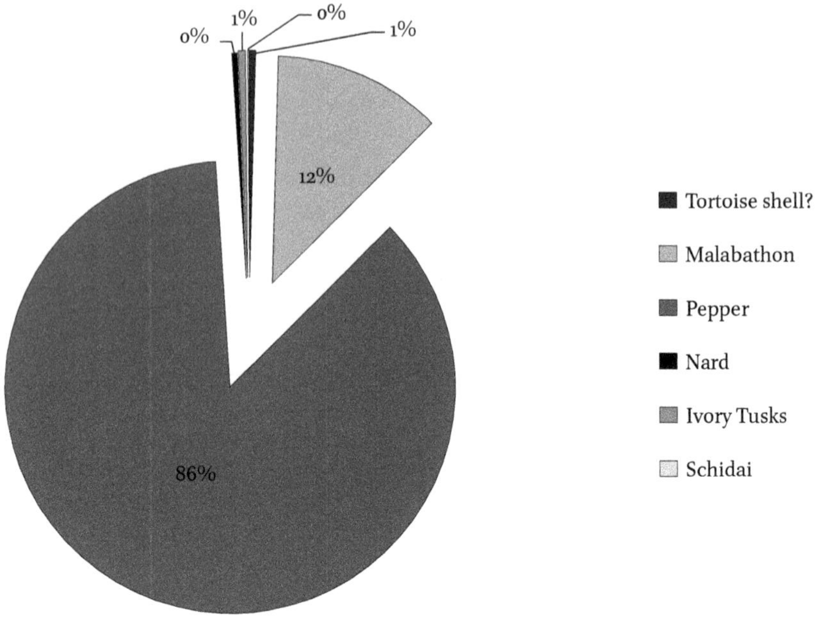

FIGURE 8.5 Hermapollon's *cargo* (*based on De Romanis 2010/2011* [*2012*]).

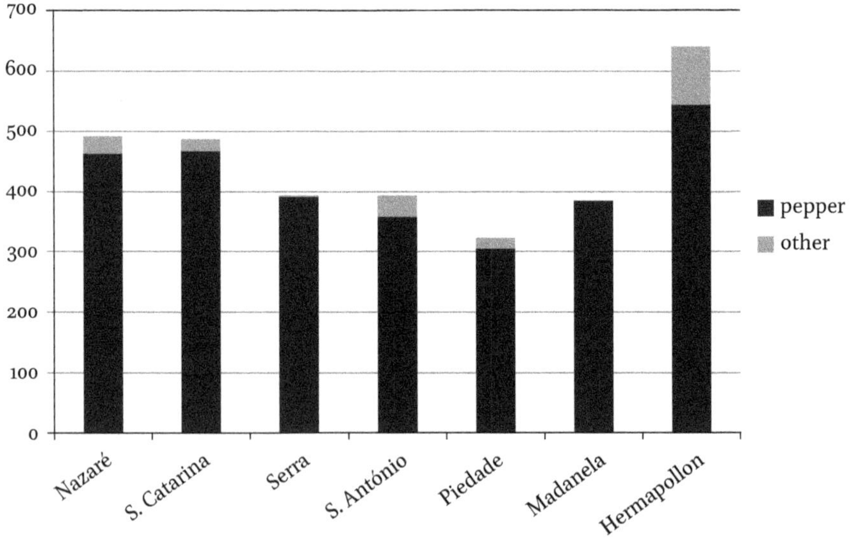

FIGURE 8.6 *Cargoes of the 1518 fleet and the* Hermapollon (*in tons*).

Moreover, a price for pepper of 6 drachmas per mina and a weight of *c*.1,860 weight talents (col. i, l. 18) for three-quarters of the malabathron on board would result in a total cargo of more than 620 tons, with pepper representing *c*.86 per cent of the entire cargo.

A comparison with the cargoes of the six ships from the 1518 fleet shows an even greater proportion accorded to pepper in the sixteenth century.

The cargo of the *Hermapollon* equals the almost 620 tons of pepper that the galleons *São Bento* and *São João* were built to carry. However, while in the sixteenth century the Portuguese ships of the *Rota do Cabo* were usually smaller than the *São Bento* and the *São João*, it is likely that the Roman pepper carriers of the first two centuries, which sailed along a much shorter and safer route than the Portuguese ships, were all about the same size as the *Hermapollon*. If early modern quantitative data offer an approximate benchmark for the volume of the ancient pepper export, and if the *Hermapollon* is representative of the size of the 'very big ships' that imported pepper from the emporia of the Limyrike, then it follows that we cannot imagine hundreds of ships like the *Hermapollon*, each importing 500 tons of pepper every year. This is not a reason to reject Strabo's testimony about the 120 ships sailing to India when Aelius Gallus (26–25 BCE) was prefect of Egypt.[34] However, such a large fleet would have included all the ships bound for any of the Indian emporia and, since they were sailing from Myos Hormos, they must have been much smaller than the pepper carriers that eventually would depart from Berenice.[35] At the time the geographer made his inquiry, the pattern of trade evidenced by Pliny,[36] by the author of the *Periplus Maris Erythraei*, by the Muziris papyrus, and by Philostratus was still to come.

When the author of the *Periplus Maris Erythraei* says that Muziris was 'flourishing thanks to both the ships that come from Ariake and the Greek ones',[37] we should visualize less than a dozen 'very big ships', surrounded by several hundred riverboats and small sea vessels that convey commodities to supply them. It is not unlikely that at the beginning of the third century CE when that pattern was coming to an end, only one such 'very big ship' still imported pepper from South India, yet its cargo would have been enough to give five to ten grams of pepper to each inhabitant of the Roman Empire.

---

34 Strabo 2.5.12.

35 De Romanis 1996, 171–183.

36 Plin., *HN* 6.101–106.

37 *Peripl. M. Rubr.* 54: 'ἡ δὲ Μούζιρις [. . .] ἀκμάζουσα δὲ τοῖς ἀπὸ τῆς Ἀριακῆς εἰς αὐτὴν ἐρχομένοις πλοίοις καὶ τοῖς Ἑλληνικοῖς.'

Mapping the Pepper Trade

The Portuguese never even conceived of having direct control of the foothill areas in central Kerala where pepper grew;[38] a pragmatic realism advocated maintaining control only of the mouth of the Periyar River and promoting relations with the *senhores* of the hinterland.[39] Nonetheless, information included in da Ca' Masser's and Quirini's reports suggests early explorations of the upstream portions of the Periyar River[40] and, most importantly, a demarcation of a region where, they maintained, all the Malabar pepper grew. It is described as a rather small mountain zone, 15 leagues (= 45 miles) in circuit (da Ca' Masser); or 50 to 60 miles in length (Quirini). It adjoins Cranganore and Cochin on the west side and the kingdom of Narsi on the east; it is controlled by a 'king', whose name is Mat(h)ac(h)aimal;[41] and it can produce 10,000 *bahar* or 30,000 to 35,000 *cantara* of pepper each year.[42]

If we turn to the *Livro que trata das cousas da Índia e do Japão*, written in 1548, we get a completely different picture. The third chapter of this work, devoted to the rivers that flow near Cochin or into Vembanad Lake, claims to be based on information by Nycolao Gomçallvez. Obviously, it also refers to the course of the Periyar River and to the lands of the *Mangate kaymal*, through which, however, no pepper is said to be transferred, but only shipmasts, a little angelim wood, and a lot of teak wood.[43] What is even more remarkable, though, is that the lord of Vadakkenkur, one of the 'kings' who controlled the rivers through which pepper came to Cochin, is called—in this text as well as in many other more or less contemporary Portuguese documents (even official ones)—*o Rey da pimenta*, 'the Pepper king', a nickname that indicates his prominent role

38 For an accurate description of the Malabar pepper-growing areas, cf. Malekandathil 2001, 40–47.

39 In 1504, Álvaro Vaz thought to overawe them by advancing upstream of the Periyar 5 or 6 leagues from Cochin (cf. *supra*, n. 1); eventually, the *Estado da Índia* established annuities for them (Malekandathil 2001, 46).

40 Labelled *o Rio da Pimenta* in Correia I 1, 418–419. The definition probably goes back to Correia's sources for 1504. This passage was brought to my attention by Prof. L.F. Thomaz.

41 Mat(h)ac(h)aimal is the rendering of *Mangate kaymal*, the title of the lord of Alengad, 'regulo quazy sujeito ao rey de Cochim' (Bocarro II 196). A *kaymal* may have at his command 100 to 10,000 Nairs: Pires II 362.

42 Da Ca' Masser 27; 33; 35; Quirini 9–10. Note that both authors confuse Calangannor with Cannanor.

43 *Cousas da India e do Japão* 44: 'De Cramguanor se toma outro rio que vay pera a serra e pasa pelo Mamguate e per o Carta da Llua he por Melcatur (Meleatur?), que sam todos estes caymays destes luguares nosos amyguos, e per este rio vem mastos e amgelyns pouquos e tequas muytas; este rio vay pera a serra dez leguoas.'

in the trade. Therefore, while around 1506 Mat(h)ac(h)aimal was believed to control all the Malabar pepper, eventually—by 1546 at the latest[44]—the king of Vadakkenkur was recognized as the one and only 'Pepper king'. It can be inferred that although most of the pepper was transferred through the Periyar River in the first years of the sixteenth century, eventually, by the second or third decade of the century, more and more pepper reached Cochin through the rivers that flowed into the Vembanad Lake from the land of Vadakkenkur.

Nycolao Gomçallvez was very well informed about the Malabar pepper trade. He mentions the presence of pepper merchants at Belur, neighboring the possessions of the 'Pepper king'.[45] He points to the importance of Jumquão Telhado, a customs house and a node for the transfer of pepper to Cochin on the southern shore of the Vembanad Lake.[46] He says that pepper produced in the nearby region of Tekkenkur was sold at a monthly fair at Kanjirappally and exported to the other side of the Western Ghats;[47] and finally he records pepper envoys to Cochin from Putamguale, on the Chalakudy River.[48]

This information is extremely important for the histories of both the early modern and ancient pepper trade. The description of the waterways that connect Cochin to its hinterland explains why Tomé Pires' estimate refers to an

---

44 It would be important to establish when such a nickname was invented. The earliest document I came across is dated 1546: Carta de Salvador de Leão para D. João De Castro. Cochim, 5 Agosto 1546, DUP VII 289–291. A serious investigation is required.

45 *Cousas da India e do Japão* 46: 'Defromte desta terra pera a bamda do sul estáa outra ilha que se chama Chembe; esta hé del rey de Pimenta; per aquy vay hum rio pera a serra que vay ter a hum luguar que se chama Belur; neste luguar de Belur morão muytos mercadores que tratão em madeyra e em pimemta pera Cochym; este rio vay pera serra dez ou doze leguoas.'

46 *Cousas da India e do Japão* 46: 'Defronte desta ilha pera a bamda do sull estáa o Jumquão Telhado, que hé de grande remda porque pasa por ele muyta pimemta e madeyra e outras mercadaryas que vão pera Cochym e de Cochym pera a serra e pera outros luguares muytos; neste Jumquão tem parte muytos rios.' The word *jumquão* means 'customs house', cf. Sassetti 145: 'al luogo di questi rii per la terra stanno regni, che impediscono il passaggio, e lo fanno fastidiosissimo co' i loro diritti, che domandano giunconi, i quali sono stati dati da' Signori delle terre ai soldati particolari, perch' e' vivano di quello.'

47 Ibid. 47: 'Destas casas del rey vay hum rio que vay ter a terra del rey de Tequa Amquete; nesta terra há muyta pimemta e pela terra demtro dez leguoas há hum luguar que se chama Quanhara Pee e se faz cada mes hũa feyra homde se guasta muyta pimenta que se leva em boys pela terra demtro. Desta feyra a Cochym averá vymtee duas ou vymte e tres leguoas; per este rio não há madeyra nenhũa.'

48 Ibid. 45–46: 'Pela bamda de leste desta terra de Parau vay outro rio que tambem torna pera o norte e vay ter a hum luguar de crystãos que se chama Putamguale, e este rio vay seys ou sete legoas pela terra demtro, e daquy vem a Cochym muyta pimenta, e tambem há madeyra d'amgelym; este luguares são del Rey de Vyamper.'

area spanning from Chettuva to Kayamkulam. It also helps to explain why in the first century CE the export of Malabar pepper was split between two major emporia: Muziris, at the delta of the Periyar,[49] and Becare-Nelkynda, located on a river that flowed less than 500 *stadioi* south of Muziris,[50] pointing to a place in the southern part of Vembanad Lake. Behind the dualism of the ancient emporia Muziris and Nelkynda lies the corresponding dualism of the pepper waterways that also structured the sixteenth century pepper trade: on one side, the Chalakudy/Periyar waterways and, on the other side, all the rivers flowing into the southern part of the Vembanad Lake: Meenachil, Manimala, Pampa, and Achankovil.

Ancient literary evidence suggests that Roman trade in the first century CE had an evolution similar to that of the Portuguese in the first decades of the sixteenth century. Pliny labels Muziris as 'the first trade centre of India', but he then adds that it was not plentiful in supplies and that another port was 'more useful'.[51] This contradiction can be understood by assuming that, just like the Portuguese in the sixteenth century, Roman traders must have first become familiar with the resources of the Chalakudy/Periyar valley, then eventually realized that the real 'pepper kingdom' was farther south. Both the author of the *Periplus Maris Erythraei* and Pliny make special mention of *Kuṭṭanādu*—Κοτταναρική/*Cottonara regio*, the lowlands close to the southern part of Vembanad Lake—the former as the land where pepper grows abundantly and the latter as the region from where pepper is conveyed.[52] Neither

49 Very likely, it included the area of the Pattanam archaeological site, whose excavations have revealed Roman pottery and artifacts: Shajan, Tomber, Selvakumar, and Cherian 2004. Nearby, at Valluvally, a considerable mid 2nd century CE hoard of Roman gold coins has been found: Sathyamurthy 1992.

50 *Peripl. M. Rubr.* 54: 'ἡ δὲ Νέλκυνδα σταδίους μὲν ἀπὸ Μουζίρεως ἀπέχει σχεδὸν πεντακοσίους, ὁμοίως διά τε ποταμοῦ καὶ διὰ θαλάσσης.' Less important was Tyndis (= Tamil Toṇḍi = Ponnāni?), located some 500 *stadioi* north of Muziris, and Naoura (= tamil Naṟavu), presumably further north. The estimated distances of Nelkynda and Tyndis from Muziris suggest that the pepper emporia of the mid 1st century CE extended in latitude just a little less than the region delimited by Tomé Pires—from Chettuva to Kayamkulam—for his estimate of the Malabar pepper production. The distances indicated by the *Periplus* recommend not locating Nelkynda near Varkala; Banaji's arguments to the contrary in this volume are dubious.

51 Plin., *HN* 6.104: 'inde vento hippalo navigant diebus XL ad primum emporium Indiae Muzirim [. . .] alius utilior portus gentis Neacyndon, qui vocatur Becare.'

52 *Peripl. M. Rubr.* 56: 'φέρεται δὲ πέπερι μονογενῶς ἐν ἑνὶ τόπῳ τούτων τῶν ἐμπορίων γεννώμενον πολὺ, τῇ λεγομένῃ Κοτταναρικῇ'; Plin., *HN* 6.105: 'regio autem, ex qua piper monoxylis lintribus Becaren convehunt, vocatur Cottonara.'

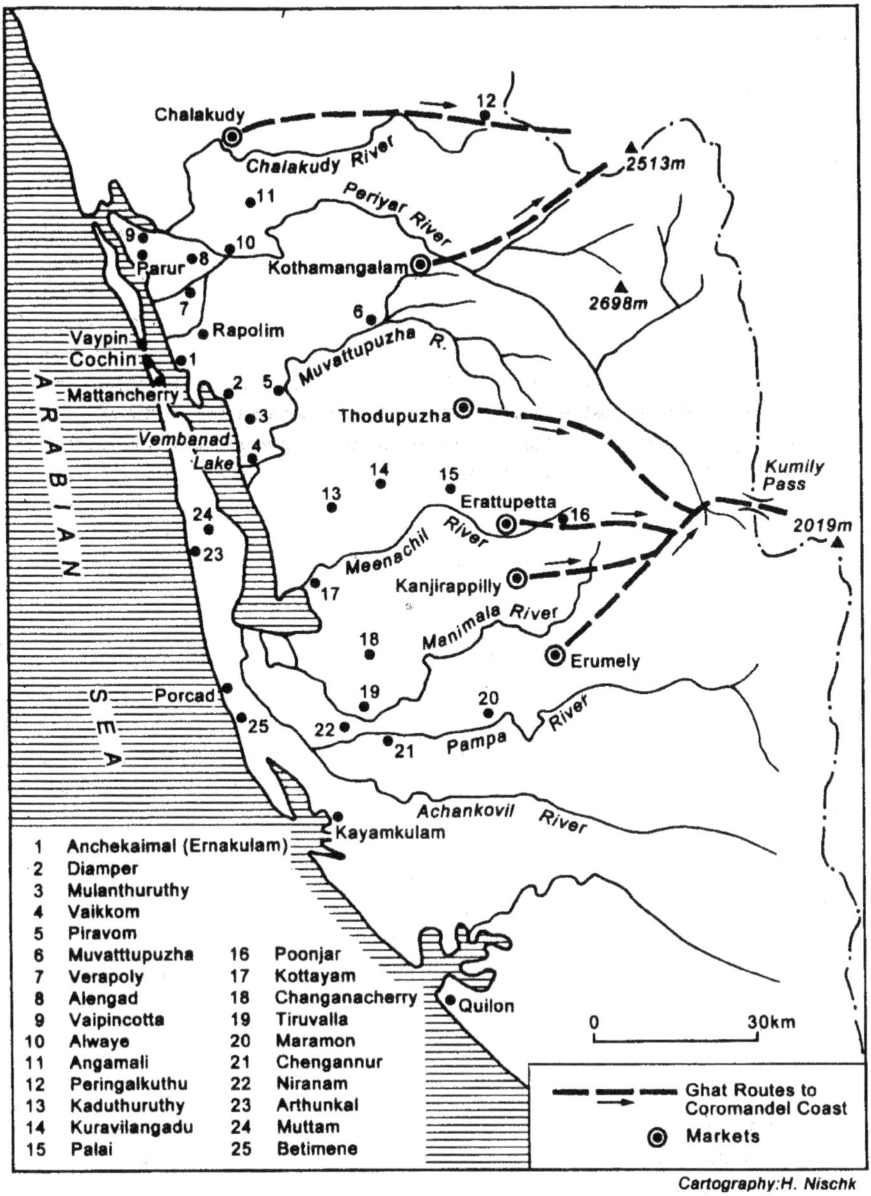

MAP 8.1 *Cochin region in the 16th century (from Malekandathil 2001).*

of them shows any awareness that the enormous amounts of pepper came mostly, if not entirely, from the highlands. Nycolao Gomçallvez knew better: pepper was collected and traded farther upstream, in the foothill regions, at Putamgale (Peringalkuthu), Belur (?), and Quanhara Pee (Kanjirappally)—all several dozen miles away from the coastal area.

Pepper, Forests, and the 'Tribe of Monkeys'

How was pepper produced in the highlands? What was the impact of production on that ecosystem? These problems have been investigated based on two very different initial assumptions and leading to two very different solutions. Jan Kieniewicz assumed that 'up to the end of the eighteenth century, pepper was exclusively grown in gardens', and 'predominantly grown by each household for its own consumption'. He posited, however, that 'at the same time' pepper 'could always be sold', since its seeds would have been 'treated as currency' and used to 'purchase foodstuffs'. This mode of production would have required the 'felling of tropical forests' in the mountain regions and the 'planting of gardens on terraces' provided with 'fine soil and sufficient irrigation'.[53]

A different perspective has been proposed by Kathleen D. Morrison, who frames the pepper production in an ecological and anthropological context characterized by the tropical forests of the Western Ghats and the communities of hunters and gatherers who lived there. Moreover, she sees its trade as the major propellant for the upland-lowland exchange, the intensity of which would have been sensitive to the stimulus provided by the external demand for pepper. [54]

Unless Nuno de Castro was grossly mistaken in estimating 25,000 or even 29,000 *bahar* as the total production of Malabar and only 2,000 to 2,500 *bahar* as its domestic consumption,[55] pepper was hardly grown chiefly for local household consumption in the sixteenth century. The size, cargo, and number of ships sailing to the Limyrike imply a comparable imbalance in the mid first century CE. How could that overproduction denote garden cultivation with felling of tropical forests, terraces, and irrigation?

If we leave aside the accounts of early European travellers about pepper cultivation in the coastal plain,[56] where production was never commercially

53 Kieniewicz 1986, 1–2.

54 Morrison 2002.

55 CA VII 175, cit. *supra* n. 5.

56 Near and even in the cities of Kollam and Calicut: Marco Polo, *Mil.* 176; *Div.* 180; Marignolli 496; Varthema 115; 125.

significant and had different modalities from the foothills, the evidence is scant. In his chapter on Cochin, fifteenth-century Chinese voyager Ma Huan mentions what is translated as (pepper) 'gardens', and people who cultivate them for a living; in the section on Calicut, he says that in the 'mountainous countryside' pepper is 'extensively cultivated'.[57] Portuguese sources of the sixteenth century evoke *lavradores* ('farmers') as suppliers of the pepper merchants.[58] All this information, however, is of little help in clarifying what exactly those 'gardens' were, how they were cultivated, and by whom.

Kieniewicz was inspired by the farmers of the southern division of British Malabar described by Buchanan, with their very small pepper gardens around their houses and their pre-harvest sales to itinerant traders from the nearby Calicut.[59] However, in the regions that supported, via Muziris and Cochin, Roman and Portuguese demand, pepper must have been cultivated quite differently.

The testimony of Johann Philipp Wesdin, also known as fra Paolino da San Bartolomeo, carries the authority of thirteen years (1776–1789) spent in Malabar, as well as his mastery of Malayalam and Sanskrit, and his travels to the interior. In his 1796 *Viaggio alle Indie Orientali*, he hints that pepper vines were planted at the bottom of trees, which means that they were cultivated. But he labels as *boschi* (woods)—the English edition has 'large forests'—the vast spaces occupied by the pepper-producing areas in places like *Aragoshe* (Arakuzha), *Porròta* (Piravom), *Palàya* (Pala), *Vaypur* (Vaipur), *Collam* (Kollam), *Muhatuge* (?), *Ràamapurata* (Ramapura), and all along the foothills of the Western Ghats.[60]

---

57 Ma Huan 135; 143; cf. also 118, regarding Pasai (Sumatra). I wish to thank Dr. Donatella Guida, who pointed out to me that in all three passages (Ma Huan, *Yingya shenglan jiaozhu*, 29, 41, 47) basically the same terms (*zhi yuan* or *zhi yuanpu*) occur and that they mean 'to establish, prepare, arrange gardens'. The last passage (related to Calicut) specifies that pepper is 'widely' or 'in large quantity' cultivated (*duo zhong*).

58 CA III 394; Barbosa 148. *Lavradores* of pepper appear also in DUP I 70.

59 Buchanan II 455: 'All the gardens are small, and all the cultivators have other property. In June, July, or August, the traders go round to the cultivators, and advance them money, on condition, that in January or February the cultivators shall deliver their pepper at a given place'; 463: 'I here [sc. Tirurangadi] examined the cultivators concerning the manner of raising the pepper vine. They say, that it does not thrive where planted close together; and therefore every man, in the garden near his house, has five or six trees only, which are intended as supports for this valuable plant.'

60 Fra Paolino 116: 'Il pepe nero piccolo è una elera che si pianta appiè de grand'alberi. Vi sono boschi intieri di pepe in *Aragoshe*, a *Porròta*, a *Palàya*, a *Vaypur*, a *Collam*, e da per tutto appiè delle montagne *Ghattes*, ove il terreno è grasso, nero, argillaceo, focoso'; 356: 'La pianta del pepe è un ellera, o vime, che si pianta presso gli alberi grandi per farla salire,

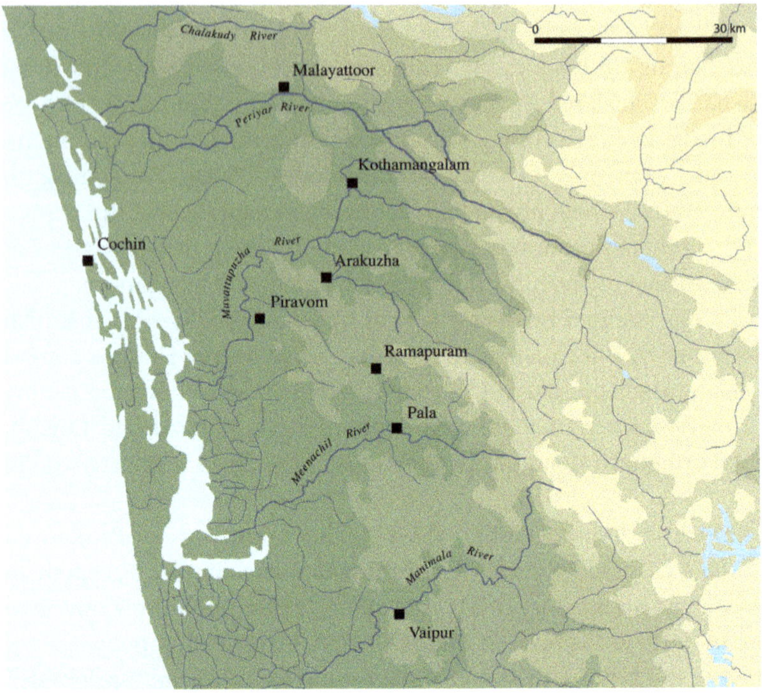

MAP 8.2 *Location of pepper forests and/or Maler encounters per fra Paolino.*

Fra Paolino's description of the pepper woods both vindicates Odorico da Pordenone's statement that pepper grew in a forest that was a good eighteen days' journey wide and identifies the venue of the overproduction of Malabar.[61] Moreover, the words *elera che si pianta* and the density of the pepper plants in the woods (*boschi interi di ellere di pepe*) leave no doubt that fra Paolino was referring to a form of pepper cultivation that did not transform a wooded area into a garden.[62] Where these woods were close to villages, one may wonder if the nearby pepper was grown and collected by villagers. Otherwhise, the

---

come le viti nella Marca. In *Aragoshe, Muhatuge, Ràmapurata, Vaipur*, ed altri luoghi del Malabar si trovano boschi interi di ellere di Pepe'. In the English edition (London 1800) only the first passage is found, p. 163: 'The small black pepper is a kind of ivy, planted for the most part at the bottom of trees, the trunks of which are tall. Large forests of it may be found at *Aragoshe, Poròtta, Valaya, Vaypur*, and every where at the foot of the Gauts, where the soil is black, rich, argillaceous, and hot'.

61 Odorico 439: 'nemus enim in quo nascitur ipsum piper continet in se bene 18 dietas et in ipso nemore sunt due civitates, una nomine Flandrina, altera vero Çinglin.'

62 Cultivation is also implied by Odorico 439: 'In hac contrata autem habetur piper per istum modum: nam primo nascitur in folia de elere, que folia iuxta magnos arbores plantantur sicut hic nostre ponuntur vites.'

pepper was likely exploited by the *Maler* ('people of the hills') described by the same fra Paolino:

> I *Maler*, che abitano le montagne di *Ghattes* sono uomini silvestri, che non comunicano cogli altri Malabari, se non una volta l'anno, quando vengono a comprare le provisioni. Io ne vidi varj a *Maleatur*, a *Codamangalam* e a *Vaypur*. Essi vanno ignudi uomini e donne, ma queste si coprono le parti con un solo foglio di *Banana*, attaccato ad un cordone, che fa il giro delle reni. Si dice, che esse si vergognano più nella loro società di mostrare il seno che questa parte, perchè dicono, che il petto cresce tardi, e che colli altri membri uno nasce dal ventre della sua madre: Quindi girano affatto ignude nei boschi, e il foglio sudetto si attacca quando vengono alli borghi sulle pianure. Gli uomini raccolgono il mele, la cera, il cardamomo, il pepe, varie erbe medicinali, il *Bezoar* dell'Antilope. Essi dormono sopra gli alberi, per non essere assaliti dalle tigri quando girano per le montagne. Le donne partoriscono sole senza assistenza delle Commari. Nei loro tugurj hanno una pietra, che rappresenta l'anima dei loro parenti defunti, hanno un Re o Capitano che chiamano *Malenràgiàva*, cioè, *Re dei Montagnoli*. Essi non hanno nè culto pubblico, nè Sacerdoti.[63]

Fra Paolino's *Maler*—collectors and sellers of honey, wax, cardamom, pepper, medical herbs, *bezoar*—embody the forager-traders of Morrison's model. They live in the forests of the Ghats, sleep in the trees, and come to sell their commodities in villages like Malayattoor, Kothamangalam and Vaipur. These villages were at the foothills of the Western Ghats[64] and close to forests[65] and navigable rivers—the Periyar River, the Muvattupuzha River, and the Manimala River, respectively.

It is remarkable that fra Paolino does not depict them as exclusively or even predominantly pepper sellers. It would seem that the *Maler* were selling pepper in quantities comparable to other forest products, which is odd considering the alleged density of pepper-rich wooded zones all along the foothills of the Western Ghats. It has to be borne in mind, however, that by the time fra Paolino witnessed the *Maler* trading in those villages of central Kerala, their role in the pepper trade must have been undermined by both the expansion of pepper cultivation into new areas and the propagation of the plantation

63 Fra Paolino 182. This passage cannot be found in the German (Berlin 1798), English (London 1800), or French (Paris 1808) edition of fra Paolino's work.

64 Fra Paolino 116.

65 Ibid. 80; 154.

system. Pepper production in the northern part of the country, insignificant in the sixteenth century, had by the late eighteenth century boomed. In the mid eighteenth century some 4,350 tons are recorded as the local annual production[66]—more than the Portuguese ever exported, and more than Marthanda Varma collected from his dominions in 1757. Moreover, in his 1800–01 travel across the British province of Malabar, Francis Buchanan saw plantations—in Telliccherry as well as in Palighat—from which he could report the exact number of pepper vines: 17,529 (7,930 productive) in Tellicherry; 13,316 (4,365 full bearing) in Palighat.[67]

Along the road, Buchanan was able to learn about the trade conducted by the *Malaya-pudy*—literally the 'hill-village-man', who was granted by the rajah of Mysore the privilege of collecting medicinal drugs—with both the *Cadar*, a community in the hills of Ani-malaya (Anaimalai), and neighboring groups from the adjacent Travancore kingdom such as the *Visuar* or *Coravan, Vucamar*, and *Munnan*.[68] The *Cadar* supplied ginger, turmeric, honey, wax, resins, barks, juices, and ivory; the other tribes offered the same items along with cardamom. After describing at length the cardamom swidden cultivation of the Travancore tribes, Buchanan casually adds: 'Wild black-pepper is also found in these hills; but is of a bad quality'.

The triumph of the plantation system recast the relationships between the people of the forests and the agriculturalists of the plains. Tamil poets of the first centuries CE were well aware that the Muziris trade was based on a commercial interaction between the coastal area and the mountain hinterland.[69] The interdependence between the Malabar highlands and the coastal plains is visually represented in the *Tabula Peutingeriana*, where Muziris and a lake (probably, Vembanad Lake) are depicted next to a range of mountains labelled *Mons Lymodus* (most likely, the Western Ghats), where the 'elephants are born'.[70]

---

66 Buchanan II 530: 'Before the invasion of *Hyder*, in the Malabar year 940 (1764/5), the country now called the province of Malabar produced annually about 15,000 *Candies* of 640 lb.'

67 Buchanan II 365; 526.

68 Ibid. II 334–337.

69 Puranāṉūṟu 343, 1–10: 'like Muciṟi (= Gr. Mouziris; Lat. Muziris), of the sea which roars like a drum, which belongs to the *Kuttuvan* with the golden garland, who offers toddy as if it were water to those who come to pour there the goods from the mountains and those from the sea (*malait tāramum kaṭal tāramum*), to those who bring ashore in the lagoon boats the "gifts" of gold brought by the ships, and to those who crowd the port in the turmoil created by the sacks of pepper piled up in the houses, and finally to those who return home having sold the fish and having heaped the paddy on the boat.'

70 On Muziris' ivory trade, see De Romanis 2014.

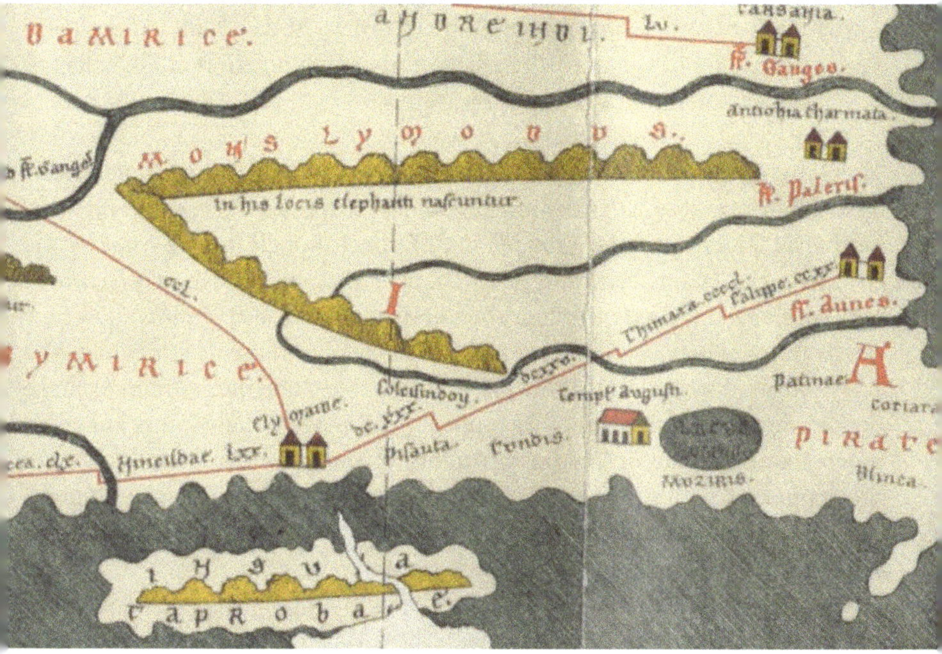

AP 8.3 *Tabula Peutingeriana seg. XI*

The only ancient western text that situates the collection of pepper in a mountain setting is, again, a passage of Philostratus' *Life of Apollonius*. If one reads it while keeping in mind fra Paolino's and Buchanan's descriptions of hill people, it may be taken as a manipulated ethnographic account:

> In the folds of the mountain, however, grow tall frankincense trees and many other kinds too, including pepper-bearing trees that are harvested by monkeys. Since the party did not fail to note what the tree looks like, I shall describe it. The pepper tree looks like the Greek willow in every respect, down to the clusters of fruit, except that it grows on precipices where it is inaccessible to humans. But they say that a tribe of monkeys lives there in the clefts and hollows of the mountain out of reach of men, and the Indians value them so highly that, when the animals are harvesting the peppers, they use dogs and weapons to keep lions away from them. [...] But the method used for the peppers is this. The Indians make their way to the trees lower down, pick the fruit, and after making little clearings around the trees collect the peppers in them, as if they were dumping it as garbage of no use to humans. The monkeys watch from their inaccessible places above, and when night comes they imitate the actions of the Indians by tearing the clusters of fruit from the trees and

> bringing them to be dumped in the clearings. At dawn the Indians carry off the piles of spice that they have gotten with no effort at all, in fact at their ease and during sleep.[71]

There are elements in this passage that may be assumed to be Philostratus' own colourful additions, such as the references to frankincense trees and lions, neither of which can be connected with India—though this may not be the case with the characterization of the pepper collectors as 'monkeys', which may have been inspired by Indian epics and folklore, whose *vānaras* show how the distinction between men and monkeys may blur in the forests. Unlike the story repeated by Isidorus of Seville,[72] Philostratus' tale did not aim to make pepper more valuable—quite the opposite. Moreover, Philostratus knew too much about India for us to presume that he invented from scratch the story of the pepper-collecting monkey.[73] He is more likely to have included in his novel a piece of Indian folklore popularized by Western traders—the same traders who used to sail with the very big ships that he so well describes.

The accounts of Philostratus and of fra Paolino support each other and make clear that the pepper trade that characterized Malabar history from Antiquity up to the early modern age was not only prodigious in quantity, requiring large seagoing vessels, but also relied in no small part on the contributions of the forest dwellers of the Western Ghats.

---

71 Philostr., *VA* 3.4: 'ἐν δὲ τοῖς κρημνοῖς τοῦ ὄρους λίβανοί τε ὑψηλοὶ πεφύκασι καὶ πολλὰ εἴδη ἕτερα καὶ τὰ δένδρα αἱ πεπερίδες, ὧν γεωργοὶ πίθηκοι, καὶ οὐδὲ ᾧ εἴκασται τοῦτο, παρεῖταί σφισιν, ὃν δὲ εἴρηται τρόπον, ἐγὼ δηλώσω· τὸ δένδρον ἡ πεπερὶς εἴκασται μὲν τῷ παρ' Ἕλλησιν ἄγνῳ τά τε ἄλλα καὶ τὸν κόρυμβον τοῦ καρποῦ, φύεται δὲ ἐν τοῖς ἀποτόμοις οὐκ ἐφικτὸς τοῖς ἀνθρώποις, οὗ λέγεται πιθήκων οἰκεῖν δῆμος ἐν μυχοῖς τοῦ ὄρους καὶ ὅ τι αὐτοῦ κοῖλον, οὓς πολλοῦ ἀξίους οἱ Ἰνδοὶ νομίζοντες, ἐπειδὴ τὸ πέπερι ἀποτρυγῶσι, τοὺς λέοντας ἀπ' αὐτῶν ἐρύκουσι κυσί τε καὶ ὅπλοις [...] τὰ γὰρ πραττόμενα περὶ τὰς πεπερίδας ὧδε ἔχει· προσελθόντες οἱ Ἰνδοὶ τοῖς κάτω δένδρεσι τὸν καρπὸν ἀποθερίσαντες ἅλως ποιοῦνται μικρὰς περὶ τὰ δένδρα καὶ τὸ πέπερι περὶ αὐτὰς ξυμφοροῦσιν οἷον ῥιπτοῦντες, ὡς ἄτιμόν τι καὶ μὴ ἐν σπουδῇ τοῖς ἀνθρώποις, οἱ δὲ ἄνωθεν καὶ ἐκ τῶν ἀβάτων ἀφεωρακότες ταῦτα, νυκτὸς γενομένης ὑποκρίνονται τὸ τῶν Ἰνδῶν ἔργον καὶ τοὺς βοστρύχους τῶν δένδρων περισπῶντες ῥιπτοῦσι φέροντες ἐς τὰς ἅλως, οἱ Ἰνδοὶ δὲ ἅμα ἡμέρᾳ σωροὺς ἀναιροῦνται τοῦ ἀρώματος οὐδὲ πονήσαντες οὐδέν, ἀλλὰ ῥᾴθυμοί τε καὶ καθεύδοντες' (trans. C.P. Jones LCL, 2005, with modifications).

72 Isid., *Etym*. 18. 8. 8, on which Freedman 2005.

73 For the *aśvamedha*, cf. Goossens 1930.

CHAPTER 9

Into the East: European Merchants in Asian Markets During the Early Modern Period

Martha Howell

Like the Romans before them, Europeans of the Middle Ages had what seemed an insatiable appetite for the luxuries that came from the markets stretching across the Indian Ocean, from eastern Africa to the South China Sea. Spices—pepper, nutmeg, mace, cinnamon, and cloves—along with textiles, dyes, jewels, gold, glassware, and metal wares from China, Japan, and India had flowed into Europe from at least the time of the Crusades. But, except for a brief period during the height of the Yuan Empire when a few European merchants like Marco Polo had travelled the Silk Road and explored the Indian Ocean's commercial routes, medieval Europeans' commerce in these luxuries was largely confined to the Mediterranean area, and Europeans were dependent on Jewish, Arab, and other Muslim intermediaries to supply them with exotic luxuries.[1]

But the collapse of the Yuan dynasty in the late fourteenth century made the Silk Road a less safe, less continuous, and less busy route to and from the East. Energy thus shifted to alternative water–land routes farther south, mostly to Red Sea routes passing through Cairo. The Egyptian city, soon to be under Ottoman control, had replaced Baghdad as the premier city of the eastern Mediterranean (Baghdad having suffered a dramatic decline thanks to regional climatic disasters and the Mongol invasion of 1258); when the Ottomans took Constantinople in 1453, virtually all the spice trade and much of the remaining luxury trade to Europe started to go through Cairo and from there into Venice, which now had almost exclusive control of Asian trade with Europe. Indeed, Venice lived so completely from the Asian trade through Cairo that it was reportedly said at the time, 'he who is lord of Malacca has his hand on the throat of Venice'.[2]

Venice's ascendency came at the expense of Genoa. After over a century of intermittent conflict, ending with a particularly ruinous series of battles between 1379 and '81, Genoa ceded the Asian luxury trade to its main rival, and

1 For an influential account of Indian Ocean commerce and European trade with Asia during the high and late Middle Ages see Abu-Lughod 1989. Also, Remie Constable 1994.

2 Attributed to Duarte Barbosa, a Portuguese writer and Portuguese India officer.

 | DOI 10.1163/9789004289536_011

instead concentrated its eastern Mediterranean activities on the slave trade out of Black Sea ports.

Although that trade would continue, Genoa's future prosperity lay with the western Mediterranean and the Atlantic. Beginning in the late thirteenth century, Genoese had been financing cargoes shipped through Gibraltar to Bruges and other northern ports, and after the Portuguese sailed around the Cape of Good Hope in 1488—thus providing a direct, if long and dangerous, route to the Indian Ocean—Genoese bankers, merchants, and sailors found countless opportunities for adventure and gain.

But it was the Portuguese who led the way to the Indian Ocean markets. For about a half-century, merchants, sailors, and investors supported by—or in direct service to—the Portuguese crown had been perfecting their navigation skills, building ever more seaworthy ships, and arming them to the teeth; now they were in a position to circumvent Cairo and the Venetians. Other Europeans would soon follow, and during the next two centuries Europeans would infiltrate Indian Ocean trade routes, taking over some of them and forever changing the history of the region. During the same centuries, Europeans went west, into the new world, so that by the end of the sixteenth century its merchants and adventurers in the subcontinent were dominating the globe.

This is well-known history, but the story of the entry of Europeans into Indian Ocean markets bears repeating in a volume focused on earlier centuries when the Romans ventured there, because, in apparent contrast to their Roman predecessors, Europeans of the early modern centuries entered the Indian Ocean not simply as participants but as predators. And it is eminently worth considering how they succeeded. After all, until this period Europeans were distinctly minor players in global commerce. Although eager consumers of Asian luxuries, they had had—and still had—little to offer in exchange except for silver, slaves, and raw materials, and until the late Middle Ages they remained imitators or adapters of commercial techniques used in the trade, not originators. Yet, soon after their arrival in the Indian Ocean, Europeans succeeded in monopolizing the Asia–Europe trade in certain commodities; not long afterwards they seized control of production and supply routes in key areas; and in the end they would emerge as colonial powers in the region. Undoubtedly, they owed their success in part to luck, but credit also has to be given to their experience in seafaring trades, their organization, their business models—and their military might. The Dutch story is the most spectacular, and in the pages to follow I will concentrate on their strategies. But the European story begins with the Portuguese.

•••

When Vasco da Gama's man stepped onto the shores of western India in 1498, he is reported to have eagerly announced that his ships were in search of 'Christians and spices'. The Portuguese found both, but not quite in the way they expected. Christians were already there, but they were men from Syria who had arrived long before, and they were not subjects of the mythical Prester John about whom medieval Europeans had fantasized for centuries—the emperor, it was said, of a fabulously rich Christian empire somewhere in India or thereabouts.[3] Although by the turn of the sixteenth century Europeans were becoming sceptical about this story, Vasco da Gama nevertheless carried a letter of introduction from the Pope to Prester John—just in case. As well as Syrian Christians, the Portuguese found pepper—the best in the world—although the vines on which it grew were not protected by poisonous snakes, as Europeans had imagined.[4]

The markets into which the Portuguese surged had long prospered.[5] The trade networks extended from east Africa to India to the islands of the Indonesian archipelago, to the straits of Malacca and the South China Sea, and on to Japan; through these networks flowed silks, dyes, jewels, gold, spices, and the other luxuries the Europeans craved, but also rice, grain, horses, armour, and timber destined for markets throughout the region.

The Portuguese managed in just a few decades to take effective control of much of the trade for European markets and, in fact, to extract profit from regional trade routes as well. Although they were dealing with sophisticated merchant communities and in some cases with warrior kingdoms, their ships and the guns they mounted were powerful enough to win them secure markets in the region and, in effect, a significant degree of control over the waterways. The crucial factor in their success, however, was that the Indian Ocean was open as it had not been for centuries, because the Chinese, who controlled a vastly more powerful state, had abruptly abandoned Indian Ocean trade over a half-century before, leaving it available to others who sought hegemony.[6]

The Portuguese thus had an easier time of it than they might have, but their ships did not go unchallenged. In fact, they fought long and hard battles with the formidable forces of the Ottomans, who were steadily expanding into the Indian Ocean from their land-based empire around the eastern Mediterranean.

---

3 For one medieval version of the story of Prester John, see *The Travels of Sir John Mandeville*.

4 For a recent analysis of these stories and the role they played in stimulating demand in Europe, see Freedman 2005.

5 For a useful collection of recent scholarship on the economy of the Indian Ocean in this period see Chaudhury and Morineau 1999.

6 For an account of this history, in brief, and references to the literature, see Prakash 1999.

Recently in possession of Egypt and Syria, the Ottomans were simultaneously seeking to position themselves at the head of a loose 'Muslim alliance' made up of the culturally distinct trading communities scattered throughout the ocean, many of them Muslim. After some costly setbacks in warfare with the Portuguese, however, the Ottomans abandoned that goal and focused on control of their land empire, although they remained a powerful presence in the Red Sea and Persian Gulf.[7]

Other Europeans would cause the Portuguese even more problems. In the early days of their forays into the Indian Ocean, the chief European rival of the Portuguese was the Spanish crown. The Treaty of Tordesillas of 1494, negotiated by the Pope, had divided the globe between the Portuguese and the Spanish, giving the former the eastern half and the latter the western. Spain was thus, in theory, denied access to most Indian Ocean markets, but the Spanish Crown had a claim in the eastern realm of that vast region via its Pacific routes. The two nations, or the merchants and seamen in their employ, thus fought over precious markets and supply routes stretching from the straits of Malacca into the spice islands of the Indonesian archipelago. Further west, however, the Portuguese initially met no serious challenges from other Europeans, and even as the English, then the Dutch, entered these waters, they were able to establish and long maintain a series of enclaves connected by maritime links to each other and to Goa, its administrative and religious centre and largest city. At its height, the Portuguese trade network stretched from Mozambique Island, north along the African coast to Mombasa, farther north to Hormuz and Muscat (which controlled access to the Persian Gulf and Basra), east to Diu and Daman in modern Gujarat, south to Bombay Island, Goa, Cochin, most of coastal Sri Lanka, across the Indian Ocean to Malacca, and beyond to Timor and Macau, the second city after Goa in the Portuguese mercantile empire.[8]

These critical outposts allowed the Portuguese to tax the existing trade in goods such as rice, cotton textiles, horses, silks, and spices via a system of passes that ships travelling through these entrepôts were compelled to purchase. At the expense of Spain, they also won control of much of the spice trade to Europe. By 1512 they had captured the tiny Banda Islands, then the world's only source of nutmeg and mace (the lacy seed coat covering the nutmeg). In the sixteenth century nutmeg was the most expensive spice, worth multiples of pepper and more than clove, cinnamon, or any of the other trea-

7 For this account, see Casale 2010.

8 The history of Europe's merchant empires during this period is examined in Tracy 1990. For the Portuguese history in the region in particular see Subrahmanyam 1996 and 1990.

sures from these islands. On the return trip from the Banda Islands, one of the Portuguese ships ran aground on the island of Ternate, which turned out to be the most important of the clove islands—and thus Europeans found the last secret source of spice.

Although during much of the sixteenth century the Portuguese controlled the supply of these spices to Europe, they did not distribute their precious cargo throughout Europe. Rather, they stopped at Lisbon, and because the local market was far too small to absorb the wealth of goods coming in from the east, they needed a European-wide distribution system. Antwerp's merchants provided it.[9]

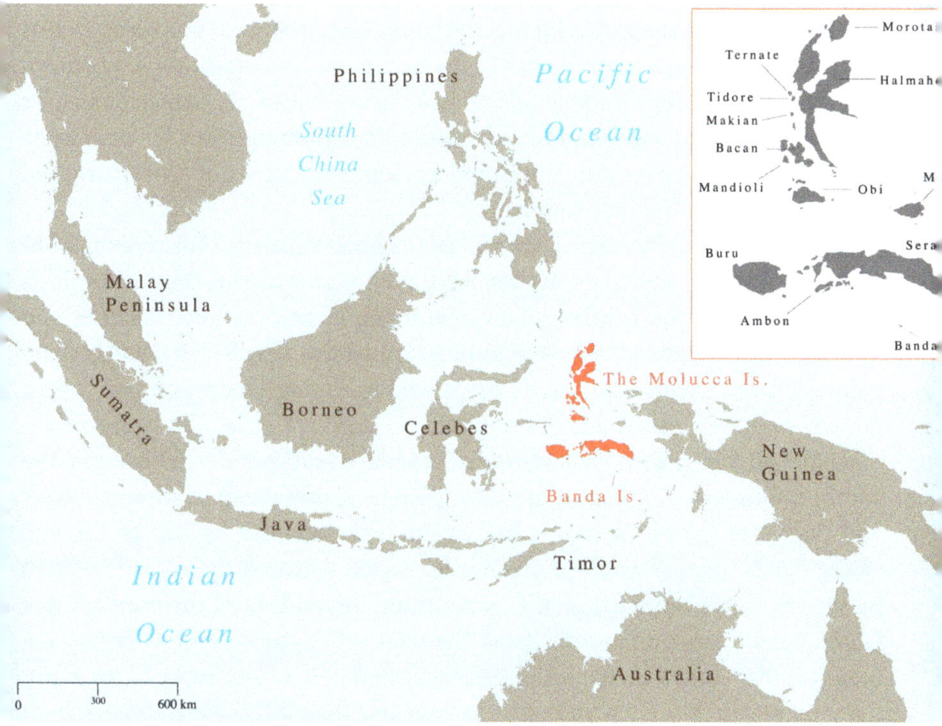

AP 9.1 *The Spice Islands*

9 For recent scholarship on these developments, see Stabel, Blondé, and Greve 2000. For the shift in European trade in particular, see Van der Wee 1999; and De Vries and Van Der Woude 1997.

Sixteenth-Century Europe

In the first half of the sixteenth century Antwerp became the richest port and mercantile centre in northern Europe—indeed, a kind of world city whose financiers and traders managed the flow of luxury goods into northern Europe and helped to finance the distribution of the region's own trade goods throughout the subcontinent and beyond; it was thus a key source of income not only for the Portuguese, but also for the Spanish. Antwerpers were famous as financiers and merchants, however, not as shipbuilders or shippers. Their neighbours to the north, in Holland and Zeeland, took that role; builders of cargo ships ideally suited for the Baltic, North Sea, and North Atlantic coastal trade, they were also the shippers of wood, naval stores, and grain from Baltic markets, much of it destined for Iberian markets. Amsterdam took the lead in this trade, building the basis for its rise in the next century. In addition to northern markets and northern trade goods, the Portuguese needed northern men, for their own small country could not supply sufficient manpower for their massive fleets; they thus recruited both officers and men from any likely corner of Europe, including the Low Countries.[10]

But in the late sixteenth century, the Lisbon–Antwerp–Amsterdam links would be broken, and the catalyst for the change was the Dutch Revolt. It began in 1568 in the southern Low Countries, in what is now Belgium and Luxembourg, as resistance by the nobles against the Spanish Hapsburgs, who controlled the entire Low Countries as well as Iberia. The aristocratic revolt quickly escalated into a battle for republican traditions led by nobles and urban magistrates, mixed with Protestant movements of various kinds.[11] Because the southern provinces, although the most populous, urbanized, commercialized, and richest of the entire realm, had fallen to the Spanish legions by the end of the 1580s, the war would thereafter be waged between the seven northern provinces, thus eventually giving us the Dutch Republic and the moniker 'the Dutch Revolt'. Holland and Zeeland, the relatively populous mercantile provinces on the North Sea, were the leaders, and that is where most of the fighting took place. When Antwerp was sacked and then fell in 1585, its merchant and artisan elites fled to places like Hamburg, Lübeck, Frankfurt am Main, and Cologne, which were outside the war zone; once the Dutch kept the Spanish at bay, these elites entered Amsterdam and other Dutch cities.

10 For details on this history, see Israel 1990.

11 For a recent study of the early years of the so-called Dutch Revolt, see Arnade 2008.

Meanwhile, in 1580, Spain gobbled up Portugal and quickly closed Lisbon to Dutch traders, leaving them little access to Asian luxuries. The markets for pepper and other spices tightened dramatically and prices soared. Although the Spanish would later be forced to open their markets to the Dutch in order to get Baltic grain and naval supplies, the distribution networks for Asian goods that had once been centred in Antwerp were now scattered. The 'Dutch', that is, the people in the seven northern provinces that were not under Spanish control, would have to find a way back into what they called the 'rich trades'. And by late in the sixteenth century they had accomplished their mission; shortly after, they would outflank both the English and the Portuguese, their European rivals in the Indian Ocean trade. Theirs is a spectacular success story, for the Dutch East Indies Company, or the VOC in its Dutch acronym (*Vereenigde Oost-Indische Compagnie*), established in 1602, was to become the largest and most profitable mega-corporation in the world. Between 1602 and 1796 it sent almost a million Europeans to work in the Asia trade on 4,785 ships, and netted for their efforts more than 2.5 million tons of Asian trade goods. By contrast, the rest of Europe combined sent only 882,412 people from 1500 to 1795 (a century longer); the fleet of the British East India Company, the VOC's nearest competitor, was a distant second with 2,690 ships and a mere one-fifth the tonnage of goods carried by the VOC. The VOC established a capital in the port city of Batavia, now Jakarta, and over the next two centuries the Company acquired additional ports as trading bases, safeguarded their interests by taking over surrounding territory, and for almost 200 years paid on average an 18 per cent annual dividend, although in early years none of this was paid in cash.[12]

An extraordinary story in its own right, it appears even more extraordinary when we consider that when the story began in 1602, the Dutch Republic was not a state. It was a collection of seven small provinces, only two of them of any real mercantile importance, and they were then—and would be for about another fifty years—at war with, and sometimes under siege by, the Spanish Habsburgs, the greatest European power of the day. Historians have offered several explanations for their success despite these circumstances, four of them central: (1) their own—and that of their southern neighbours'—mercantile history (2) the state–business partnership that we know as the Dutch East Indies company (the VOC); (3) their brutality; and (4) the novel business model they developed for the Indian Ocean trade.

12 For an exhaustive study of the VOC, see Gaastra 2003.

Mercantile Histories

The Dutch had long been merchants, shipbuilders, and seamen; in the sixteenth and seventeenth centuries they dominated Baltic trade, which included shipping grain and naval stores to European markets in the Mediterranean, and transporting sugar, salt, and various bulk goods north. The grain trade was key, for it was a necessary commodity in the rapidly expanding markets in western and southern Europe, especially in the sixteenth-century Low Countries themselves, where cities were again growing, where much land was devoted to market farming, dairying, and pasturage rather than large-scale grain production, and where land was relatively scarce. Grain and other Baltic products such as tar, hemp, flax, and wood were destined not only for the Low Countries, but also for England, Spain, and Portugal via Amsterdam, the port that had succeeded in surpassing Lübeck and other Hanseatic towns as the primary trans-shipment point for Baltic goods. No wonder that the Dutch referred to the Baltic trade as their 'mother trade', relegating the 'rich trades' of luxury goods to second place in their hierarchy of economic importance. The Dutch were also masters of the herring trade and were already encroaching upon early English efforts to get into the Muscovy trade, a source of gold, silks, and other luxuries from central and eastern Asia. Indeed by 1600 the Dutch had replaced the English in that rich market, were finishing English cloth for markets in Europe, and had seen the revival of textile production in some of their own cities. In short, at that time they had easier access to the luxury goods available in southern markets than did the English.[13]

Some scholars have explained the Dutch success in the Indian Ocean trade as a 'natural' outcome of this mercantile history, and certainly Dutch expertise in the carrying trades in the north and on the north–south European route served them well. But travel to the Indian Ocean required different kinds of ships. The famous flyships or *fluyts* that had given the Dutch supremacy in European trade because of their speed and low cost were not themselves big enough for those long, rough voyages, and they were not heavily armed enough to fight their way into those markets. In order to compete, the Dutch had to refit and redesign the *fluyt*.

---

13 For a summary of this history and an argument that it was a key factor in the success of the VOC, see Israel 1990.

Business Organization

The Dutch also had to organize themselves for ventures into more distant markets, beginning with the south Atlantic and African coast, where they had little experience. Merchants from Antwerp, who had relocated to Zeeland following the revolt, helped provide that entry. They were instrumental in setting up the so-called Guinea trade with West Africa, and initiated Dutch involvement in the Western Hemisphere, which in the end produced the Dutch West Indies Company (the *Geoctroyeerde Westindische Compagnie* or GWIC; commonly known as the GWC or in the English acronym the WIC). It established outposts throughout the Caribbean and in parts of Latin America, briefly including the Portuguese colony of Brazil, which the Dutch held from 1630 to 1654.

Merchants from southern cities in the Low Countries, such as Antwerp, were also instrumental in establishing the Indian Ocean trade. But breaking into the lucrative Asian markets was not just a simple matter of undercutting Portuguese shippers, because the Portuguese closely guarded the route around Africa. In fact, the Dutch did not have enough information about shipping lanes to attempt the voyage until 1596, when a Dutchman from Haarlem, Jan Huyghen van Linschoten, who had served on Portuguese voyages, published his travelogue of the Indies. Prospects for the Dutch were further enhanced by a rise in the price of pepper following the depredations of the English privateers who were systematically harassing ships from Portugal (now part of Spain). One by one, harbour towns in what is now The Netherlands, essentially in Zeeland and Holland, began to organize so-called 'voor-compagnies' to finance expeditions to trade in the East Indies, not only bypassing Portugal, but also competing with it and any other state that got in the way. Each separate company financed a fleet of heavily armed ships to sail together for the East Indies.

These independent voyage fleets, set up for only a single round-trip, were liquidated on return; investment was thus a very high-risk venture, in part because of the usual dangers of piracy, disease, and shipwreck. In addition, the interplay of the inelastic demand and relatively elastic supply of spices meant enormous risk for financiers. Further, this system put Dutch merchants at each other's throats, making everyone a competitor. In an attempt to eliminate such mutually destructive competition from markets, the English had in 1600 formed a cartel that was given a monopoly on supplying markets in Europe: their famous East India Company. The Dutch were to copy that model with their VOC, but in addition they did something the English would not do until 1657: they formed a semi-permanent joint-stock company that funded all voyages and shared the profits over many years. In this way, they spread the risks of a single voyage over many voyages, in effect providing a kind of insurance to investors.[14]

The VOC was thus a novelty in its day. Given a twenty-one-year monopoly over the Asian trade by the nascent Dutch government, and set up as a joint-stock company, it attracted roughly 6.5 million florins in initial capitalization from over 1,800 investors, most of whom were merchants and many of whom were from the south. Management of the company was vested in seventeen directors (the *Heren XVII*) chosen from among the largest shareholders—which meant merchants in Amsterdam and Zeeland. The VOC was thus the first multinational corporation in the world and arguably also the world's first mega-corporation, possessing quasi-governmental powers, including the ability to wage war, imprison and execute convicts, negotiate treaties, coin money, and establish colonies. Other European countries would also form East India companies—everyone from Portugal to Sweden to Austria—but none was ever as successful in the spice trade as the VOC.

By 1670 it was the richest corporation in the world, paying its shareholders an annual dividend of 40 per cent on their investment despite financing 50,000 employees, 30,000 fighting men, and 200 ships, most of them armed. Outside of Europe the VOC became a virtual country unto itself, with the spice trade the centrepiece of its business plan. Until 1619, its headquarters were in Ambon, the centre of the spice production areas, thereafter in Jakarta, which the Dutch would rename Batavia. From there the Dutch conducted an inter-Ocean trade that would produce a huge portion of their profits over the next century and a half.

Commerce as Violence

Although much of the VOC's success can be attributed to their business organization and, as we shall see, to their business model for Indian Ocean trade, there is no doubt that they triumphed because they were willing to fight for control of markets, and fight with so little restraint that they earned a reputation for brutality unusual even for Europeans of this age.[15] The Dutch were

14 For fuller histories of these events, see Gaastra 2003; Boxer 1970; Chaudhuri and Israel 1991.

15 For this argument and additional references, see 'The Economics of Violence' in Pomeranz and Topik 2006.

not the first to equate commerce with violence. Before them, the Spanish and Portuguese had battled in the Spice Islands and the Ottomans had waged furious war with the Portuguese for control of the Red Sea and Straits of Hormuz.

The English were to become the most formidable opponent of the Dutch in the Spice Islands. Indeed, from 1611 to 1617, the two northern European enterprises competed for markets, intermittently battling, and although diplomatic agreements in Europe in 1620 ushered in a period of cooperation, this ended in 1623 with the notorious but disputed incident, the Amboyna massacre, in which ten Englishmen were arrested, tried, and beheaded for conspiracy against the Dutch government. Although the incident caused outrage in Europe and a diplomatic crisis there, the European response did not change the course of events in the Spice Islands: the English withdrew from most of their activities there (except trading in Bantam) and focused on other Asian interests. This infamous incident, and several more to follow, have earned the VOC the reputation as the most brutal of the European interlopers in the Indian Ocean trade—in a period known for its brutality.

Whatever the ambiguity of the story in Ambon, there is little dispute about how the Dutch took exclusive control of Jakarta. This city had long hosted European traders, including the English and the Dutch. By 1619, however, Dutch relations with their hosts had deteriorated; the local prince was allied with the British and together they attacked the Dutch fort. The Dutch won the battle, drove the British out, and took Jakarta as their own. The victory consolidated Dutch power in the region, and they renamed the city 'Batavia'.

The VOC went on to try to monopolize the nutmeg, mace, and clove trades by driving out competitors and preventing the cultivation of the crops on any islands but those where they originated, and which the Dutch controlled or sought to control. Sometimes they bought these rights, but if they couldn't do that they stopped at little. Thus, in what probably stands as the most horrendous example of Dutch methods, Batavia's Governor-General, Jan Pieterszoon Coen, convinced the recalcitrant Bandanese of his firm's God-given right to monopolize the nutmeg trade by ordering the slaughter of every male over the age of fifteen whom he could capture. The population of the isles is estimated to have been about 15,000 before the VOC arrived; fifteen years later it was said to be 600. Once in control there and elsewhere in the Spice Islands, the Dutch sought to assure that these islands remained the sole source of nutmeg, mace, and cloves. Indeed, by 1681, the VOC had destroyed three-quarters of all nutmeg trees in unwanted areas and reorganized farms into plantations. It imposed the death penalty on anyone caught growing, stealing, or possessing nutmeg or clove plants without authorization.

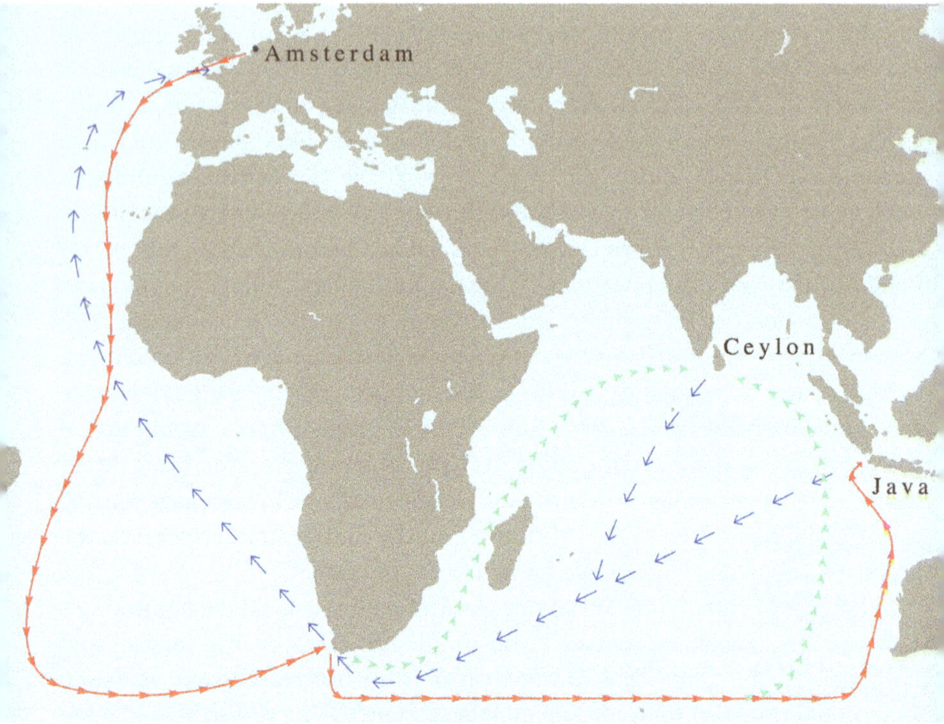

P 9.2 *The trade routes of the VOC in the Indian Ocean.*

Business Model

Coen, deservedly condemned as the author of the massacre in Banten, was, however, a master business strategist, and the business model he devised for Indian Ocean trade counts as the fourth, and in some historians' accounts, the chief reason for the success of the VOC.[16] A major problem in the European trade with Asia at the time was that the Europeans could offer few goods that Asian consumers wanted, except silver and gold. European traders therefore had to pay for spices with precious metals, and these were in short supply in northern Europe, since Spain (now joined with Portugal) controlled the American silver and gold mines; the Dutch and the English had to rely on trade surpluses or piracy to get any share of the loot, and although they succeeded in moving much Spanish silver to their treasuries, they were unwilling—and

16 Om Prakash has most influentially made this case. See, in addition to his other publications, Prakash 1994 and Prakash 1998.

unable—to sustain the Asia trade with silver and gold alone. Coen provided the solution: an intra-Asiatic trade system, whose profits could be used to finance the spice trade with Europe.

The VOC traded throughout Asia, taking advantage of price differentials among the various markets—for example, trading for silver where silver was undervalued and taking it to places where it was more highly valued. A case in point: until 1688, when Japan banned the export of silver, it was the source of a plentiful and relatively inexpensive supply of this precious metal, along with gold. In return, the Dutch supplied the Japanese with Chinese silk, textiles from Europe, spices from the Dutch-controlled East Indies, hides from Thailand and Taiwan, and ivory from Africa and South-East Asia. Silk, cotton, porcelain, and textiles obtained from India and China were also traded within Asia for spices or brought back to Europe; spices themselves also went to Asian markets as well as to Europe. In many historians' accounts, this arbitrage trade, managed out of Batavia—now not just a port and a fort but also a bustling administrative city—was the 'secret' of Dutch success. Although the Portuguese also participated in intra-Ocean trade, they did not operate on this scale or with such success in these waters, whether in voyages financed by the Crown itself or in those managed by private traders authorized by the Crown. Instead, the Portuguese concentrated on taxing the trade with their system of passes, and on preserving the European spice trade for themselves. The Dutch were even more aggressive about trying to monopolize the spice trade to Europe, especially for nutmeg, mace, and cloves, but they fashioned a different, and more successful, role for themselves as Indian Ocean traders.

In the long run this system obviated the need for exports of precious metals from Europe, and the VOC was wildly profitable during the seventeenth century even though in the first few decades they did not pay cash dividends, but reinvested most profits in building the inter-Ocean trade. In the course of the century, however, their position weakened as the English and French began to institute mercantilist strategies (for instance, the Navigation Acts in England). In addition, despite the VOC's extreme precautions, the French got hold of clove seedlings and transplanted the crop to the Seychelles, Réunion, and especially Zanzibar, which later became the world's largest producer of cloves. By the end of the eighteenth century these rivals had broken the Dutch monopoly for good.

By that time the VOC was already a mockery of its original if ghastly self. As early as the end of the seventeenth century, its volume of trade was declining annually. In addition, the firm's overhead was huge—its tens of thousands of employees, garrisons, and war-ships cost a fortune to maintain. Further, decades of easy rents had created a corrupt and inefficient beast. By 1735, the spice trade brought in less income than the textile trade, a clear sign that the VOC had lost control of that once lucrative market. In 1799, what was arguably the most vicious corporation of them all met its final end—the VOC went bankrupt.

The demise of the VOC marked more, however, than the end of what had become a corrupt institution with a bad reputation. It also marked the end of an era in the spice trade, indeed in world trade more generally. Trade routes that spanned oceans were becoming commonplace and, as such, competitive. The Dutch had done their best to buck the trend, even destroying their stocks so that supplies were kept scarce and prices high. Indeed, according to one observer, the streets of Amsterdam were 'flooded with nutmeg butter' as the VOC ruthlessly destroyed supplies. But it was in vain. Spices were no longer hard to come by, and their exotic qualities no longer so appreciated. Monopolies, as one scholar has put it, had given way to markets.

Afterword

Elio Lo Cascio

The exceptional Muziris papyrus is the indisputable cornerstone of this book, not only because it is cited, commented upon, or mentioned in most chapters, but also because it provides us with a seemingly reliable assessment of the qualitative and, more importantly, quantitative dimension of the maritime trade that tied the Roman Empire to the Indian subcontinent. The merchandise loaded aboard the *Hermapollon* that is listed in the papyrus suggests which items were traded and which kinds of goods were imported from India in a well-defined time period that corresponds with the peak of this transnational trade, after a century and a half of quantitative growth.

What emerges in many essays of the book—starting from the introduction briefly outlining the modern debate on the relevance of the India trade for the Roman economy (from Huet to Cantillon, to Montesquieu and Gibbon, to the debate of present times)—is indeed the diachronic dimension of the topic. Despite its explicit comparativist approach, or perhaps because of it, this volume does not aim to single out the 'structural' elements of this trade, nor does it insist, as a consequence, on its environmental or geographic preconditions. Rather, it seeks to appreciate those historical elements that signal an evolution—albeit an evolution that is anything but linear, since the first efflorescence of this trade is situated in the two and a half centuries that followed the Augustan revolution, which gave rise to a series of favourable circumstances: the annexation of Egypt; the (re)discovery of the pattern of the monsoons; the spread of shipbuilding techniques and skills from the Mediterranean to the Red Sea; and the creation or, rather, multiplication of roads linking the Nile Valley to the Red Sea. Such an intensity in mercantile relations with the East would emerge once again only with the premodern commercial expansion of European nations, starting with the Portuguese maritime enterprises. In their introduction De Romanis and Maiuro emphasize how the prevailing historiographic approach, which minimizes the quantitative dimensions of Roman trade with India, reflects a view of history that is linear and progressive and, as a consequence, denies any possibility of comparative analysis between the Roman economy and that of early modern European states.

Documents such as the Muziris papyrus seem to demonstrate, on the contrary, that the alleged gap between the Roman economy and those of the most developed premodern European states—at least, as far as the financial

 | DOI 10.1163/9789004289536_012

relevance of overseas imports is concerned—is not as unbridgeable as usually thought. This is the underlying argument of De Romanis' chapter comparing the expanding Portuguese interests in the commerce of pepper in the sixteenth century with the same commerce in Roman times. The danger of a circular argument is of course always present. In a complex argument De Romanis quantifies the freight cargo of the *Hermapollon* based on a specific reading of a number in the papyrus: the price of pepper per mina is taken to be 6 drachmas instead of 24, as argued by other scholars. The next step in his reasoning, however—the quantification of the demand for pepper acquired by trade with the Muziris region, and thus the overall number of cargoes and their loading capacities (also on the basis of a passage of Strabo that cannot be easily rejected)—is in fact based on the assumption that the quantity of pepper exported to Europe during the sixteenth century must be comparable to the quantities traded during the Roman Empire in the second century.

The relevance of Indo-Mediterranean trade within the more general framework of the Roman economy and its performance, measured through necessarily rough estimates of the State's budget and GDP, is highlighted most explicitly in Wilson's chapter about the role of the State in trade. One of the building blocks of his analysis, once again based on the evidence from the Muziris papyrus, is the enormous financial gain for imperial coffers as a result of the customs duties imposed on Indian merchandise. According to Wilson it is precisely the impact of these trade revenues that sparked the interest of the Roman State in Indian commerce and its commercial routes—an interest expressed by the provision of infrastructures to improve transport conditions and by rulings to facilitate and protect that commerce. The infrastructures are, first and foremost, the roads that tie the Nile Valley to the Red Sea, known both archaeologically and through references in the literary (Strabo, Pliny, the *Itineraria*, etc.), papyrological, and epigraphic sources. The two roads from Coptos, to Berenice and to Myos Hormos, are particularly noteworthy because of the associated facilities of wells and cisterns (the *hydreumata*).

One chapter in the history of the imperial policy benefitting the India trade is the (re)opening of the canal between Clysma and the Red Sea in Trajanic times. Two opposing arguments are laid out in the volume regarding the practical use of this canal: while Wilson sees the references to the canal in the literary *testimonia* as trustworthy with regard to its use, albeit limited to specific periods of the year and dependent on the flooding of the Nile, Aubert instead casts a good deal of doubt on the *testimonia*. Aubert's main and most substantive argument relies on a principle of economy: had the canal been used regularly, there would have been no need to build and maintain the roads from Coptos to the Red Sea harbours. It is true that these roads were used for other reasons as well, but it seems beyond doubt that their upkeep was meant primarily to support commercial activities along the Red Sea. Indeed, the (re)discovery of the monsoon winds had already contributed to the exponential growth in the number of ships sailing to the East by the Augustan age, according to a famous passage of Strabo (the interpretation of which is presented in two slightly different ways in this volume: one by Wilson, who believes that these ships were as sizeable as the *Hermapollon*, and the other by De Romanis, who argues that the average size of ships sailing to the East grew over time).

At any rate, new developments during Trajanic times lend weight to the argument that a more general and self-conscious policy of the promotion of commerce along the Red Sea occurred as a consequence of the annexation of the Nabataean kingdom and the takeover of its interests in that area. This is the topic of Nappo's chapter, and his conclusions, while conjectural, are nevertheless plausible. In addition to the presence of a Roman fleet in the Red Sea from the moment of the conquest of the region, a series of other innovations characterize the age of Trajan and subsequent decades, including the settlement of a military garrison in the Farasan Islands, well beyond the line of Roman occupation in Egypt.

The developments in late Antiquity are the topic of Banaji's chapter, which provides an altogether much more continuist image of the India trade with regard to its quantitative dimension, although it signals remarkable differences with the Roman model when it comes to the analysis of the social actors. The role of Sasanid mediators with the Byzantine Empire, as pointed out in a well-known passage by Procopius, or that of the Indian actors as maritime transporters, is an entirely new phenomenon which first appeared during late Antiquity. Of course, Banaji's conclusions are consistent with his overall vision of both the economic conditions during late Antiquity and the reasons for and modalities of the expansion of Islam. The very learned and erudite description of southern Indian harbours is fundamental to the argument, according to which the temporal continuity of commerce necessarily implies the reshuffling of harbours. The other important conclusion is the definition of 'precocious capitalism' as the economic dimension typical of merchants responsible for the Indo-Mediterranean trade.

Can 'precocious capitalism' also describe the commercial activities carried out in these areas in Roman times? The chapter by Schörle focuses on just one specific activity, pearl fishing and commerce, and insists on the usefulness of the notion of 'vertical integration' as a market strategy—meaning the involvement of businessmen belonging to important Puteolan and later Ostian merchant families (the Peticii, Annii, and Calpurnii), who were, as merchants and shipowners, actors in this early form of commercial capitalism. Pearls were indeed imported from India through the gulf and the Red Sea, although they must have been fished in the Red Sea as well, if we are to interpret the mention of pearls as an allusion to both pearl fishing and pearl trading in the two Eastern Desert epigraphic dedications in which pearls are listed along with quarries and mines as activities overseen by the tribune of the third legion, P. Juventius Rufus. If we accept this reading, we should be prepared to surmise that the Roman State took care not only to demand dues on commercial profits from the sale of pearls as a form of fiscal exaction, but to institute rulings that protected and encouraged fishing activities as well.

Puteoli, as a hub where commercial interests with the Red Sea are located, is the central topic of Terpstra's chapter on the Nabataean community in the Greek and Roman Mediterranean, and its importance is indeed reflected in the epigraphic evidence. Terpstra's chapter analyses several aspects of this topic, all tangential to the core themes of the book, with an allusive reference to matters of economic history only at the end of his essay. Noteworthy, however, is his survey of the documents attesting to the Nabataean presence in the eastern Mediterranean and in Italy, and it is certainly remarkable that this geographic overview points to Puteoli as a particularly dense spot. But the conclusion, which suggests that there may have been Nabataean communities comparable in size and importance to that of Puteoli in other knots of the international trade network—such as the caravan cities or harbours where Nabataean presence is attested—can hardly be accepted, as Terpstra himself seems to argue, when he says that 'there seems to have been something peculiar about it' (*scil.* the Puteolan community of Nabataeans). The best parallel is obviously with trading communities of other peoples and cities, as studied by Terpstra himself. Other important observations in this chapter include those concerning the impact of institutional factors on this commerce, as is also discussed in other essays of the volume.

Another essay with a programmatic comparative approach, and regarding a crucial component of the Mediterranean trade with the East—namely gold—is the chapter by Falk. In this case, it is not only the dimension of time that conditioned the direction of commercial fluxes, but also that of space. Northwestern India produced significant quantities of gold that were exported to the Mediterranean area or paid as tribute to the Achaemenid kings. This area of ancient India adopted an articulated metrological system based on weight standards consistent with those of the Mediterranean region which thus seems to prove the existence of complex relations between those areas. In Southern India, by contrast, imported gold was transformed into coins imitating Roman ones in weight and metal content; this practice was in fact a cultural borrowing of sorts, since the coins were valued only for their intrinsic metal content, and hence cannot be described as counterfeit Roman coins. When we ask why this happened, we can surmise only that it was the presence and popularity of Roman coins that suggested the opportunity to turn available gold into local currency modelled after the Roman prototypes.

The concluding essay by Howell offers a lucid and, in many respects, less controversial overview of commercial interactions between Europe and the East in modern times, and their impact on the evolution of European economies. It starts with the Portuguese expansion that filled the vacuum left by Chinese merchants, but focuses mainly on the forms and modalities of the Dutch presence in the East. If a difference from the precedent of Roman commercial expansion is to be noted, it lies in the fact that the modern Europeans arrived and acted as 'predators', whereas the Romans were 'participants'. An important new development is the creation of companies (the VOC in particular) with mega-corporation qualities, promoting reliable financial support for commercial ventures, allowing a large share of profits, and diversifying the risks among individual investors. The companies, in fact, behave as if they were states, exerting functions that are the prerogative of states, and they act brutally, protecting and defending their commercial interests with extensive recourse to violence. The VOC moreover adopts a business model that brilliantly solves the issue of the lack of appeal of Western merchandise in the East (other than gold and silver) by creating commercial circuits within Eastern regions, whose profits are just as useful for financing the trade in spices.

Continuity and discontinuity, similarity and alterity, characterize Indo-Mediterranean trade over time. This volume takes these polarities well into account by presenting, evaluating, and analysing an array of sources that are quite impressive in variety and richness.

References

Archival Sources

Arquivo Nacional da Torre do Tombo,
- Cartas dos Vice-Reys da Índia 16
- Cartas Missivas III 377 & 367 (= Bouchon 1976)
- Colecção de São Lourenço II ff. 339–340 v (= DUP VII 289–291)
- Colecção São Lourenço III f. 412 (= Cartas de Rui Gonçalves de Caminha)
- Colecção São Lourenço IV ff. 329–330
- Corpo Cronólogico, P. I., M. 10, D. 53
  - P. I., M. 12, D. 13 (= CA I 83–84)
  - P. I., M. 13, D. 108 (= CA I 118–121)
  - P. I., M. 13, D. 113 (= CA III 380–406)
  - P. I., M. 86, D. 94
  - P. I., M. 103, D. 31
  - P. II., M. 79, D. 59 (= CA VII 172–186)
- Gaveta 15, M. 2, D. 36 (= CA III 256–267)
- Núcleo Antigo 705 (= Bouchon 1977)

Biblioteca da Ajuda
- Livro das mercês que fez o Senhor D. João de Castro, ff. 59–64v

Fürstlich und Gräflich Fuggersches Familien- und Stiftungsarchiv
- MSS Codex no. 46.1. ff. 33–38 (= Mathew 1997, 256–269)
- MSS Codex no. 46.1. ff. 50–51

Greek and Latin authors, as well as inscriptions, papyri, ostraca, and encyclopaedias of classical scholarship, are cited, when possible, in abbreviated forms according to the conventions established by the *Oxford Classical Dictionary* (4th edition). European, Arabic, Persian, and Chinese sources are quoted with the simple name of the author or the title of the work, followed by the page in the editions or translations quoted below.

Medieval and Early Modern Literary Sources

Al-Idrīsī (1836–40; repr. 1975), Nuzhat al-mushtāq fī ikhtirāq al-āfāq. *La géographie d'Édrisi. Tr. de l'arabe en français d'après deux manuscrits de la Bibliothèque du roi et accompagnée de notes, par P. Amédée Jaubert*, trans P.-A. Jaubert, 2 vols (Paris, repr. Amsterdam).

Al-Maqrizi, Ahmad Ibn Ali (1895), Mawāʿiz wa-al-iʿtibār fī dhikr al khiṭaṭ wa-al-āthār. *Description topographique et historique de l'Égypte I* trans. U Bouriant (Paris).

Al-Muqaddasī, Muḥammad b. Aḥmad (2001), *The Best Divisions for Knowledge of the Regions: A Translation of Aḥsan al-Taqāsīm fi Maʿrifat al-Aqālīm*, trans. B.A. Collins (Reading, UK).

Ananias of Širak (1992), *The Geography of Ananias of Širak (Ašxarhacʿoycʿ): The Long and the Short Recensions. Introduction, Translation, and Commentary by R.H. Hewsen* (Wiesbaden).

Barbosa, Duarte (1946), *Livro em que dá relação do que viu e ouviu no Oriente. Introdução e notas de A.R. Machado* (Lisboa).

Bocarro, António (1992), *O livro das plantas de todas as fortalezas, cidades e povoações do Estado da Índia Oriental (ed. I. Cid), I–III* (Lisboa).

Buchanan, Francis (1807), *Journey from Madras through the Countries of Mysore, Canara, and Malabar, vol. I–II* (London).

Ca' Masser, Leonardo da (1845), 'Relazione di Leonardo da Ca' Masser alla Serenissima Repubblica di Venezia sopra il commercio dei Portoghesi nell' India dopo la scoperta del capo di buona speranza (1497–1506)', *Archivio Storico Italiano. Appendice. Tomo II.* (Firenze), 13–51.

Caminha, Rui Gonçalves de (1989), *Cartas de Rui Gonçalves de Caminha; [comentário, Luís de Albuquerque]* (Lisboa).

Cantillon, Richard (1755), *Essai sur la nature du commerce en général* (London).

Correia, Gaspar (1858–1863), *Lendas da Índia* 3 t. 6 v. (Lisboa).

Corsali, Andrea (1563), 'Allo Illustrissimo Principe & Signor il Signor Duca Lorenzo de Medici, Della nauigatione del mar Rosso & sino persico sino a Cochin città nella India, scritta alli XVIII di Settembre MDXVII', in G.B. Ramusio (ed.), *Delle navigationi et viaggi, I* (Venezia), 181–89.

Costa, Francisco da (1963), 'Relatório sobre o trato da pimenta', *DUP III* (Lisboa), 293–379.

Dīnawarī (1888), 'Akhbār al-ṭiwāl', in V. Guirgass (ed.), (Leiden).

Gomes de Brito, Bernardo (1735–1736), *Historia tragico-maritima*, 2 vols. (Lisboa).

Hauqal, Ibn (1938–1939), *Kitāb Ṣurat al-ʿarḍ = Liber imaginis terrae* (ed. J.H. Kramers) (2nd edn. 1967; Leiden).

Huan, Ma (1955), *Yingya shenglan jiaozhu*, in Feng Chen jun (ed.), (Beijing).

———, (1970), *Ying-yai sheng-lan: 'The Overall Survey of the Ocean's Shores' [1433]*, trans. J.V.G. Mills (ed.), (Cambridge).

Ibn al-Balki (1912), *Description of the Province of Fars in Persia at the Beginning of the Fourteenth Century A.D. from the MS. of Ibn al-Balkhi in the British Museum*, trans G. Le Strange (London).

Ibn Baṭṭūṭa, Muḥammad ibn ʿAbdallāh (1958–2000), *The Travels of Ibn Baṭṭūṭa A.D. 1325–1354*, trans. H.A.R. Gibb (London).

——— (1960), *Riḥlat Ibn Baṯṯūṭa* (Beirut).
Ibn Khurradādhbih, 'Ubayd Allāh ibn 'Abdallāh (1889), Kitāb al-Masālik wa l-Mamālik', in M.J. de Goeje (ed.) *Liber viarum et regnorum* (Leiden).
Ibn Mājid (1971), *Arab Navigation in the Indian Ocean Before the Coming of the Portuguese, Being a Translation of Kitāb al-Fawā'id fī uṣūl al-baḥr wa'l-qawā'id of Aḥmad b. Mājid al-Najdī*, trans G.R. Tibbets (London).
'Livro que trata das cousas da Índia e do Japão', (1960) *Boletim da Biblioteca da Universidade de Coimbra* 24, 1–138, in A. de Almeida Calado (ed.) (Coimbra).
Marignolli, Giovanni de' (1882), 'Chronicon', in J. Emler (ed.), *Fontes rerum Bohemicarum, III* (Praze), 492–604.
Mas'ūdī (1861–1877), *Les prairies d'or, Texte et Traduction par C. Barbier de Meynard et Pavet de Courteille*, 9 vols. (Paris).
Mustawfi, Hamd-Allah (1919), *The Geographical Part of the Nuzhat al-Qulūb composed by Hamd-Allah Mustawfi of Qazwin in 740 (1340)*, trans. G. Le Strange (London).
Odorico da Pordenone (1929), 'Relatio', in A. van den Wyngaert (ed.) Sinica Franciscana: Itinera et relationes Fratrum Minorum saeculi xiii et XIV, *Vol. I* (Firenze), 413–495.
Pacheco Pereira, Duarte (1892), *Esmeraldo de situ orbis* (Lisboa).
Pires, Tomé (1944), *The Suma Oriental of Tomé Pires: An Account of the East, from the Red Sea to Japan, Written in Malacca and India in 1512–1515*, trans. A. Cortesão, 2 vols. (London).
Polo, Marco (1982), *Milione: Divisament dou Monde* (a cura di G. Ronchi) (Milano).
Quirini, Vincenzo (1863), 'Relazione', *Relazioni degli ambasciatori veneti al Senato; raccolte, annotate ed edite da E. Albèri* (XV; Firenze), 5–19.
S. Bartolomeo, fra Paolino da (1796), *Viaggio alle Indie Orientali* (Roma).
Santa Cruz, Alvaro de Baçan (1959), 'Parecer al Rey Don Felipe segundo sobre la navegacion de la India de Portugal', in J. Gentil da Silva (ed.), *Alguns elementos para a história do comércio da Índia de Portugal existentes na Biblioteca Nacional de Madrid, Anais. Estudos de História e Geografia da Expansão Portuguesa* (5; Lisbon), 53–59.
Sanuto, Marino (1879–1903), *I diarii di Marino Sanuto (MCCCCXCVI–MDXXXIII) dall'autografo Marciano ital. cl. VII codd. CDXIX–CDLXXVII* (Venezia).
Sassetti, Filippo (1995), *Lettere dall'India, 1583–1588* (a cura di A. Dei) (Roma).
Sebastião, King of Portugal (1816), *Leis, e Provisões, que El Rei Dom Sebastião nosso senhor fez depois que começou a governar* (2nd edn.; Coimbra).
Seure, Chevalier de (1895), 'Lettre au Roy (30/1/1559)', in E. Falgairolle (ed.), *Le chevalier de Seur ambassadeur de France en Portugal au XVIe siècle* (18), 49–85.
Varthema, Ludovico de (1991), *Itinerario dallo Egypto alla India* (a cura di E. Musacchio) (Bologna).
Xuanzang (1884), *Si-Yu-Ki. Buddhist Records of the Western world. Translated from the Chinese of Hiuen Tsiang (A.D. 629) by S. Beal* (London).

Bibliography

Abraham, M. (1988), *Two Medieval Merchant Guilds of South India* (New Delhi).

Abram, D. (1999), *South India, the Rough Guide* (London).

Adams, C.E.P. (2007), *Land Transport in Roman Egypt: A Study of Economics and Administration in a Roman Province* (Oxford and New York).

Adams, L.A. (1989), 'The Indian Imitations of Roman *Aurei*', *Journal of the Society for Ancient Numismatics*, 17 (4), 68–76.

Amadasi Guzzo, M.G. (1988), 'Iscrizione dedicatoria Nabatea', *Archeologia Laziale*, 9, 67–68.

Anonymous (1884) *Gazetteer of the Hoshiarpur District, 1883–1884*.

Arnade, P.J. (2008), *Beggars, Iconoclasts, and Civic Patriots: The Political Culture of the Dutch Revolt* (Ithaca).

Asthana, S. (1984), 'Harappan Trade in Metals and Minerals: A Regional Approach', in B.B. Lal and S.P. Gupta (eds.), *Frontiers of the Indus Civilization; Sir Mortimer Wheeler Commemoration Volume* (New Delhi).

Aubert, J.-J. (2004a), 'Aux origines du canal de Suez? Le canal du Nil à Mer Rouge revisité', in M. Clavel-Lévèque and E. Hermon (eds.), *Espaces intégrés et ressources naturelles dans l'Empire Romain: actes du colloque de l'Université de Laval-Québec, 5–8 mars 2003* (Paris), 219–52.

——— (2004b) [2005], 'Utopie ou mégalomanie? Le canal antique du Nil à la Mer Rouge/Canal de Trajan ou l'histoire d'une gageure', *Au Fil de l'eau, Bulletin de la Société Neuchâteloise de Géographie*, 48 (2004), 93–107.

——— (2013), 'Trajan's Canal', in R.S. Bagnall (ed.), *The Encyclopedia of Ancient History* (12; Leiden), 6815–16.

Aubin, J. (1953), 'Les princes d'Ormuz du XIIIe au XVe siècle', *Journal Asiatique*, 241, 77–138.

——— (1973), 'Francisco de Albuquerque, un juif castillan au service de l'Inde Portugaise (1510–15)', *Arquivos do Centro Cultural Português*e, 7, 175–88.

——— (1987), 'L'apprentissage de l'Inde: Cochin, 1503–1504', *Moyen Orient et Océan Indien*, 4, 1–96.

Bagnall, R.S., A. Bülow-Jacobsen, and H. Cuvigny (2001), 'Security and Water on the Eastern Desert Roads: The Prefect Iulius Ursus and the Construction of Praesidia Under Vespasian', *Journal of Roman Archaeology*, 14 (1), 325–33.

Bagnall, R.S., et al. (1996), 'A Ptolemaic Inscription from Bir 'Iayyan', *Chronique d'Égypte* 71 (142), 317–30.

Ball, J., and G.W. Murray (1942), *Egypt in the Classical Geographers* (Cairo).

Bandyopadhyay, S. (2007–08), 'Epigraphic Evidence for the Commoners' Use of Gold Coins', *Journal of Ancient Indian History*, 24, 70–72.

Bang, P.F. (2008), *The Roman Bazaar: A Comparative Study of Trade and Markets in a Tributary Empire* (Cambridge, UK).

Bauzou, T. (2000), 'La Gaza romaine (69 avant J.-C.–403 après J.C.)', in J.B. Humbert (ed.), *Gaza méditerranéenne: Histoire et archéologie en Palestine* (Paris), 47–69.

Begley, V. (1996), *The Ancient Port of Arikamedu: New Excavations and Researches 1989–1992*, 2 vols. (Pondicherry).

Berghaus, P. (1998), 'Republican and Early Roman Imperial *Denarii* from India', in A. Kumar Jha and S. Garg (eds.), Ex Moneta*: Essays on Numismatics, History and Archaeology in Honour of Dr. David W. MacDowall* (1; New Delhi), 119–27.

——— (2006), 'Strange Mould Links out of the Tirukkoilur Hoard', in R. Nagaswamy (ed.), *Sangam: Numismatic and Cultural History—Essays in Honour of Dr. R. Krishnamurthy* (Chennai), 11–20.

Bietak, M. (1975), *Tell el-Dab'a II* (Wien).

Biffi, N. (2002), *Il Medio Oriente di Strabone: Libro XVI della Geografia* (Bari).

Birley, A.R. (2000), *Marcus Aurelius, A Biography* (London).

Blet-Lemarquand, M. (2006), 'Analysis of Kushana Gold Coins: Debasement and Provenance Study', in F. De Romanis and S. Sorda (eds.), *Dal denarius al dinar—L'oriente e la moneta Romana (Atti dell'incontro di studio, Roma 16–18 settembre 2004)* (Roma), 155–71.

Bopearachchi, O. (2006), 'Chronologie et généalogie des premiers rois kushans: nouvelles données', *CRAI*, 1433–47.

——— (2008), 'Les premiers souverains kouchans: chronologie et iconographie monétaire', *Journal des Savants*, 3–56.

Bouchon, G. (1976), 'L'inventaire de la cargaison rapportée de l'Inde en 1505', *Mare Luso-indicum*, 3, 101–36.

——— (1977), *Navires et cargaison: Retour de l'Inde en 1518 = Cadérno dos ofiçiaes da India da carreguaçam das naos que vieram o anno bcxviij* (Paris).

——— (1988), 'Un microcosme: Calicut au 16e siècle', in D. Lombard and J. Aubin (eds.), *Marchands et hommes d'affaires asiatiques dans l'Océan Indien et la Mer de Chine 13e–20e siècles* (Paris), 53–56.

Bourdon, C. (1925), *Anciens canaux, anciens sites et ports de Suez* (Cairo).

Bowersock, G.W. (1983), *Roman Arabia* (Cambridge, MA).

Bowman, A.K. (2010), 'Trade and the Flag: Alexandria, Egypt and the Imperial House', in D. Robinson and A. Wilson (eds.), *Alexandria and the North-Western Delta* (Oxford).

Braudel, F. (1972), *The Mediterranean and the Mediterranean World in the Age of Philip II*, 2 vols. (London).

Broekaert, W. (2012), 'Vertical Integration in the Roman Economy', *Ancient Society*, 42, 109–25.

Brown, P. (1971), *The World of Late Antiquity: From Marcus Aurelius to Muhammad* (London).

Brun, J.P. (2003), 'Chronologie de l'équipement de la route à l'époque gréco-romaine', in H. Cuvigny (ed.), *La route de Myos Hormos: L'armée romaine dans le désert oriental d'Égypte, 1* (Cairo), 187–234.

Bruneau, P. (1970), *Recherches sur les cultes de Délos a l'époque hellénistique et a l'époque impériale* (Paris).

Brunt, P.A. (1978), 'Laus Imperii', in P.D.A. Garnsey and C.R. Whittaker (eds.), *Imperialism in the Ancient World* (London), 159–91.

Bruyère, B. (1966), *Fouilles de Clysma-Qolzoum (Suez), 1930–1932* (Cairo).

Buschmann, K. (1991), 'Motiv und Ziel des Aelius-Gallus-Zuges nach Südarabien', *Die Welt des Orients*, 22, 85–93.

Butler, H.E. (1909), *The Apologia and Florida of Apuleius of Madaura* (Oxford).

Butzer K. (1975), 'Delta', *LÄ* 1043–52.

Calderini, A. (1920), 'Ricerche sul regime delle acque nell'Egitto greco–romano', *Aegyptus* 1, 37–62.

——— (1940), 'I precedenti del Canale di Suez nell'antichità', *Aegyptus*, 20, 214–31.

Caley, E.R. (1926), 'The Stockholm Papyrus: An English Translation with Brief Notes', *Journal of Chemical Education*, 4 (8), 979–1002.

Camodeca, G. (1977), 'L'ordinamento in regiones e i vici di Puteoli', *Puteoli, studi di storia antica*, 1, 62–98.

——— (1979), 'La gens Annia puteolana in età giulio-claudia: potere politico e interessi commerciali', *Puteoli, studi di storia antica*, 3, 17–34.

——— et al. (2001), 'Ricerche sul vicus Lartidianus di Puteoli', in P.A. Gianfrotta and F. Maniscalco (eds.), *Forma Maris: Forum internazionale di archeologia subacquea* (Napoli).

Carswell, J. (1985), 'Sri Lanka and China', in A.R.B. Amerasinghe and S.J. Sumanasekera Banda (eds.), Festschrift 1985: James Thevathasan Rutnam, (Sri Lanka).

Carter, R. (2005), 'The History and Prehistory of Pearling in the Persian Gulf', *Journal of the Economic and Social History of the Orient*, 48 (2), 139–209.

Casale, G. (2010), *The Ottoman Age of Exploration* (Oxford and New York).

Casson, L. (1971), *Ships and Seamanship in the Ancient World* (Princeton, NJ).

——— (1980), 'Rome's Trade with the East: The Sea Voyage to Africa and India', *Transactions of the American Philological Association* 110, 21–36.

——— (1986), '*P. Vindob.* G. 40.822 and the Shipping of the Goods from India', *BASP*, 23, 73–9.

——— (1989), *The Periplus Maris Erythraei: Text with Introduction, Translation, and Commentary* (Princeton, NJ).

——— (1990), 'New Light on Maritime Loans: *P. Vindob. G* 40822', *ZPE*, 84, 195–206.

Cereti, C.G. (2003), 'Le croci di San Tommaso e la letteratura cristiana in lingue medio-iraniche', in M.V. Fontana and B. Genito (eds.), *Studi in Onore di Umberto Scerrato* (2; Napoli).
Chakravarti, R. (1998), 'Coastal Trade and Voyages in Konkan: The Early Medieval Scenario', *The Indian Economic and Social History Review*, 35 (2), 97–123.
Champakalakshmi, R. (1996), *Trade, Ideology, and Urbanization: South India 300 BC to AD 1300* (Delhi and New York).
Charpentier, V., C.S. Phillips, and S. Méry (2012), 'Pearl Fishing in the Ancient World: 7500 BP', *Arabian Archaeology and Epigraphy* 23, 1–6.
Chatterjee, B. (1997), 'Provenance of Kushan gold in Ethiopia: An Explanation', *Journal of the Numismatic Society of India*, 59, 62–65.
Chaudhuri, K.N. and I.J. Israel (1991), 'The English and Dutch East India Companies and the Glorious Revolution of 1688', in J.I. Jonathan (ed.), *The Anglo-Dutch Moment: Essays on the Glorious Revolution and its World Impact* (Cambridge), 407–38.
Chaudhury, S. and M. Morineau (1999), *Merchants, Companies, and Trade: Europe and Asia in the Early Modern Era* (London and New York).
Chaussende, D. (2011), 'Compte rendu', *Etudes Chinoises* 28, 267–75.
Chehade, J. (1987), 'Zur Schmuckdarstellungen auf Palmyrenischen Grabreliefs', in E.M. Ruprechtsberger (ed.), *Palmyra: Geschichte, Kunst und Kultur der Syrischen Oasenstadt* (Linz), 193–99.
Cherpion, N., J.P. Corteggiani, and J.F. Gout (2007), *Le tombeau de Pétosiris à Touna el-Gebel: Relevé photographique* (Cairo).
Clédat, M.J. (1912), 'Fouilles à Qasr-Gheit (mai 1911)', *Annales du Service des Antiquités de l'Égypte* 12, 145–68.
Clermont-Ganneau, C.S. (1906), 'Un épitrope nabatéen à Milet', *Recueil d'Archéologie Orientale*, 7, 305–29.
——— (1924), 'Les Nabatéens en Égypte', *Recueil d'Archéologie Orientale*, 8, 229–57.
Cohen, G.M. (2006), *The Hellenistic Settlements in Syria, the Red Sea Basin, and North Africa* (Berkeley).
Cohen, R. (1982), 'New Light on the Date of the Petra–Gaza Road', *The Biblical Archaeologist* 45 (4), 240–47.
Cooper, J.P. (2009), 'Egypt's Nile–Red Sea Canals: Chronology, Location, Seasonality and Function', in L. Blue, et al. (eds.), *Connected Hinterlands: Proceedings of Red Sea Project IV (Bar International Series: Society for Arabian Studies Monographs 8)* (Oxford), 195–209.
——— (2011), 'No Easy Option: Nile Versus Red Sea in Ancient and Mediaeval North–South Navigation', in W.V. Harris and K. Iara (eds.), *Maritime Technology in the Ancient Economy: Ship-Design and Navigation* (Portsmouth, RI), 189–210.
Costa, L.F. (1997), *Naus e Galeões na Ribeira de Lisboa: A construção naval no século XVI para a Rota do Cabo* (Cascais).

Cotton, H.M. (2000), '*The legio* VI *Ferrata*', in Y. le Bohec and C. Wolff (eds.), *Les Legions de Rome sous le Haut-Empire: Actes du Congrès de Lyon (17–19 septembre 1998)* (Lyon), 351–357.

Cracco, G. (1967), *Società e Stato nel Medioevo veneziano: (secoli XII–XIV)* (Florence).

Cuvigny, H. (2003a), *La Route de Myos Hormos: L'Armée Romaine dans le Désert Oriental d'Égypte*, 2 vols., Cairo.

——— (2003b), 'La société civile des praesidia', in H. Cuvigny (ed.), *La Route de Myos Hormos: L'Armée Romaine dans le Désert Oriental d'Égypte* (2; Cairo), 361–97.

——— (2003c), 'Le fonctionnement du réseau', in H. Cuvigny (ed.), *La Route de Myos Hormos: L'Armée Romaine dans le Désert Oriental d'Égypte* (2; Cairo), 295–353.

——— (2010), 'Femmes tournantes: remarques sur la prostitution dans les garnisons romaines du désert de Bérénice', ZPE, 172, 159–66.

D'Arms, J.H. (1974), 'Puteoli in the Second Century of the Roman Empire: A Social and Economic Study', JRS, 64, 104–24.

Dames, M.L. (1989), *The Book of Duarte Barbosa: An Account of the Countries Bordering on the Indian Ocean and Their Inhabitants*, 2 vols. (New Delhi).

Daris, S. (1956), 'Note per la storia dell'esercito romano in Egitto. I. I reparti', *Aegyptus*, 36, 235–46.

——— (2000), 'Legio II Traiana Fortis', in Y. Le Bohec and C. Wolff (eds.), *Les Légions de Rome sous le Haut-Empire* (Lyon), 359–63.

De Romanis, F. (1993), 'Puteoli e l'Oriente', in F. Zevi (ed.), *Puteoli* (Naples), 61–72.

——— (1996), *Cassia, cinnamomo, ossidiana: uomini e merci tra Oceano indiano e Mediterraneo* (Roma).

——— (1998), 'Commercio, metrologia, fiscalità. Su *P. Vindob. G.* 40.822 verso', *Mélanges de l'École Française de Rome, Antiquité* 110 (1), 11–60.

——— (2000), 'Esportazioni di corallo mediterraneo in India nell'età ellenistico-romana', in C. Rondi-Costanzo, J.P. Morel, and D. Ugolini (eds.), *Corallo di ieri, corallo di oggi: Atti del convegno, Ravello, Villa Rufolo, 13–15 dicembre 1996* (Bari), 211–16.

——— (2001), 'Lysas e il tempo: ulteriori considerazioni su AEp, 1954, 121a', *Epigraphica*, 63, 9–36.

——— (2002), 'Τραιανὸς ποταμός. Mediterraneo e Mar Rosso da Traiano a Maometto', in R. Villari (ed.), *Controllo degli stretti e insediamenti militari nel Mediterraneo* (Roma e Bari), 21–70.

——— (2006), '*Aurei* after the Trade: Western Taxes and Eastern Gifts', in F. De Romanis and S. Sorda (eds.), *Dal denarius al dinar. L'Oriente e la moneta romana. Atti dell'Incontro di studio, Roma, 16–18 settembre 2004* (Roma), 54–82.

——— (2010/2011) [2012], 'Playing Sudoku on the Verso of the "Muziris Papyrus": Pepper, Malabathron and Tortoise Shell in the Cargo of the Hermapollon', *Journal of Ancient Indian History*, 27, 75–101.

——— (2012), 'On Dachinabades and Limyrike in the *Periplus Maris Erythraei*', in J.-Fr. Salles, J.-B. Yon, and M.-Fr. Boussac (eds.), *Autour du Périple de la mer Érythrée* (*Topoi. Supplément*) 11, 329–40.

De Vries, J. and A. Van Der Woude (1997), *The First Modern Economy: Success, Failure, and Perseverance of the Dutch Economy, 1500–1815* (Cambridge).

Desanges, J. (1984), 'Rome et les riverains de la mer Rouge au IIIᵉ siècle de notre ère', *Ktema*, 9, 249–60.

Devijiver, H. (1974), 'The Roman Army in Egypt with Special Reference to the Militiae Equestres', in H. Temporini and W. Haase (eds.), *Aufstieg und Niedergang der römischen Welt* (2.1; Berlin), 452–92.

Di Meglio, R.R. (1970), 'Arab Trade with Indonesia and the Malay Peninsula from the 8th to the 16th Century', in D.S. Richards (ed.), *Islam and the Trade of Asia: A Colloquium* (Oxford), 105–36.

Domaszewski, A. von (1981), *Die Rangordnung des römischen Heeres*, 3rd edn. (Bonn).

Donkin, R.A. (1998), *Beyond Price: Pearls and Pearl-Fishing: Origins to the Age of Discoveries* (Philadelphia).

Dubois, C. (1907), *Pouzzoles antique (histoire et topographie)* (Paris).

Duncan-Jones, R.P. (1994), *Money and Government in the Roman Empire* (Cambridge, UK).

——— (2006), 'Roman Customs Dues: a Comparative View', *Latomus. Revue d'études latines*, 65 (1), 3–16.

Eadie, J.W. (1985), 'Artifacts of Annexation: Trajan's Grand Strategy and Arabia', in J.W. Eadie, C.G. Starr, and J. Ober (eds.), *The Craft of the Ancient Historian: Essays in Honor of Chester G. Starr* (Lanham, MD), 407–23.

——— (1986), 'The Evolution of the Roman Frontier in Arabia', in P. Freedman and D. Kennedy (eds.), *The Defence of the Roman and Byzantine East* (Oxford), 243–52.

——— (1989), 'Strategies of Economic Development in the Roman East: The Red Sea Trade Revisited', in D.H. French and C.S. Lightfoot (eds.), *The Eastern Frontier of the Roman Empire, Part I* (Oxford), 113–20.

Elliot, H.M. and J. Dowson (1867–1877), *The History of India, as Told by its Own Historians: The Muhammadan Period*, 8 vols. (London).

Erickson-Gini, T. (2006), 'Down to the Sea: Nabataean Colonisation in the Negev Highlands', in P. Bienkowski and K. Galor (eds.), *Crossing the Rift: Routes, Resources, Settlement Patterns and Interaction in the Wadi Arabah* (Oxford), 157–66.

Errington, E. (1998), 'Gandharan Stupa Deposits', *Arts of Asia*, 28 (2), 80–87.

Evans, K.G. (1995), 'Alexander the Alabarch: Roman and Jew', in E.H.J. Lovering (ed.), *Society of Biblical Literature: 1995 Seminar Papers* (Atlanta), 576.

Falk, H. (1997), 'Refining Gold in Ancient India: ad JUB 3.17,3', *Acta Orientalia*, 58, 47–51.

——— (2000), 'Measuring Time in Mesopotamia and Ancient India', *Zeitschrift der Deutschen Morgenländischen Gesellschaft*, 150, 107–32.
——— (2003), 'A Copper Plate Donation Record and Some Seals from Kashmir Smast', *Beiträge zur Allgemeinen und Vergleichenden Archäologie* 23, 1–19.
——— (2014), 'The First Century Copper-Plates of Helagupta from Gandhāra Hailing Maitreya', *Annual Report of the International Research Institute for Advanced Buddhology* 17.
Faville, E. (1902–03), 'La stèle de Pithom', *Zeitschrift für ägyptische Sprache und Altertumskunde*, 40, 66–75.
Fiema, Z.T. (1987), 'The Roman Annexation of Arabia: A General Perspective', *Ancient World*, 15, 25–35.
Flinterman, J.-J. (1997), 'The Date of Lucian's Visit to Abonuteichos', *ZPE*, 119, 280–3.
Fonseca, H.Q. da (1989), *Os Portugueses no Mar. Memórias Históricas e Arqueológicas das Naus de Portugal* (2nd edn.; Lisboa).
Foraboschi, D. and A. Gara (1989), 'Le direttrici del commercio alessandrino', *Quaderni ticinesi di numismatica e antichità classiche*, 18, 280–2.
Freedman, P. (2005), 'Spices and Late-Medieval Ideas of Scarcity and Value', *Speculum*, 80 (4), 1209–27.
Freeman, P. (1996), 'The Annexation of Arabia and Imperial Grand Strategy', in D.L. Kennedy (ed.), *The Roman Army in the East* (*JRA Suppl. 18*) (Ann Arbor), 91–118.
Fuks, A. (1951), 'Notes on the Archive of Nicanor', *JJP*, 5, 207–16.
Gaastra, F. (2003), *The Dutch East India Company: Expansion and Decline* (Zutphen).
Ganguly, D.K. (1989), 'The Satamana Metallic Currency', in D.C. Bhattacharyya and D. Handa (eds.), *Prācī-Prabhā: Perspectives in Indology* (*Essays in Honour of Professor B.N. Mukherjee*) (New Delhi), 91–100.
Gates, J.E. (2006), 'Hidden Passage: Graeco-Roman Roads in Egypt's Eastern Desert', in E.C. Robertson, et al. (eds.), *Space and Spatial Analysis in Archaeology* (Calgary), 315–22.
Gawlikowski, M. (1994), 'Palmyra as a Trading Centre', *Iraq*, 56, 27–33.
——— (2003), 'The Nabataean Temple at Qasrawet', in Z. Hawass and L.P. Brock (eds.), *Egyptology at the Dawn of the Twenty-First Century* (Cairo), 195–99.
Gianfrotta, P.A. (2008), 'Il Commercio Marittimo in Età Tardo-Repubblicana: Merci, Mercanti, Infrastrutture', in J. Pérez Ballester and G.P. Berlanga (eds.), *Comercio, Redistribución y Fondeaderos. La navegacíon a vela en el Mediterráneo* (València), 65–78.
Göbl, R. (1960), 'Roman Patterns for Kushāṇa Coins', *Journal of the Numismatic Society of India*, 22, 75–95.
Godinho, V.M. (1981–1983), *Os descobrimentos e a economia mundial*, 4 vols., 2nd edn. (Lisboa).
Goitein, S.D. and M.A. Friedman (2008), *India Traders of the Middle Ages: Documents from the Cairo Geniza ('India book'), part I* (Leiden).

Goossens, R. (1930), 'Un texte grec relatif à l'Asvamedha', *Journal Asiatique* 217, 280–85.

Graf, D.F. (1978), 'The Saracens and the Defence of the Arabian Frontier', *BASOR*, 229, 1–29.

——— (1996), 'The Roman East from the Chinese Perspective', *International Colloquium on Palmyra and the Silk Road (Les annales archéologiques arabes syriennes vol. 42)* (Damascus), 199–216.

——— (2007), 'The Nabataeans under Roman Rule (After AD 106)', in K.D. Politis (ed.), *The World of the Nabataeans* (Stuttgart), 173–86.

Greif, A. (2006), *Institutions and the Path to the Modern Economy: Lessons from Medieval Trade* (Cambridge).

Hamilton-Dyer, S. (2011), 'Faunal Remains', in D. Peacock and L. Blue (eds.), *Myos Hormos–Quseir al-Qadim: Roman and Islamic Ports on the Red Sea. Volume 2: Finds from the Excavations 1999–2003* (Oxford), 245–88.

Hammond, P.C. (1979), 'Nabataean', in D.S. Whitcomb and J.H. Johnson (eds.), *Quseir al-Qadim 1978 Preliminary Report* (Cairo), 245–47.

Hansman, J. (1973), 'A Periplus of Magan and Meluḫḫa', *Bulletin of the School of Oriental and African Studies*, 36, 554–87.

Harrauer, H. and P. Sijpesteijn (1985), 'Ein neues Dokument zu Roms Indienhandel, *P. Vindob.* G 40.822', *Anzeiger d. Österreichischen Akad. d. Wissenschaften, Phil.-Hist. Klasse*, 122, 124–55.

Hayek, F.A. (1991), *The Trend of Economic Thinking: Essays on Political Economists and Economic History* (London).

Healey, J.F. (2001), *The Religion of the Nabataeans: A Conspectus* (Leiden).

Hemmy, A.S. (1938), 'System of Weights', in E.J.H. Mackay (ed.), *Further Excavations at Mohenjo-Daro* (New Delhi), 604–12.

Hill, J. (2009), *Through the Jade Gate to Rome: A Study of the Silk Routes during the Later Han Dynasty 1st to 2nd Centuries CE* (Charleston).

Hirth, F. (Leipsic and Munich, 1885; repr. 1975), *China and the Roman Orient* (Chicago).

Ho, C. (2001), 'The Ceramic Boom in Minnan During Song and Yuan Times', in A. Schottenhammer (ed.), *The Emporium of the World: Maritime Quanzhou, 1000–1400* (Leiden), 237–81.

Höckmann, O. (1985), *Antike Seefahrt* (München).

Holladay, J.S., Jr. (1999a), 'Tell el-Maskhuta', in K.A. Bard (ed.), *Encyclopedia of the Archaeology of Ancient Egypt* (London and New York), 786–89.

——— (1999b), 'Wadi Tumilat', in K.A. Bard (ed.), *Encyclopedia of the Archaeology of Ancient Egypt* (London and New York), 878–81.

——— (ed.), (1982), *Tell el-Maskhuta: Preliminary Report on the Wadi Tumilat Project 1978–1979* (Malibu).

Horden, P. and N. Purcell (2000), *The Corrupting Sea: A Study of Mediterranean History* (Oxford).

Hornell, J. (1914), *The Sacred Chank of India: A Monograph of the Indian Conch (Turbinella Pyrum)* (Madras).

Horton, M.C. (1996a), 'Early Maritime Trade and Settlement Along the Coasts of Eastern Africa', in J. Reade (ed.), *The Indian Ocean in Antiquity* (London and New York), 439–59.

——— (1996b), *Shanga: The Archaeology of a Muslim Trading Community on the Coast of East Africa* (London).

——— (2003), 'Islam, Archaeology, and Swahili Identity', in D. Whitcomb (ed.), *Changing Social Identity with the Spread of Islam: Archaeological Perspectives* (Chicago), 67–88.

Humbert, J.-B. (ed.), (2000), *Gaza méditerranéenne: Histoire et archéologie en Palestine* (Paris).

Isaac, B. (1992), *The Limits of the Empire* (revised edn.; Oxford).

Israel, J.I. (1990), *Dutch Primacy in World Trade: 1585–1740* (Oxford).

Jain, V.K. (1990), *Trade and Traders in Western India, A.D. 1000–1300* (New Delhi).

Jameson, S. (1968), 'Chronology of the Campaigns of Aelius Gallus and C. Petronius', *JRS*, 58, 71–84.

Jomard, E.-F. (ed.), (1809–1828), *Description de l'Egypte ou Recueil des observations et des recherches qui ont été faites en Egypte pendant l'expédition de l'armée française, publié par les ordres de sa majesté l'empereur Napoléon le Grand* (Paris).

Jones, R.N., et al. (1988), 'A Second Nabataean Inscription from Tell esh-Shuqafiya', *Bulletin of the American Schools of Oriental Research* 269, 47–57.

Jördens, A. (2007), 'Neues zum Trajanskanal', in T. Purola, J. Frösen, and E. Salmenkivi (eds.), *Proceedings of the 24th International Congress of Papyrology, Helsinki, 1–7 August, 2004. Vol. 1, with appendices by A. Jördens (478–80), P. Heilporn (480–82), and R. Duttenhöfer (483–85)* 469–78.

——— (2009), *Statthalterliche Verwaltung in der römischen Kaiserzeit. Studien zum praefectus Aegypti* (Stuttgart).

Jung-Pang, Lo (1970), 'Chinese Shipping and East–West Trade from the Tenth to the Fourteenth Century', in M. Mollat (ed.), *Sociétés et compagnies de commerce en Orient et dans l'Océan Indien* (Paris), 167–76.

Karashima, N. (2009), *Ancient to Medieval: South Indian Society in Transition* (New Delhi).

Kennedy, D.L. (1980), '*Legio VI Ferrata*: The Annexation and Early Garrison of Arabia', *HSCP* 84, 283–309.

——— (1985), 'The Composition of a Military Work Party in Roman Egypt (*ILS* 2483: Coptos)', *Journal of Egyptian Archaeology* 71, 156–60.

Keppie, L. (1986), 'Legions in the East from Augustus to Trajan', in P.W.M. Freeman and D.L. Kennedy (eds.), *The Defence of the Roman and Byzantine East* (*BAR International Series 297*) (Oxford), 411–29.

Kienast, D. (1966), *Untersuchungen zu den Kreigsflotten der romischen Kaiserzeit* (Bonn).

Kieniewicz, J. (1996), 'Pepper Gardens and Market in Precolonial Malabar', in M.N. Pearson (ed.), *Spices in the Indian Ocean World* (Brookfield, VT).

Kirkbride, D. (1990), 'The Nabataeans, Trajan and the *Periplus*', *Aram* 2, 253–65.

Kortenbeutel, H. (1931), *Der ägyptische Süd- und Osthandel in der Politik der Ptolemäer und römischen Kaiser* (Berlin).

Krishnamurthy, R. (2000), 'A Roman Coin Bronze Die from Karur, Tamilnadu, India', in B. Kluge and B. Weisser (eds.), *XII. Internationaler Numismatischer Kongress Berlin 1997: Akten-Proceedings—Actes I.* (Berlin), 552–53.

——— (2005), 'Some Roman Republican *Denarii* from Karur in South India', in C. Marcos, C. Alfaro, and P. Otero (eds.), *XIII Congreso Internacional de Numismática, Madrid 15–19 Septiembre, Actas—Proceedings—Actes, Vol. I* (Madrid), 625–28.

Krzywinski, J. (2007), 'Water Harvesting in the Eastern Desert of Egypt', in E.H. Seland (ed.), *The Indian Ocean in the Ancient Period: Definite Places, Translocal Exchange* (*BAR International Series 1593*) (Oxford), 45–57.

Kulke, H. (1999), 'Rivalry and Competition in the Bay of Bengal in the Eleventh Century and its Bearing on Indian Ocean Studies', in O. Prakash and D. Lombard (eds.), *Commerce and Culture in the Bay of Bengal 1500–1800* (New Delhi), 17–36.

Kunz, G.F. and C.H. Stevenson (1908), *The Book Of The Pearl: The History, Art, Science, And Industry Of The Queen Of Gems* (New York).

Lacerenza, G. (1994), 'Due nuove iscrizioni del tempio di Dusares dell'antica Puteoli', *Annali dell'Istituto Universitario Orientale di Napoli* 54, 15–17.

——— (1988/1989), 'Il dio Dusares a Puteoli', *Puteoli, Studi di Storia Antica* 12/13 119–49.

Lauffer, S. (1971), *Diokletians Preisedikt* (Berlin).

Levi Della Vida, G. (1938), 'Una bilingue greco-nabatea a Coo', *Clara Rhodos* 9, 137–48.

Lewis, M.J.T. (1997), *Millstone and Hammer: The Origins of Water Power* (Yorkshire).

Lima Felner, R.J. (1868), *O Livro dos Pesos, Medidas e Moedas por Antonio Nunes* (Lisboa).

Littmann, E. and D. Meredith (1953), 'Nabataean Inscriptions from Egypt, I', *Bulletin of the School of Oriental and African Studies* 15 (1), 1–28.

——— (1954), 'Nabataean Inscriptions from Egypt, II', *Bulletin of the School of Oriental and African Studies* 16 (2), 211–46.

Luther, A. (1999), 'Medo nectis catenas? Die Expedition des Aelius Gallus im Rahmen der augusteischen Partherpolitik', *Orbis Terrarum* 5, 157–182.

MacDowall, D.W. (1960), 'The Weight Standards of the Gold and Copper Coinages of the Kushāṇa Dynasty from Vima Kadphises to Vāsudeva', *Journal of the Numismatic Society of India* 22, 63–74.

——— (1991), 'Indian Imports of Roman Silver Coins', in A.K. Jha (ed.), *Coinage, Trade and Economy: The 3rd International Colloquium, January 8th–11th 1991* (Anjaneri) 145–63.

——— (1997), 'Western Impact on the Coinage of the Great Kushans', in R. Allchin, et al. (eds.), *Gandharan Art in Context. East–West Exchanges at the Crossroads of Asia* (New Delhi), 231–43.

MacDowall Hellings, T.C.L. (1998), 'The Defacement of Roman *Aurei* Exported to India', in A.K. Jha and S. Garg (eds.), Ex Moneta: *Essays on Numismatics, History and Archaeology in Honour of Dr. David W. MacDowall, Vol. 1* (New Delhi), 129–44.

Mainkar, V.B. (1984), 'Metrology in the Indus Civilization', in B.B. Lal and S.P. Gupta (eds.), *Frontiers of the Indus Civilization: Sir Mortimer Wheeler Commemoration Volume* (New Delhi), 141–51.

Maiuri, A. (1938/1939), 'Statuetta eburnea di arte indiana a Pompei', *Le Arti* 2, 111–15.

Majumdar, R.C. (1960), *The Classical Accounts of India* (Calcutta).

Malekandathil, P. (2001), *Portuguese Cochin and the Maritime Trade of India 1500–1633* (New Delhi).

Malouta, M. and A.I. Wilson (2013), 'Mechanical Irrigation: Water-Lifting Devices in the Archaeological Evidence and in the Egyptian Papyri', in A. Bowman and A. Wilson (eds.), *The Roman Agricultural Economy: Organization, Investment, and Production* (Oxford), 273–306.

Maqbul Ahmad, S. (1954), *India and the Neighbouring Territories as Described by the Sharif al-Idrisi in his Kitāb Nuzhat al-mushtāq fi'khtirāq al-āfāq of Sharīf al-Idrīsī: Part 1 (Arabic text)* (Aligarh).

——— (1960), *India and the Neighbouring Territories in the Kitāb Nuzhat al-Mushtāq fi'khtirāq al-Āfāq of Sharīf al-Idrīsī* (Leiden).

——— (1989), *Arabic Classical Accounts of India and China* (Shimla).

Marek, C. (1993), 'Die Expedition des Aelius Gallus nach Arabien im Jahre 25 v. Chr.', *Chiron* 23, 121–156.

Margariti, R.E. (2007), *Aden and the Indian Ocean Trade: 150 Years in the Life of a Medieval Arabian Port* (Chapel Hill).

Mathew, K.S. (1997), *Indo-Portuguese Trade and the Fuggers of Germany: Sixteenth Century* (New Delhi).

Mayerson, P. (1992), 'The Island of Iotabê in the Byzantine Sources: A Reprise', *Bulletin of the American Schools of Oriental Research* 287, 1–4.

——— (1993), 'A Confusion of Indias: Asian India and African India in the Byzantine Sources', *JAOS*, 113, 169–74.

——— (1995a), 'A Note on Iotabe and Several Other Islands in the Red Sea', *Bulletin of the American Schools of Oriental Research* 298, 33–35.

——— (1995b), 'Aelius Gallus at Cleopatris (Suez) and on the Red Sea', *Greek, Roman and Byzantine Studies* 36, 17–24.

——— (1996), 'The Port of Clysma (Suez) in Transition from Roman to Arab Rule', *Journal of Near Eastern Studies*, 55 (2), 119–26.

McCrindle, J.W. (1885), *Ancient India as Described by Ptolemy* (London).

Medas, S. (2004), 'Lemboi e Liburnae', in L. Braccesi (ed.), *La Pirateria nel Mondo Antico* (Roma), 129–38.

Meredith, D. (1953), 'Annius Plocamus: Two inscriptions from the Berenice Road', *JRS*, 43, 38–40.

Messeri, G. (2004–5), 'Un nuovo trierarco e la presenza della flotta romana nel Mar Rosso', *Analecta Papyrologica* 16–17, 69–73.

Metcalf, W.E. (1979), 'Roman *Aurei* from India', *American Numismatic Society Museum Notes* 24, 123–27.

Michaelides, D. (1995), 'Cyprus and the Persian Gulf in the Hellenistic and Roman Periods: The Case of *Pinctada margaritifera*', in V. Karageorghis and D. Michaelides (eds.), *Cyprus and the Sea. International Symposium organized by the Cyprus Ports Authority and the Archaeological Research Unit of the University of Cyprus, 25–26 September. Nicosia 1993* (Nicosia), 211–26.

Minorsky, V. (1937), *Hudūd al-ʿĀlam: The Regions of the World. A Persian Geography 372 A.H.–982 A.D.* (London).

Monteix, N. (2013), '"Caius Lucretius [...], marchand de couleurs de la rue des fabricants de courroies." Réflexions critiques sur les concentrations de métiers à Rome', in A. Esposito and G.M. Sanidas (eds.), *'Quartiers' artisanaux en Grèce ancienne: Une perspective Méditerranéenne* (333–52).

Mordini, A. (1967), 'Gold Kushana Coins in the Convent of Dabra Dammo', *Journal of the Numismatic Society of India* 29, 19–25.

Morelli, F. (2011), 'Dal Mar Rosso ad Alessandria: Il verso (ma anche il recto) del "papiro di Muziris" (*SB* XVIII 13167)', *Tyche* 26, 199–234.

Morgan, P. (1991), 'New Thoughts on Old Hormuz: Chinese Ceramics in the Hormuz Region in the Thirteenth and Fourteenth Centuries', *Iran* 29 67–83.

Morley, N. (2007), *Trade in Classical Antiquity* (Cambridge).

Morrison, K.D. (2002), 'Pepper in the Hills: Upland–Lowland Exchange and the Intensification of the Spice Trade', in K.D. Morrison and L.L. Junker (eds.) *Forager-Traders in South and Southeast Asia*, (Cambridge),105–30.

Mukund, K. (1999), *The Trading World of the Tamil Merchant: Evolution of Merchant Capitalism in the Coromandel* (London).

Murray, G.W. (1925), 'The Roman Roads and Stations in the Eastern Desert of Egypt', *The Journal of Egyptian Archaeology* 11, 138–50.

Nagaswamy, R. (1991), 'Alagankulam: An Indo-Roman Trading Port', in C. Margabandhu, et al. (eds.), *Indian Archaeological Heritage: Shri K.V. Soundara Rajan Felicitation, Volume II* (Delhi), 247–54.

——— (1995), *Roman Karur* (Madras).

Nappo, D. (2009), 'Roman Policy in the Red Sea between Anastasius and Justinian', in L.K. Blue, et al. (eds.), *Connected Hinterlands: Proceedings of Red Sea Project IV held at the University of Southampton, September 2008* (Oxford), 71–77.

Nizami, K.A. (1994), 'Early Arab Contact with South Asia', *Journal of Islamic Studies* 5 (1), 52–69.

Oertel, F. (1964), 'Das Problem des antiken Suezkanals', in K. Repgen and S. Skalweit (eds.), *Spiegel der Geschichte, Festgabe für Max Braubach zum 10. April 1964* (Münster), 18–51.

Ogden, J. (1996), 'The Pearl in Classical Jewellery', *Jewellery Studies* 7, 37–42.

Oleson, J.P. (1984), *Greek and Roman Mechanical Water-Lifting Devices: The History of a Technology* (*Phoenix Supplementary Volume*) (Toronto).

Oren, E.D. (1982), 'Excavations at Qasrawet in North-Western Sinai: Preliminary Report', *Israel Exploration Journal* 32 (1), 203–11.

Papi, E. (2002), 'La turba inpia: artigiani e commercianti del Foro Romano e dintorni (i sec. a.C.–64 d.C.)', *JRA*, 15 (1), 45–62.

Parker, G. (2008), *The Making of Roman India* (Cambridge).

Parker, S.T. (1986), *Romans and Saracens: A History of the Arabian Frontier* (Winona Lake).

——— (1996), 'The Roman 'Aqaba Project: The 1994 Campaign', *ADAJ* 40, 231–57.

——— (1998), 'The Roman 'Aqaba Project: The 1996 Campaign', *ADAJ* 42, 375–94.

——— (2000), 'The Roman 'Aqaba Project: The 1998 Campaign', *ADAJ*, 44, 373–94.

——— (2002), 'The Roman 'Aqaba Project: The 2000 Campaign', *ADAJ*, 46, 409–28.

——— (2003), 'The Roman 'Aqaba Project: The 2002 Campaign', *ADAJ* 47, 321–33.

——— (2009), 'The Roman Port of Aila: Economic Connections with the Red Sea Litoral', in L.K. Blue, et al. (eds.), *Connected Hinterlands: Proceedings of Red Sea Project IV Held at the University of Southampton, September 2008* (Oxford), 79–89.

Peacock, D. (1993), 'The Site of Myos Hormos: A View from Space', *JRA*, 6, 226–32.

Pearson, M.N. (2007), *The Indian Ocean* (London).

Pekáry, T. (1968), *Untersuchungen zu den römischen Reichsstrassen* (Bonn).

Petruso, K.M. (1981), 'Early Weights and Weighing in Egypt and the Indus Valley', *M Bulletin: Museum of Fine Arts* (79; Boston), 44–51.

Phillipson, D.W. (2009) 'Aksum, the entrepôt, and highland Ethiopia, 3rd–12th centuries', in M.M. Mango (ed.), Byzantine Trade, 4th–12th Centuries. The Archaeology of Local, Regional and International Exchange. (Ashgate), 353–68.

Piacentini, V.F. (1992), *Merchants, Merchandise and Military Power in the Persian Gulf (Sūriyānj/Shahriyāj-Sīrāf)* (Rome).

Pleket H. (1990), 'Wirtschaft', in F. Vittinghoff (ed.), *Handbuch der Europäischen Wirtschafts-und Sozialgeschichte, I.* (Köln) 25–160.

Pomeranz, K. and S. Topik (2006), *The World that Trade Created: Society, Culture, and the World Economy, 1400 to the Present* (New York).

Posener, G. (1938), 'Le canal du Nil à la Mer Rouge avant les Ptolémées', *CE*, 13, 258–73.

Potts, D.T. (1994), 'Augustus, Aelius Gallus and the *Periplus*: A Re-Interpretation of the Coinage of San'â' Class B', in N. Nebes (ed.), *Arabia Felix: Beiträge zur Sprache und Kultur des vorislamischen Arabien. Festschrift Walter W. Müller zum 60. Geburtstag.* (Wiesbaden), 212–22.

Power, T. (2012), *The Red Sea from Byzantium to the Caliphate: AD 500–1000* (Cairo and New York).

Prakash, O. (1994), *Precious Metals and Commerce: The Dutch East India Company in the Indian Ocean Trade* (Brookfield, VT).

——— (1998), *European Commercial Enterprise in Pre-Colonial India: The New Cambridge History of India, Vol. II* (Cambridge).

——— (1999), 'The Portuguese and the Dutch in Asian Maritime Trade: A Comparative Analysis', in S. Chaudhury and M. Morineau (eds.), *Merchants, Companies and Trade: Europe and Asia in the Early Modern Era* (Cambridge) 175–88.

Prange, S.R. (2011), ' "Measuring by the Bushel": Reweighing the Indian Ocean Pepper Trade', *Historical Research* 84 (224), 212–35.

Purpura, G. (1996), 'Testimonianze storiche e archeologiche di traffici marittimi di libri e documenti', *ASGP* 44, 368–75.

——— (2005), 'Osservazioni sulla pesca del corallo rosso nell'antichità', *Archaeologia Maritima Mediterranea*, 2, 93–106.

Rajan, K. (1996), 'Early Maritime Activities of the Tamils', in H.P. Ray and J.-F. Salles (eds.), *Tradition and Archaeology: Early Maritime Contacts in the Indian Ocean* (Delhi), 96–108.

Raman, K.V. (1988), 'Port Towns of Tamilnadu: Some Field Data and the Prospects of Maritime Archaeology', in S.R. Rao (ed.), *Marine Archaeology of Indian Ocean Countries* (Goa).

Rao, S.R. (1985), *Lothal: A Harappan Port Town (1955–62: Memoirs of the Archaeological Survey of India)* (New Delhi).

Raschke, M.G. (1978), 'New Studies in Roman Commerce with the East', in H. Temporini and W. Haase (eds.), *Aufstieg und Niedergang der römischen Welt, II.9.2* (Berlin), 604–1378.

Rathbone, D.W. (2000), 'The "Muziris" Papyrus (*SB* XVIII 13167): Financing Roman Trade with India', in M. Abd-el-Ghani, S.Z. Bassiouni, and W.A. Farag (eds.), *Alexandrian Studies II in Honor of Mostafa el Abbadi, Societé Archéologique d'Alexandrie* (Alexandria), 39–50.

——— (2002), 'Koptos the Emporion: Economy and Society, I–III AD', in M.-F. Boussac (ed.), *Autour de Coptos: Actes du colloque organisé au Musée des Beaux-Arts de Lyons (17–18 mars 2000)* (Lyon), 179–98.

——— (2007), 'Roman Egypt', in R. Saller I. Morris and W. Scheidel (eds.), *The Cambridge Economic History of the Greco-Roman World* (Cambridge), 698–719.

Rau, W. (1973), *Metalle und Metallgeräte im vedischen Indien* (Wiesbaden).
Raven, E.M. (2006), 'Kuṣāṇa Echoes and the "Indianization" of Early Gupta Gold Coin Design', in F. De Romanis and S. Sorda (eds.), *Dal denarius al dinar: L'oriente e la moneta Romana. Atti dell'incontro di studio, Roma 16–18 settembre 2004* (Roma), 201–37.
Ray, H.P. (2003), *The Archaeology of Seafaring in Ancient South Asia* (Cambridge).
Redmount, C.A. (1995), 'The Wadi Tumilat and the "Canal of the Pharaohs" ', *Journal of Near Eastern Studies* 54 (2), 127–35.
——— (1989), 'On an Egyptian/Asiatic Frontier: An Archaeological History of the Wadi Tumilat' (Unpublished Ph.D. dissertation, University of Chicago).
Rey-Coquais, J.-P. (1978), 'Syrie romaine, de Pompée à Dioclétien', *JRS*, 68, 44–73.
Roaf, M. (1982), 'Weights on the Dilmun Standard', *Iraq*, 44, 137–41.
Robert, L. (1940), 'ΠΕΤΡΑΙΟΣ onomastique et géographie', *Hellenica: Recueil d'épigraphie, de numismatique et d'antiquités grecques, vol. 1.* (Paris), 121–26.
Roche, M.-J. (1996), 'Remarques sur les Nabatéens en Méditerranée', *Semitica* 45, 73–99.
Rostovtzev, M. (1931), 'Review of Greek *Ostraka* of the Bodleian Library', *Gnomon* 7, 23–26.
Rougé, J. (1957), 'Ad ciconias nixas', *Revue des Études Anciennes* 59, 320–28.
Rougelle, A. (1996), 'Medieval Trade Networks in the Western Indian Ocean (8th–14th Centuries)', in H.P. Ray and J.-F. Salles (eds.), *Tradition and Archaeology: Early Maritime Contacts in the Indian Ocean* (Delhi), 159–80.
Ruffing, K. (1993), 'Das Nikanor-Archiv und der römische Süd- und Osthandel', *Münstersche Beiträge zur Antiken Handelsgeschichte* 12, 1–26.
Ruggiero, M. (1888), *Degli scavi di antichità nelle province di Terraferma dell'antico regno di Napoli dal 1743–1876* (Naples).
Sachet, I. (2000), 'La céramique fine de Gaza: Une fenêtre ouverte sur les voies commerciales', in J.-B. Humbert (ed.), *Gaza Méditerranéenne: Histoire et archéologie en Palestine* (Paris), 51–53.
Sachs, C. and M. Blet-Lemarquand (2005), 'Le monnayage d'or des Kouchans et de leurs successeurs nomades: altération et chronologie', in C. Marcos, C. Alfaro, and P. Otero (eds.), *XIII Congreso Internacional de Numismática, Madrid 15–19 Septiembre, Actas—Proceedings—Actes, II.* (Madrid), 1659–67.
Salomon, R. (1990), 'A Kharoṣṭhī Inscription on a Silver Goblet', *Bulletin of the Asia Institute*, 4, 149–57.
Salonen, A. (1965), *Die Hausgeräte der alten Mesopotamier nach sumerisch-akkadischen Quellen* (Helsinki).
Sastri, K.A. Nilakanta (1939), *Foreign Notices of South India: From Megasthenes to Ma Huan* (Madras).
Sathyamurthy, T. (1992), *Catalogue of Roman Gold Coins in the Collections of Department of Archaeology, Kerala* (Thiruvanthapuram).

Scheidel, W. (ed.), (2009a), *Rome and China: Comparative Perspectives on Ancient World Empires* (Oxford).

——— (2009b), 'In Search of Roman Economic Growth', *JRA*, 22 (1), 46–70.

Schneider, P. (2004), *L'Éthiopie et l'Inde: Interférences et confusions aux extrémités du monde antique* (Rome).

Schoff, W.H. (1912), *The* Periplus *of the Erythraean Sea: Travel and Trade in the Indian Ocean, by a Merchant of the First Century* (New York).

Schörle, K. (2008), 'The Roman Exploitation of the Eastern Desert of Egypt', (University of Oxford).

——— (2010), 'From Harbour to Desert: An Integrated Interface on the Red Sea and its Impact on the Eastern Egyptian Desert', *Bolletino di Archeologia Online* <http://www.bollettinodiarcheologiaonline.beniculturali.it/bao_document/articoli/5_SCHÖRLE.pdf>, accessed.

Schroeder, L. von (1895), 'Das Kāṭhaka, seine Handschriften, seine Accentuation und seine Beziehung zu den indischen Lexikographen und Grammatikern', *Zeitschrift der Deutschen Morgenländischen Gesellschaft* 49, 145–71.

Seland, E.H. (2012), 'The *Liber Pontificalis* and Red Sea Trade of the Early to Mid 4th Century AD', in D.A. Agius, et al. (eds.), *Navigated Spaces, Connected Places: Proceedings of Red Sea Project V Held at the University of Exeter, 16–19 September 2010* (Oxford), 117–26.

Selvakumar, V., K.P. Shahjan, and R. Tomber (2010), 'Archaeological Investigations at Pattanam, Kerala: New Evidence for the Location of Ancient Muziris', in L. Blue, R. Tomber, and S. Abraham (eds.), *Migration, Trade and Peoples, Part 1; Indian Commerce and the Archaeology of Western India* (London), 29–41.

Seshadri, G. (2009), 'New Perspectives on Nagapattinam: The Medieval Port City in the Context of Political, Religious and Commercial Exchanges between South India, Southeast Asia, and China', in K. Kesavapany, H. Kulke, and V. Sakhuja (eds.), *Nagapattinam to Suvarnadwipa: Reflections on the Chola Naval Expeditions to Southeast Asia* (Singapore), 102–34.

Sewell, R. (1904), 'Roman Coins Found in India', *Journal of the Royal Asiatic Society* 591–637.

Shajan, K.P., et al. (2004), 'Locating the Ancient Port of Muziris: Fresh Findings from Pattanam', *Journal of Roman Archaeology* 17, 313–20.

Sheehan, P. (2012), 'The Port of Babylon in Egypt', in D.A. Agius, et al. (eds.), *Navigated Spaces, Connected Places: Proceedings of Red Sea Project V Held at the University of Exeter, 16–19 September 2010*, (*BAR International Series 2346*) (Oxford), 103–15.

Shinde, V., S. Gupta, and D. Rajgor (2002), 'An Archaeological Reconnaissance of the Konkan Coast from Bharuch to Janjira', *Man and Environment* 27 (1), 73–82.

Sicker, M. (2000), *The Pre-Islamic Middle East* (Westport).

Sidebotham, S.E. (1986a), *Roman Economic Policy in the Erythra Thalassa 30 B.C.–A.D. 217* (Leiden).
——— (1986b), 'Aelius Gallus and Arabia', *Latomus* 45 (3), 590–602.
——— (1996), 'An Overview of Archaeological Work in the Eastern Desert and Along the Red Sea Coast by the University of Delaware—Leiden University, 1987–1995', *Topoi* 6 (2), 773–83.
——— (1997), 'Caravans Across the Eastern Desert of Egypt: Recent Discoveries on the Berenice–Apollinopolis Magna–Coptos Roads', in A. Avanzini (ed.), *Profumi d'Arabia: Atti del Convegno* (Roma), 385–93.
——— (1999), 'Survey of the Hinterland', in S.E. Sidebotham and W.Z. Wendrich (eds.), *Berenike 1997: Report of the 1997 Excavations at Berenike and the Survey of the Eastern Desert, Including Excavations at Shenshef* (*CNWS Special Series*) (Leiden), 349–69.
——— (2000), 'Survey of the Hinterland', in S.E. Sidebotham and W.Z. Wendrich (eds.), *Berenike 1998. Report of the 1998 Excavations at Berenike (Egyptian Red Sea coast) and the Survey of the Eastern Desert* (*CNWS Special Series*) (Leiden), 354–77.
——— (2002a), 'From Berenike to Koptos: Recent Results of the Desert Route Survey', in M.-F. Boussac (ed.), *Autour de Coptos: Actes du colloque organisé au Musée des Beaux-Arts de Lyon* (Lyon), 415–38.
——— (2002b), 'Late Roman Berenike', *JARCE* 39, 217–40.
——— (2007), 'Chapter 4: Excavations', in S.E. Sidebotham and W. Wendrich (eds.), *Berenike 1999/2000: Report on the Excavations at Berenike, Including Excavations in the Wadi Kalalat and Siket, and the Survey of the Mons Smaragdus Region* (Los Angeles), 30–165.
——— (2011), *Berenike and the Ancient Maritime Spice Route* (Berkeley, Los Angeles, and London).
——— M. Hense, and H.M. Nouwens (2008), *The Red Land: The Illustrated Archaeology of Egypt's Eastern Desert* (Cairo).
——— and W.Z. Wendrich (1995), *Berenike 1994: Preliminary Report of the 1994 Excavations at Berenike (Egyptian Red Sea Coast) and the Survey of the Eastern Desert* (Leiden).
——— (1996), *Berenike 1995: Preliminary Report of the 1995 Excavations at Berenike (Egyptian Red Sea Coast) and the survey of the Eastern Desert* (Leiden).
——— (1998), *Berenike 1996: Report of the 1996 Excavations at Berenike (Egyptian Red Sea Coast) and the Survey of the Eastern Desert* (Leiden).
——— 1999), 'Interpretative Summary and Conclusion', in S.E. Sidebotham and W.Z. Wendrich (eds.), *Berenike 1997: Report of the 1997 Excavations at Berenike and the Survey of the Egyptian Eastern Desert, Including Excavations at Shenshef* (Leiden), 445–56.
——— (2000), *Berenike 1998: Report of the 1998 Excavations at Berenike (Egyptian Red Sea Coast) and the Survey of the Eastern Desert, Including Excavations in Wadi Kalalat* (Leiden).

——— (2007), *Berenike 1999/2000: Report on the Excavations at Berenike, Including Excavations in Wadi Kalalat and Siket, and the Survey of the Mons Smaragdus Region* (Los Angeles).

——— and R.E. Zitterkopf (1995), 'Routes Through the Eastern Desert of Egypt', *Expedition: Bulletin of the University Museum of the University of Pennsylvania* 37 (2), 39.

——— (1996), 'Survey of the Hinterland', in S.E. Sidebotham and W.Z. Wendrich (eds.), *Berenike 1995: Preliminary Report of the 1995 Excavations at Berenike (Egyptian Red Sea Coast) and the Survey of the Eastern Desert* (Leiden), 357–409.

——— and J.A. Riley (1991), 'Survey of the Abu Sha'ar–Nile Road', *American Journal of Archaeology* 95 (4), 571–622.

Sijpesteijn, P.J. (1963), 'Der Τραιανός ποταμός', *Aegyptus* 43, 70–83.

Silver, M. (2009), 'Glimpses of Vertical Integration/Disintegration in Ancient Rome', *Ancient Society* 39, 171–84.

Singer, C. (2007), 'The Incense Kingdoms of Yemen: An Outline History of the South Arabian Incense Trade', in D. Peacock and D. Williams (eds.), *Food for the Gods: New Light on the Ancient Incense Trade* (Oxford), 4–27.

Siviero, R. (1954), *Gli ori e le ambre del museo nazionale di Napoli* (Sansoni).

Skinner, F.G. (1954), 'Measures and Weights', in E.J. Holmyard, C. Singer, and A.R. Hall (eds.), *A History of Technology, Vol. 1* (Oxford), 774–84.

——— (1967), *Weights and Measures: Their Ancient Origins and Their Development in Great Britain up to AD 1855* (London).

Sleeswyk, A.W. (1979), 'Vitruvius' waywiser', *Archives Internationales d'Histoire des Sciences* 29, 11.

——— (1981), 'Vitruvius' Odometer', *Scientific American* 245 (October), 158–71.

——— (1990), 'Archimedes' Odometer and Waterclock', *Ancient Technology*, 23–37.

Sogliano, A. (1890), 'Di un'epigrafe dedicatoria ad Adriano', *N.d.sc.*, 17–18.

Sonnabend, H. (1999), 'Kanal', in H. Sonnabend (ed.), *Mensch und Landschaft in der Antike. Lexikon der historischen Geographie* (Stuttgart and Weimar), 243.

Soundara Rajan, K.V. (1994), *Kaveripattinnam Excavations 1963–73: A Port City on the Tamilnadu Coast* (New Delhi).

Speidel, M.A. (2000), 'Sold und Wirtschaftslage der römischen Soldaten', in B. Dobson, G. Alföldy, and W. Eck (eds.), *Kaiser, Heer und Gesellschaft in der römischen Kaiserzeit. Gedenkschrift für Eric Birley* (Stuttgart), 65–96.

Speidel, M.P. (1977), 'The Roman Army in Arabia', in H. Temporini and W. Haase (eds.), *Aufstieg und Niedergang der römischen Welt, II.8* (Berlin), 688–730.

Spijkerman, A. (1978), *The Coins of the Decapolis and Provincia Arabia* (Jerusalem).

Stabel, P., B. Blondé, and A. Greve (2000), *International Trade in the Low Countries (14th–16th Centuries)* (Garant).

Starcky, J. (1955a), 'The Nabataeans: A Historical Sketch', *Biblical Archaeologist* 18, 84–106.

——— (1955b), 'Enno Littmann: Nabataean Inscriptions from Egypt', *Syria* 32 (1), 150–57.

Stephen, S. Jeyaseela (1997), *The Coromandel Coast and its Hinterland: Economy, Society and Political System, A.D. 1500–1600* (New Delhi).

Stern, S.M. (1967), 'Rāmisht of Sīrāf, a Merchant Millionaire of the Twelfth Century', *JRAS*, (April), 10–14.

Steuernagel, D. (2004), *Kult und Alltag in römischen Hafenstädten: Soziale Prozesse in archäologischer Perspektive* (Stuttgart).

Strack, E. (2008), 'Introduction', in P.C. Southgate and J.S. Lucas (eds.), *The Pearl Oyster* (Amsterdam), 1–35.

Strobel, K. (1988), 'Zur Fragen der frühen Geschichte der römischen Provinz Arabia und zu einigen Problemen der Legionsdislokation im Osten des Imperium Romanum zu Beginn des 2. Jh. n.Chr', *ZPE* 71, 251–80.

Stronach, D. (1965), 'Excavations at Pasagardae: Third Preliminary Report', *Iran* 3, 9–40.

Strugnell, J. (1959), 'The Nabataean Goddess Al-Kutba' and Her Sanctuaries', *Bulletin of the American Schools of Oriental Research* 156, 29–36.

Stückelberger, A. and G. Graßhoff (2006), *Klaudios Ptolemaios: Handbuch der Geographie*, 2 vols. (Basel).

Subrahmanyam, S. (1993), *The Portuguese Empire in Asia, 1500–1700: A Political and Economic History* (London and New York).

——— (1996), *Merchant Networks in the Early Modern World* (Brookfield, VT).

——— (1990), *The Political Economy of Commerce: Southern India, 1500–1650* (Cambridge).

Suresh, S. (2004), *Symbols of Trade: Roman and Pseudo-Roman Objects Found in India* (New Delhi).

Takmer, B. (2007), '*Lex Portorii provinciae Lyciae*: Ein Vorbericht über die Zollinschrift aus Andriake von neronischer Zeit', *Gephyra: Journal for the Ancient History and Cultures of the Eastern Mediterranean* 4, 1–22.

Tchernia, A. (1992), 'Le dromadaire des Peticii et le commerce oriental', *MEFRA* 104, 293–301.

——— (2005), 'Winds and Coins: From the Supposed Discovery of the Monsoon to the *Denarii* of Tiberius', in F. De Romanis and A. Tchernia (eds.), *Crossings. Early Mediterranean Contacts with India* (New Delhi), 250–76.

——— (2011a), 'L'utilisation des gros tonnages', in W.V. Harris and K. Iara (eds.), *Maritime Technology in the Ancient Economy: Ship-Design and Navigation* (Portsmouth), 83–88.

——— (2011b), *Les Romains et le commerce* (Naples).

Terpstra, T.T. (2013), *Trading Communities in the Roman World, A Micro-Economic and Institutional Perspective* (Leiden).

Thomas, E. (1874), *Ancient Indian Weights* (London, repr. Varanasi).

Thomas, R.I. (2011), 'Fishing Activity', in D.P.S. Peacock and L. Blue (eds.), *Myos Hormos–Quseir al-Qadim: Roman and Islamic Ports on the Red Sea. Volume 2: Finds from the Excavations 1999–2003* (Oxford), 211–20.

Thomaz, L.F.F.R. (1988), 'Malaka et ses communautés marchandes au tournant du 16e siècle', in D. Lombard and J. Aubin (eds.), *Marchands et hommes d'affaires asiatiques dans l'Océan Indien et la Mer de Chine 13e–20e siècles* (Paris), 31–48.

Thür, G. (1987), 'Hypotheken-Urkunden eines Seedarlehens für eine Reise nach Muziris und Apographe für die Tetarte in Alexandria (zu *P.Vindob. G* 40.822)', *Tyche* 2, 229–45.

——— (1988), 'Zum Seedarlehen κατὰ Μουζεῖριν', *Tyche* 3, 229–33.

Toll, C. (1994), 'Two Nabataean Ostraca from Egypt', *Bulletin de l'Institut Français d'Archéologie Orientale*, 94, 381–82.

Tomber, R. (2008), *Indo-Roman Trade: From Pots to Pepper* (London).

Tracy, J. (1990), *The Rise of Merchant Empires* (Cambridge).

Tran tam Tinh, V. (1972), *Le culte des divinités orientales en Campanie en dehors de Pompéi, de Stabies et d'Herculanum* (Leiden).

Trombley, F.R. (2009), Amr B. Al-'ās's Refurbishment of Trajan's Canal: Red Sea Contacts in the Aphrodito and Apollōnonas Anō Papyri', in L. Blue, et al. (eds.), *Connected Hinterlands: Proceedings of Red Sea Project IV, Held at the University of Southampton, September 2008* (BAR *International Series 2052*) (Oxford), 99–109.

Tuplin, C. (1991), 'Darius' Suez Canal and Persian Imperialism', in H. Sancisi-Weerdenburg and A. Kuhrt (eds.), *Achaemenid History VI, Asia Minor and Egypt: Old Culture in a New Empire* (Leiden), 237–83.

Turner, E.G. (1954), 'Tiberius Iulius Alexander', *Journal of Roman Studies*, 44, 54–64.

Van der Wee, H. (1993), 'Structural Change in European Long-Distance Trade, and Particularly in the Re-Export Trade from South to North, 1350–1700', in J.D. Tracy (ed.), *The Rise of Merchant Empires: Long-Distance Trade in the Early Modern World, 1350–1750*, 14–33.

Van Neer, W. and A. Ervynck (1998), 'The Faunal Remains', in S. Sidebotham and W. Wendrich (eds.), *Berenike '96: Report of the excavations at Berenike (Egyptian Red Sea Coast) and the Survey of the Eastern Desert* (Leiden), 349–88.

——— (1999), 'Faunal Remains from Shenshef and Kalalat', in S. Sidebotham and W. Wendrich (eds.), *Report of the 1997 Excavations at Berenike and the Survey of the Egyptian Eastern Desert, Including Excavations at Shenshef* (Leiden), 431–44.

Vasunia, P. (2011), 'The Comparative Study of Empires', *JRS*, 101, 222–37.

Vats, M.S. (1940), *Excations at Harappā, Being an Account of Archaeological Excavations at Harappā Carried out Between the Years 1920–21 and 1933–34*, 2 vols. (Delhi).

Villeneuve, F. (2004), 'Une inscription latine sur l'archipel Farasan, Arabie Séoudite, sud de la Mer Rouge', *Comptes Rendus des Séances de l'Académie des Inscriptions et Belles-Lettres*, 419–29.

——— (2007), 'L'armée romaine en mer Rouge et autour de la mer Rouge aux IIe et IIIe siècles apr. J.-C: À propos des inscriptions de Farasân', in A. Lewin (ed.), *The Late Roman Army in the Near East from Diocletian to the Arab conquest* (Oxford), 13–27.

——— (2009) 'Les îles Farasan et la mer Rouge', <http://www.mae.u-paris10.fr/arscan/Les-iles-Farasan-et-la-mer-Rouge.html>, accessed.

——— C. Philipps, and W. Facey (2004), 'Une inscription latine de l'archipel Farasan (sud de la mer Rouge) et son contexte archéologique et historique', *Arabia* 2, 143–90.

Wallace-Hadrill, A. (2008), *Rome's Cultural Revolution* (Cambridge and New York).

Ward, W. (2007), 'Aila and Clysma: The Rise of Northern Ports in the Red Sea in Late Antiquity', in J. Starkey, et al. (eds.), *Natural Resources and Cultural Connections of the Red Sea* (*British Archaeological Reports International Series 2007*), 161–71.

Wenning, R. (1987), *Die Nabatäer—Denkmäler und Geschichte: Eine Bestandesaufnahme des archäologischen Befundes* (Freiburg).

——— (2007), 'The Nabataeans in History', in K.D. Politis (ed.), *The World of the Nabataeans* (Stuttgart), 25–53.

Whitehouse, D. and A. Williamson (1973), 'Sasanian Maritime Trade', *Iran*, 11, 29–49.

Wilkinson, J. (1971), *Egeria's Travels* (London).

Wilkinson, J.C. (1979), 'Ṣuḥār (Sohar) in the Early Islamic Period: The Written Evidence', in M. Taddei (ed.), *South Asian Archaeology 1977* (Naples), 887–907.

Williamson, A. (1972), 'Persian Gulf Commerce in the Sassanian Period and the First Two Centuries of Islam', *Bastan Chenassi va Honar-e Iran* 9–10, 97–109.

Wilson, A.I. (2008), 'Economy and Trade', in E. Bispham (ed.), *The Roman Era* (Oxford), 170–202.

——— (2009), 'Indicators for Roman Economic Growth: A Response to Walter Scheidel', *Journal of Roman Archaeology* 22 (1), 71–82.

Wissmann, H. von (1976), 'Die *Geschichte* des Sabaerreichs und der Feldzug des *Aelius Gallus*', *ANRW* 2 9.1, 308–544.

Young, G.K. (2001), *Rome's Eastern Trade: International Commerce and Imperial Policy 31 BC–AD 305* (London and New York).

Yule, Sir H. (1915), *Cathay and the Way Thither: Being a Collection of Medieval Notices of China*, 4 vols. (revised edn. by H. Cordier; London).

Zayadine, F. (1985), 'Caravan Routes between Egypt and Nabataea and the Voyage of Sultan Baibars to Petra in 1276', in A. Hadidi (ed.), *Studies in the History and Archaeology of Jordan II* (Amman), 159–71.

——— (2007), 'The Spice Trade from South Arabia and India to Nabataea and Palestine', in K.D. Politis (ed.), *The World of the Nabataeans* (Stuttgart), 201–15.

Zitterkopf, R.E. and S.E. Sidebotham (1989), 'Stations and Towers on the Quseir–Nile Road', *The Journal of Egyptian Archaeology* 75, 155–89.

Index of Sources

Juridical Sources

Ostraca and Papyri

Greek and Latin Inscriptions

Other Early Modern Documentary Evidence

General Index

www.ingramcontent.com/pod-product-compliance
Ingram Content Group UK Ltd.
Pitfield, Milton Keynes, MK11 3LW, UK
UKHW022208051026
15624UKWH00001B/57

9 789004 289192